.

Assessing Urban Design

Assessing Urban Design

Historical Ambience on the Waterfront

Richard W. Berman

LEXINGTON BOOKS

A Division of
ROWMAN & LITTLEFIELD PUBLISHERS, INC.
Lanham • Boulder • New York • Toronto • Oxford

LEXINGTON BOOKS

A division of Rowman & Littlefield Publishers, Inc.
A wholly owned subsidiary of The Rowman & Littlefield Publishing Group, Inc.
4501 Forbes Boulevard, Suite 200
Lanham, MD 20706

PO Box 317
Oxford
OX2 9RU, UK

Copyright © 2006 by Richard W. Berman

British Library Cataloguing in Publication Information Available

Library of Congress Cataloging-in-Publication Data

Berman, Richard W., 1958-
  Assessing urban design : historical ambience on the waterfront / Richard W. Berman.
    p. cm.
  Includes bibliographical references and index.
  ISBN-13: 978-0-7391-1217-5 (cloth : alk. paper)
  ISBN-10: 0-7391-1217-1 (cloth : alk. paper)
  1. Urban renewal—Pennsylvania—Philadelphia. 2. Urban renewal—Japan—
Yokohama-shi. 3. Waterfronts—Pennsylvania—Philadelphia. 4. Waterfronts—
Japan—Yokohama-shi. 5. Historic districts—Pennsylvania—Philadelphia. 6. Historic
districts—Japan—Yokohama-shi.   I. Title.
  HT177.P47B47 2006
  711'.42—dc22   2005034099

Printed in the United States of America

♾™ The paper used in this publication meets the minimum requirements of American
National Standard for Information Sciences—Permanence of Paper for Printed Library
Materials, ANSI/NISO Z39.48–1992.

To My Parents

Contents

Figures

Tables

Acknowledgments

I would like to thank all those involved in providing support and guidance during the research and writing of this book. First and foremost, my parents who have supported any endeavor I have ever tried, this only being the most recent. Their love and encouragement always make difficult projects seem easier.

This work was formerly written as a dissertation at the University of Pennsylvania. I wish to thank Seymour Mandelbaum, who is all a dissertation advisor should be. His flexibility in allowing me to explore different issues, and encouragement to "seize the day" when interesting opportunities came up, made this a far richer experience than it might have been. His knowledge and guidance throughout have been invaluable.

David DeLong and Robert St. George have given useful suggestions at key moments during the research and writing of this work, which I very much appreciate.

I am indebted to the members of WAVE (Waterfront Vitalization and Environmental Research Center) in Japan who supported and assisted my research abroad. Their knowledge, guidance, and hospitality made my seven weeks in Japan a true pleasure.

Many Penn Alumni in Japan made me feel at home during my stay and I am grateful to them all. Yoshiki Morimoto, in particular, provided insights and friendship that made Japanese culture far more understandable and enjoyable for me.

Finally, I would like to thank the many other friends and colleagues, teachers and students, who have graciously shared their time and ideas with me along the way.

R. W. B.

Introduction

As an architect, I have watched my own tastes change, particularly during my initial academic training. My respect for much historical construction was initially dampened during architecture school. It was gradually rekindled during a number of years of professional practice and most recently, additional academic study.

I have become particularly sensitive to the fact that designers' tastes and public tastes do not always mesh, and have therefore become more hesitant to impose my own "expert" opinions on others. Rapoport has noted that "one of the hallmarks of man-environment research is the realization that designers and users are very different in their reactions to environments, their preferences, and so on, partly because their schemata vary. It is thus users' meaning that is important, not architects' or critics'."[1]

The experts on architecture are as valid a subgroup of the general public as any other group. Their decisions are not necessarily based on personal preferences, but rather they try to capture broad significance through their "expert" opinions. The flaw is that this expert knowledge that gives some people a deep understanding of a subject can inherently separate their understanding and judgments from the rest of the population. Judgements of experts and non-experts may sometimes naturally overlap. At other times empathy by experts for non-expert viewpoints may be employed. Still, there are many times that those non-expert viewpoints can get lost, if the design or planning process does not deliberately incorporate them within it.

Architects and designers often try to "educate" with their designs and lead rather than merely accommodate public tastes. However, many in the public may not appreciate what might be considered "high design." If it is designed for that very same public, is a design truly doing what the larger program requires of it? This is a particularly relevant question in the case of urban design and design for public, rather than private consumption.

I am not suggesting a totally populist design aesthetic, but rather a constant awareness of public tastes by architects and other experts during the process of planning and design. This awareness should also extend to other scenarios involving the management of the public built environment. This includes selections of structures for preservation, and the types of preservation to be undertaken.

This research does not focus on the differences between designer and user preferences. Rather, it searches for what is behind the preferences, with a particular emphasis on the "lay" user.

The book touches on issues of urban design, planning, architecture, historic preservation and tourism. However, only a few questions are at the core of this research. How do people perceive urban design? What is it about the design that influences our perceptions? What is it about ourselves that leads us to "read" shared settings differently?

I have approached these questions from two directions:

1)   A reflective consideration of three bodies of literature: urban design, preservation, and tourism. The authors selected allow for a variety of insights into the perception and awareness of the built environment.

2)   An empirical study of "lay" respondents at roughly comparable waterfront sites in Philadelphia and Yokohama.

Chapter 1 discusses the distinct and the unique. The relevance and meanings of these terms are stated. How a site is perceived as distinct is then discussed. The next chapters further explore how differences are perceived, grouped, and enhanced. Chapter 2 looks at predictability and surprise. This concept ties closely into that of the distinct. Chapter 3 uses the concept of packaging as another way of looking at urban environments.

Chapter 4 deals with the idea of historical ambience. This is described as a subset of the distinct. It is not based on expert viewpoints (e.g., architect, planner, preservation specialist). Rather, it comes from the viewpoint of the more typical user, one not focusing on the built environment professionally.

Chapter 5 begins the discussion of the empirical research. By surveying a number of individuals as to sites they like, some insights were gained about people's preferences. Historical ambience was of particular concern in my analysis.

Chapter 6 describes a survey conducted in Philadelphia, near and along the Delaware River. Images of a number of sites were shown to individuals in the area to judge their preferences. The analysis procedure is described and the findings stated. Chapter 7 describes a similar survey done along the waterfront of Yokohama, Japan. Again, the analysis and findings are discussed.

Conclusions are in Chapter 8. This begins with a comparison of the findings of the Philadelphia and Yokohama studies. The survey and analysis techniques used in these two studies are then critiqued. Finally, the implications of this research are explored.

Chapter One

The Distinct and the Unique

Relevance of Concepts

This chapter will discuss both actual differences between environments ("uniqueness") and individuals' perceptions of those differences ("distinctness"). The concept of the distinct allows an alternative way to look at the attraction of environments.

The distinct is integral to an understanding of the idea of historical ambience, which is explored in a later chapter. Historical ambience does not exist independently. It only exists in relation to and in its distinctness from an adjacent ambience. A historical ambience does not rely on the uniqueness of its elements. Rather, it relies on people's perceptions of that uniqueness. These perceptions may then attract or repel observers.

Alexander has described a "specific, morphological character" that old towns take on through their gradual growth over the years.[1] Though some cities begin with a strong plan (e.g., Philadelphia) and others without (e.g., Yokohama), all cities are eventually comprised of gradual accretions over time.

Time often allows the character of a town, district, or city to develop as distinct from others, though it does not guarantee it. The changes that occur over time can also homogenize an area, reducing qualities that set it off from the surroundings. Choices of which structures to demolish, add on to, restore, or adapt, all contribute to one area's distinctness from another. The quantity, scale and style of new structures also affect an area's visual character.

Today's global economy often creates a degree of similarity of forms within different geographic locations. Due to increasing economies of scale in the construction of buildings, and the resulting use of repetitive modular units of construction, many structures built in recent years have taken on an increased homogeneity in appearance. [2] National and international distribution networks for products also contribute to this phenomenon.

In the past, building forms frequently varied in response to climatic conditions. Technologies such as heating, air conditioning, and electricity have now removed certain constraints imposed by the weather, and thereby removed some diversity of forms between different geographic locations.

There has been an increase in free time available for travel in this century, as well as an increasing tendency to commoditize travel and tourist experiences. There has also been a simultaneous increase in the ability for those living in industrialized societies to look upon a variety of tourist experiences with ease. This combination of factors is making everyone at different times and to different degrees, a tourist.

The term "tourist" is used in two overlapping ways in this essay. The first is the more traditional meaning of a person who takes a tour for recreation, "visiting a number of places for their objects of interest, scenery, or the like."[3] This notion is then expanded to include experiences encountered everyday. Urry writes, "The way in which tourism has been historically separated from other activities, such as shopping, sport, culture, architecture and so on, is dissolving. The result of such a process is a universalizing of the tourist gaze."[4]

MacCannell argues that "the differentiations of the modern world have the same structure as tourist attractions: elements dislodged from their original natural, historical and cultural contexts fit together with other such displaced or modernized things and people. The differentiations are the attractions."[5]

We always perceive things within a certain context, as if through a frame. MacCannell uses the term framing in regards to the viewing of tourist sites.[6] The tourist gaze is the viewing of a site through a frame, whether mental or physical, that creates a certain separation between what is being viewed and the viewer. The view of a site through a tour bus window, or through media (such as videos, books, or the Internet) has increased the ease in which a wide variety of once exotic sites can now be scanned. This has, however, reduced the immediacy of contact of the experience.[7] The diminishing uniqueness of the physical appearance of environments is then compounded by an increasingly well traveled public.

Tourism results from the division of the everyday and the extraordinary.[8] However, what were once considered unique and extraordinary sites for most people have now become part of their everyday vocabulary, even if only on a secondary level (that of experience filtered through mass media). Extraordinary sites to be seen, collected and experienced have become that much rarer.

Many locations are now trying to emphasize their uniqueness and capitalize on the qualities and physical forms that set them apart from other towns and cities. The goals are to improve the appearance of their locations to attract visitors and businesses, as well as to satisfy local residents. A site lacking visual distinctness is less likely to attract tourists.[9] Therefore, visual distinctness can provide a marketing advantage. Tunbridge and Ashworth suggest that "all tourism is heavily dependent upon the generation and promotion of particular place images. The place images supporting heritage and cultural tourism may, in turn, be valued for their beneficial impacts upon other unrelated activities, such as amenity-sensitive white collar employers, or, more broadly, for their support for civic consciousness and self-confidence."[10]

The lure of the unique and distinct likely exists across cultures. Differences in the degree of attraction due to varying Japanese and American sensitivities to these factors will be discussed in later chapters. How universal the attractions of the distinct and unique really are, would take additional studies in a broad range of locations.

Definitions

The concept of "distinct" is a prerequisite for the attraction of an area, whether it is perceived as distinct from the surroundings by being a waterfront area, an area with a historical ambience, or an area with any other strongly distinguishing characteristics. The simple idea being that you have to notice a specific area or environment before you can be attracted to it.[11] This does not preclude a person haphazardly wandering into an undifferentiated area and liking or disliking it. However, when intentionally choosing where to travel to and visit, attributes that distinguish one destination from another often guide the choice.

The term "unique" as defined by the Oxford English Dictionary as "a thing, fact, or circumstance which by reason of exceptional or special qualities stands alone and is without equal or parallel in its kind." Since the mid-1800s the term has also taken on "the wider meaning of "uncommon, unusual, remarkable."""[12]

Distinct, however, does not necessarily mean "without equal" or even "uncommon." Distinct, is defined in the same dictionary as: "Distinguished or separated from others by nature or qualities; possessing differentiating characteristics; individually peculiar; different in quality or kind; not alike. . . . Clearly perceptible or discernible by the senses or the mind."[13]

These perceptions of distinctness will many times overlap the qualities of uniqueness. Different individuals will notice and be attracted or repelled by different things with a variety of degrees of uniqueness.

Uniqueness is based on the object or environment itself and the degree of difference of this entity to that. Every object is unique by some degree, whether by location, relationship to other objects, exterior form, interior form, or function. This creates a continuum of uniqueness from slight to drastic, and from local to universal.

Distinctness is based on the perceptions of individuals. These perceptions of an area's unique characteristics and differences from other areas, may also vary from subtle to extreme.

Distinct refers to an individual's perception of how discernible one object or environment is from another. Jackson has used the word "visible" with a very similar meaning that I am using for the word "distinct." "The word means of course something more than that an object can be seen. It means that it is conspicuous, that it is distinct from its surroundings, and that as a form it can be understood at a glance; and in this sense it is obvious that not all objects in the landscape are really visible."[14]

Lynch writes concerning a similar, though broader concept of identity, "A workable image requires first the identification of an object, which implies its distinction from other things, its recognition as a separable entity. This is called identity, not in the sense of equality with something else, but with the meaning of individuality or oneness."[15]

Distinct is what is noticed and discernible. It depends on the attributes of the object or environment being observed, as well as the sensitivity of the observer for noticing these attributes. Unique exists at different levels relating to spheres of travel from local to worldwide. An object or environment may be distinct for observers, but only locally unique.

An example is the "Red Brick Warehouses" of Yokohama. No matter how frequently these types of brick buildings might be seen along the

Philadelphia waterfront, in Yokohama, they are rare if not unique. From the observers' viewpoints however, initially the warehouses are perceived as visually distinct from the surrounding buildings. They are set apart from their most immediate surroundings.

However, the distinct sites' attributes may or may not remain unique at a more distant sphere beyond that of the local. In Japan, the same type warehouse may exist along another waterfront. Then, the "Red Brick Warehouses" might not be considered unique in Japan by exterior form alone. However, when adapted for a particular use, such as a restaurant or retail store, the forms and functions may combine to retain the site's uniqueness.

Is the site unique for the individual? The answer might affect the interest of the potential tourist to the site. The attraction may lessen if within the individual's particular network of travels and experience, a location with similar qualities is found elsewhere and possibly closer to home. Depending on the number of converted brick warehouses encompassed in an individual's network of travels, the attraction of Yokohama's brick warehouses may be lessened for that person.

Each individual's network of travels is different. They are controlled by available means of transportation (foot, bicycle, train, plane, car, etc.), the desire to travel, and the ability to pay. Those with the money, time, and desire to travel broadly may find the perceived uniqueness of their local area reduced. For an individual, the uniqueness of an object, how rare it is, depends on the individual's sphere of travels and experiences. Distinctness lies more within an individual's perceptiveness. Though perceptiveness may be affected by experience, it also can exist more independently, as a function of human traits of an individual (e.g., the ability to discern differences in color).

A small historic area within a larger historic area will not be as noticeable to the visitor as a historic area within a larger contemporary area or a contemporary area within a larger historical area. Norberg-Schulz states that "the "identity" of a place is determined by location, general spatial configuration and characterizing articulation . . . some places get their identity from a particularly interesting location, whereas the man-made components are rather insignificant. Others, instead, may be situated in a dull landscape, but possess a well-defined configuration and a distinct character."[16]

The differences become more noticeable as the scarcity of a type increases. Some examples of this given by Norberg-Schulz are arcades in

Italy. In Venice there are only two arcades so they each take on extra importance. In contrast, Bologna, has arcades throughout, so they offer less surprise and draw less attention.[17]

The tourist or traveler seeks something different from that individual's local environment and everyday experiences.[18] One of the objectives of traveling is to see, buy, or otherwise experience something that you might not have the chance to, at home. It is a search for a certain level of uniqueness. People search for the unique within their personal subset created by their sphere of knowledge and travels. Within these spheres, some individuals may be attracted to extreme one-of-a-kind uniqueness (i.e., Landmark Tower, the tallest building in Japan with a unique silhouette), others to only slightly unusual levels (i.e., Landmark Center, a mall and large atrium with a curved escalator between floors).

Just as people decorate and personalize the insides of their bedrooms or offices to make them somehow distinct from surrounding rooms and suited to themselves, they also choose sites to visit that define their tastes and personalities. Individuals also gather tourism experiences to add meaning to their lives.[19]

People may ally themselves with certain groups in the process, or show their individuality within or from those groups. Hughes declares that "despite the global diffusion of consumer capitalism individuals continue to exercise strategies of personal identification. Territorial signifiers, or myths, may be used in support of this."[20]

An example might be Americans who visited a particular area abroad. The location may have been visited at different times. Different personal experiences of the visit accompany each individual. Yet the site itself, the object of the gaze, is a shared communal item of this group of individuals who have seen or otherwise experienced it. If the individuals have an opportunity to allude to it, this common ground may serve to link them together, even if only for a short time.

Polarities and Boundaries

The term distinct means "separated from others." It inherently creates polarities of this or that, the distinct object and the surroundings that it is distinct from. Just the term "waterfront" implies a difference from the surroundings. Locations from that standpoint are then described as being along the water's edge or not. The polarity of waterfront and non-waterfront is set up by the term. A boundary between the two is created whether physically defined or mentally constructed.

The water is a natural location that is sometimes used by nearby sites as a means of identifying, separating and making it understood to be somehow distinct from other nearby areas. Other features that may be used to describe an area include mountains, deserts, valleys, etc. These features can be natural or man-made. Rivers can be rerouted, such as occurred in Providence, re-exposing and recreating a waterfront. The edges of the water can be pushed or pulled by digging or by landfill, to shift the boundaries between land and water (such as in Battery Park City).

The boundaries themselves, though geographically discrete, may be perceived more fluidly. There is property that is on the water's edge and property that is not. A waterfront area, however, may actually be used to describe an area larger than that directly fronting the water. It may extend one or more blocks in from the water. Highways, major roadways, or train tracks may define this outer edge of the waterfront area. The stronger the boundaries, the more separate and distinct from the rest of the city.

There is an artificiality in the creation of these polarities, however. Early in his career, Alexander wrote about the human mind's predilection for understanding and representing complicated entities, like cities, in terms of trees. He explained that these trees are an analogy for a given object being in one set or another (this branch or that), but never within two or more sets simultaneously. "Because the mind's first function is to reduce the ambiguity and overlap in a confusing situation, and because to this end it is endowed with a basic intolerance for ambiguity - that structures like the city, which do require overlapping sets within them, are nevertheless persistently conceived as trees."

He further wrote that planners and designers found this conceptual simplicity useful for their actions, though "the humanity and richness of the living city" was sacrificed in its realization.[21]

This creation of polarities may have a positive effect as well. Jackson has said that "boundaries stabilize social relationships. They make residents out of the homeless, neighbors out of strangers, strangers out of enemies." The marking of boundaries has the positive function of indicating to people places where certain behaviors may be contained. By doing so, it tends to reduce conflict.[22]

The creation of special sites and areas within a city simplifies tourism. Distinct areas with clear-cut boundaries are easier for a person to grasp than the less contrived, more complex inter-relationships of the city. A potentially overwhelming city becomes far smaller and more manageable and knowable for a visitor at this reduced scale of a network of tourist attractions.

Sensing the Distinct

Sensing the distinct involves receiving sensory input and then perceiving that input as corresponding to an object or environment different from others. A strong silhouette (visible against the sky, the trees, the water, or other fairly continuous backdrops) may clearly identify an object or structure as separate and different from the immediate surroundings. A strikingly different shape or color of one object from the surroundings will also emphasize distinctness.

Lynch states that landmarks "become more easily identifiable, more likely to be chosen as significant, if they have a clear form; if they contrast with their background; and if there is some prominence of spatial location. Figure-background contrast seems to be the principal factor."[23]

Lynch further wrote that "in another sense, subjects might single out landmarks for their cleanliness in a dirty city . . . or for their newness in an old city."[24] Sites felt to be unique locations to whatever degree, which are perceived as distinct from their surroundings, might also include basic characteristic groupings of individual sites such as waterfronts or areas with a historical ambience.

Urry points out "that there has to be something distinctive to be gazed upon, that the signs collected by tourists have to be visually extraordinary." Elsewhere he explains that the tourist gaze, which inherently searches for things different than the everyday, can comprise: unique objects, signs, social life in unusual contexts (e.g., in different cultures), familiar tasks in unusual environments, and other things out of the ordinary.[25]

Hiss discusses the concept of simultaneous perception in his book, *The Experience of Place*. He wrote that we all have an underlying awareness of locations hardwired into our systems, whether we are focused on the space, or more likely on a totally separate task at hand.[26] The locations may be noticed subconsciously, or in some cases when the locations are distinct, may be consciously noted.

When two contrasting areas are juxtaposed, the boundary area heightens the visual attentions of people.[27] This may be another reason for the attraction of waterfront areas. The contrast of land and water heightens people's awareness of the environment.

A view of water available from one site or group of sites and not from another, may also serve as a distinguishing characteristic. Tuan suggests that "the feeling of spaciousness feeds on contrast."[28] The feeling of spaciousness that a view of a large body of water may provide is noted more by the user when it is in contrast to dense compact settings. The users' sensitivities are heightened.

Penn's Landing, a public gathering space along the Delaware River, is useful for illustration. The surrounding blocks on the city side are generally low scale, but dense. The water is not visible from most street level locations.

When approaching Penn's Landing over the Walnut Street pedestrian bridge, the boundary of the highway beneath can be both seen and heard. As this is crossed, the view opens up and the water becomes visible. The spaciousness of the scene is heightened through this progression. Without the contrast, Penn's Landing might not feel so spacious, nor the Delaware River so broad.

The sea (and large bodies of water in general) allows horizontality to be experienced in environments filled with verticality. Water allows movement that is not constricted by streets and sidewalks, whether the movement is actually experienced, or just imagined by onlookers along a waterside promenade. Bodies of water may also allow distant, rather than close views of an environment. The horizon line that is infrequently seen within a city may be revealed. The contrast of a natural setting (or at least one minimally altered by man) seen against the man-made city is also exposed.

Gaining the same effect as boundaries of contrasting areas, some specific sites such as certain plazas and atriums, tend to focus our senses on the location. This focus then heightens the sense of differentiation of these sites from surrounding areas. Hiss has discussed Grand Central Station in such a context. "Grand Central not only is easy to experience but also offers a special kind of experience—one that seems to amplify our perceptive reach, allowing us to notice aspects of our mental activity that are normally veiled."[29]

In less striking locales, more subtle levels of differences may be sensed. Jackson describes the underlying similarity of many American landscapes. This similarity, upon further examination, actually reveals differences and deviations, just at a more subtle level requiring a sharpened degree of awareness. This then is a sensitivity gained more by a resident passing the scene frequently, than a visitor only viewing it once or twice.[30]

A seemingly obvious, yet very pertinent statement is that people notice what interests them. The different interests and sensitivities of visitors and locals demonstrates this. The cultural background, personality, and intent of the individual then comes into play, rather than just the physical properties of one site differing from another. Moscardo wrote that "people are most likely to be mindful when they have an opportunity to control and influence a situation, when they believe the available information is relevant to them, and/or when there is variety, novelty or surprise in a situation."[31]

There are an infinite number of characteristics that may be perceived as discernible and thereby useful for visually distinguishing one object from another. Some examples are sets of distinctions that can be made between objects that look stylistically different. There is another in objects with different scale or massing. There is also a more subtle distinction that can be made between objects with a patina and objects without. Different colored surfaces with different degrees of reflectivity (matte or polished surfaces) can also be used to visually distinguish one object from another.

Empirical research on perception indicates that multiple senses, not just the visual, are important for an individual's orientation in an environment.[32] Similarly, multiple senses are involved when discerning a distinct environment. Is the bench you just sat down on warm or cool, rigid or resilient? Is the ground you just walked over hard or soft, smooth or uneven? Sounds such as the wind whistling through a courtyard, voices echoing within a cathedral, or waves breaking on the shoreline may contribute to the perception and understanding of an environment. Smells may also be significant for distinguishing one site from another. For instance, the scent of salt air near the ocean, or flowers in a garden.

Just as visual contrasts serve to heighten awareness of locations, so may contrasts within other sensory inputs. The contrast in feel is apparent when walking from a hard city sidewalk onto a resilient wooden boardwalk. The absence of the sounds of traffic may be more easily noted when passing from a noisy city intersection, over to a quiet waterfront park. Smells may be more easily discerned when contrasting car fumes at that same busy intersection at one moment, with the salt air of the ocean the next.

Contrasts can be lost in time, however. Once on a waterfront promenade for a prolonged period, the distinctness of the area may become less noted. Time allows people to become accustomed to their surroundings, and gradually the novelty wears off.

Incongruities between form and use (typically associated with the particular form) may also heighten attention to a site or series of sites. A church used as a nightclub or condominium is such an example. This may not be easy to sense from the exterior facade alone. However, a specific plaque or sign, and the dress and actions of the people flowing in and out the front door, may emphasize the specialness of the setting. A residence used as a house museum may also attract notice. Again, the physical characteristics of the exterior may not be noticeably distinct from the surrounding structures, but the number of people entering and leaving (compared to a typical residence) make it unusual.

Chapter Two

Predictability and Surprise

Variations within the Predictable

The exteriors of physical structures, their massing, fenestrations, materials, patterns, colors, details, and signage of the buildings, streets, sidewalks and street furniture, all create much of the urban environment we initially sense and give meaning to. They are the physical features that create what is sometimes termed, an "ambience." This ambience will occur in an area (sometimes defined as a district, sometimes not) that contains a consistent set of features that are not consistent in the surrounding areas.[1] These features act as clues that can be sensed by individuals.

"The physical characteristics that determine districts," are described by Lynch as "thematic continuities which may consist of an endless variety of components: texture, space, form, detail, symbol, building type, use, activity, inhabitants, degree of maintenance, topography. In a closely built city such as Boston, homogeneity of facade—material, modeling, ornament, color, skyline, especially fenestration—were all basic clues in identifying major districts."[2]

Order (a discernible pattern) in these landscape features is sensed and then creates a predictable framework within which to judge the environment. "Variations within" this pattern or theme are perceived as adding a level of interest without contradicting the distinct nature of the district. "Variations from" this pattern are perceived as surprise. The balance of order and variety creates the forms that will or will not be perceived as distinct districts.

Too much order creates monotony at one end of the spectrum. This order may distinguish an area from the surrounding areas, but it also may appear unrelenting, contrived, disorienting and uninteresting within.

13

At the other extreme is an area with too much variation. There is no visual identity within it. It lacks a theme to distinguish it from surrounding areas, unless its lack of order can count as an identifying characteristic. This might be the case if all the contiguous areas surrounding it have predictable identities. By comparison with these areas, then, its difference and distinctness might lie in its disorder.[3]

An area with too much variation may also create a type of monotony. It may appear unrelenting and disorienting due to the lack of easily discernible landmarks within it. The area leaves too much room for internal variation, lacking a discernible pattern to vary from. If everything is different from each other, then they are all the same in a way.

In discussing the meanings of differences, Rapoport points out that

> in U.S. suburbs, houses must not be too different—a modern house in an area of traditional houses is seen as an aesthetic intrusion, but the aesthetic conflict mainly has to do both with the meaning of style and with the deviation from the norm. This also applies to excessive uniformity. . . . It is the meaning of the subtle differences within an accepted system that is important in communication group identity, status, and other associational aspects of the environment while accepting the prevailing norms.[4]

Rapoport further wrote that in churches and other buildings of special buildings, "One's attention is first drawn to elements that differ from the context. They thus become noticeable, strongly suggesting that they have special significance."[5]

Referring to buildings from earlier eras compared to contemporary buildings, Alexander indicates that contemporary buildings have too little variety within them. They lack the "special balance between "order" and "disorder"" that these earlier buildings have which he admires. This concept can then be easily projected onto the larger physical fabric as well. Steele feels that "in many instances, modern society is tending to destroy the rich variety of places, replacing them with homogenized efficient settings that have no variety, surprise, or traces of their own history and development."[6]

In a similar vein, Norberg-Schulz suggests that "the modern environment in fact offers very little of the surprises and discoveries which make the experience of old towns so facinating [sic]." He uses the terms "theme" and "variation" to explain how towns grow over time. Through this process a town may remove older structures and add new ones, yet still retain a strong visual identity as a whole.[7]

In his book, *The Evaluative Image of the City*, Nasar mentions a previous 1993 study by Marsh that described preferences (for non-architects) of building types. Buildings with a certain balance of order and variety, those simulating a nineteenth century style were selected. Nasar then surmised that "older buildings and areas may have the preferred mix of order and variety."[8]

It is this case of variety within the distinct that is frequently considered a positive attribute. Simple Philadelphia rowhouses exemplify this quality. They are frequently all brick, yet patterns and details often vary from building to building. Each rowhouse is distinct from its neighbors, yet generally within expectations of what might be there. That is, distinct but not dissonant.

Street layouts may also encompass levels of variety within a distinct framework. Philadelphia exemplifies this with its combination of a planned, orderly grid of streets (laid out in 1682) and an unplanned alleyway system that subdivides this grid. Alan Jacobs, referring to the ubiquitous city grids of many American towns, wrote that the subtleties within an otherwise monotonous pattern are key to orientation and interest for those moving through it.[9] The relative uniformity of a grid or any pattern emphasizes any variation within it. What appears a potentially monotonous grid of streets within Philadelphia at first glance, eventually reveals its variations.

Some of this variation lies in the alleyways. They grew over time, and are more organic than planned. These alleyways subdivide streets at locations that often cannot be predicted. They usually run east-west, but occasionally run north-south. Sometimes one subdivides a major block, sometimes two or none at all. This balance of planned and unplanned, expected and unexpected, rigid and relaxed, contributes to the richness of Philadelphia's streets.

Variations from the Predictable

The concepts of consonance and dissonance, discussed further in the chapter on historical ambience, also relates to variety and surprise within the distinct. Consonance does not necessarily mean uniformity. There can be degrees of variation within a consonant set of structures and the set of structure may still retain a coherent larger identity. A level of variety (variations on a theme) can enrich a distinct area composed of predominantly consonant structures. A small proportion of dissonant structures can provide a level of surprise (the unexpected) within this larger whole.

Sites perceived as dissonant are surprises. The concept of dissonance is that of surprise by radical contrast with the surroundings, like a dilapidated shack amidst a block of elegant mansions, or a single mansion among a multitude of shacks. The setting highlights the differences between it and the object that it surrounds (for better or worse). The distinctness of both the object and the setting are enhanced by the contrast. A single historical building in a dissonant setting of contemporary buildings heightens the sense of distinctness, of separateness of the old building from the new ones.

"Holdouts" are buildings that remain standing while structures that surround them are torn down to allow for typically larger scale construction from the surrounding assembled lots. They exemplify dissonance to an extreme. In the case of holdouts, this contrast is an unwanted result, since the remaining property typically has been held from the developer by an owner that did not wish to sell.

The results of holdouts, in the view of the developer that co-authored the book *Holdouts*, are only negative. He feels that their existence indicate absurdity and signs of greed on the part of individuals retaining those remaining properties. Another view, discussed in the book's preface by Lindsay (which I share) is that holdouts generally add diversity and surprise to the landscape. It does this both in its own remaining existence and in the responses to its existence that new construction surrounding it is forced to make. Lindsay writes, "Some holdouts maintain that by literally standing their ground, they can make as important a contribution to urban life as a new development. The smaller shop or townhouse in the appropriate location, they say, may lend a grace note of diversity to a city's architectural fabric and offer a scale certain commentators term "human.""[10]

A holdout may also provide a physical trace of the previous context of the area, which may then further differentiate that area from its surroundings. The connection to the past for those that used to know the old look of the area and for those new to the area, is also retained.

Holdouts create an element of surprise, the surprise of a remnant of the past, still surviving, showing the passersby an example of how things used to look in the area. It is a radical break, but typically this dissonant element is a small enough proportion of the larger area so as to add an element of surprise rather than confusion into the built environment. It also is an example of the unexpected diversity that cannot be designed into an area, as part of a building code, aesthetic guidelines or pattern language. Rather it requires the benefits and conflicts of time to evolve and gain this visual richness.

Even buildings that hold out, and are then torn down, can leave unexpected imprints on the remaining buildings.[11] Though the dissonant object is gone, some sense a break from the norm remains, such as an unexplained notch in a building that is the negative of the previous building on the site, or a material or detail that is used on the new construction that alluded to the earlier structure.

Examples of surprise may also be found within the larger layout of a city. Philadelphia can be used as an example of surprise, as it was for variety.

Basically any unique element in the predictable framework created by a gridded city can provide a degree of surprise. Examples within Philadelphia's Center City are the green squares interspersed throughout the city grid (e.g., Rittenhouse or Washington Square), or the diagonal cut through the grid (i.e., Benjamin Franklin Parkway). These features provide identity to the localized areas that surround them and orientation for those people passing through the larger city.

Abstractly, on the plans of a map, these areas of surprise can be used to identify the different areas. To those driving or walking through the streets and experiencing the environment more directly, the parks provide open space and resting places in a relatively dense city. They serve as focal points providing identity to their surrounding areas and surprise within the larger framework of Philadelphia's street system.

Within the squares of Philadelphia, the degree of surprise is lessened by the repetition of the number of squares. Elements perceived as extraordinary within a smaller context, may be part of a more predictable pattern at a larger scale. The squares of Philadelphia, within the larger view of Center City, become part of a more predictable "series" of squares.

A balance between order and variety contributes to a rich physical environment. This needs to occur within a district and between districts. If every district is extremely different from every other within a city (i.e. Chinatown, Little Italy, Waterfront, etc.) then the city that these districts lie within, may not hold a distinctive larger character. The city might have too much variety, with a lack of a focus to hold it together in people's minds.

If the entire city lacks internal districts and themes, then it can become monotonous. Rapoport wrote, "Without noticeable differences-contrasts-meaning is more difficult to read."[12] The interest and diversity may exist within it, but the level may be too subtle for the typical short term visitor/tourist. These visitor/tourists have become an integral part of the economic fabric of many cities, and need to be attracted and satisfied during their stays. The challenge, then, is how to "theme" without oversimplifying, so as to keep both visitors and locals satisfied with the right level of interest, with the optimum complexity of the mix.

Variations through Historic Preservation

Preservation, rehabilitation, and restoration, can each contribute to the perceived distinctness of portions of the environment. A group of historical structures may create a distinct larger district. As individual structures, they may add variety or surprise within a district.

Preservation retains the existing historic fabric, focusing on maintenance and repairs. Rehabilitation is more flexible in its approach. It can include elements of preservation and adaptive use.[13]

Restoration involves the retention and adjustment of an original structure to exemplify an earlier period of its historical development. The identity of the structure is then focused on the moment(s) of time that it is visually brought back to.[14] These factors combine to enhance the setting's rarity. This may involve retention of the original use, introduction of a new use that fits within the existing setting, or conversion into a museum demonstrating its earlier use.

Preservation and restoration of structures can be used to enhance distinctness. It is the distinctness of a structure or a visually consistent series of structures, against a backdrop that does not appear similarly historical, that sets it apart. The structure is distinct in its insistence on holding on to past forms (and possibly past functions) while frequently the surrounding structures or districts do not. Where an individual building remains as a holdout, an icon, or anything in between, it frequently creates an element of surprise within the larger urban fabric.

When preservation or restoration involves a series of structures creating a district, whether officially designated or not, it will likely demonstrate a certain level of internal variety, though not necessarily surprise. The internal variety existing among the structures is most likely the result of construction by different builders at slightly different time periods. For restoration in particular, the element of surprise may have been edited out once the various structures were visually brought back to a specific time period. This action, however, may help package the area into a more distinct whole.

Rehabilitation within a larger district may be more difficult to discern as distinct, due to the modifications made to the structures. More extreme variations may exist within this area since it is less constrained. Juxtapositions of entire structures and additions from different time periods, along with different uses, may create an element of surprise within such a district.

The term adaptive use means the retention of an original structure, the facade at the least, and adjustments made to fit a new use. Frequently a by-product (and sometimes a primary goal) of this is the creation of a unique setting. Setting in this usage means the combination of structure with use. The structure or the use individually, may not necessarily be unique. The combination of the two, however, might contribute to the rarity of the overall setting.

Lowenthal argues that adaptive use allows old structures to remain standing. "We refashion antiquities most radically, sometimes altering them beyond recognition, in adapting them to present-day purposes. But without adaptive reuse most old artifacts would soon perish. Had the Parthenon not served variously as a mosque, a harem, even as a powder magazine, it would have succumbed to plunder and decay."[15]

Adaptive use of buildings sometimes creates odd combinations of external forms and internal functions. A few examples within Philadelphia include a restaurant in the external structure of a firehouse (Jack's Firehouse), a clothing store in a mansion (Urban Outfitters), and a drugstore in an old theater (CVS). However, these quirky juxtapositions of form and function may serve to enhance the identity of a particular setting by adding a level of interest or playfulness. Where the exterior may only be slightly distinct from the immediate surroundings, the entire setting of exterior and interior forms and functions creates a strongly distinct and possibly unique package.

These juxtapositions may even become a driving force behind the marketing of a company, providing a distinct image and hopefully a competitive advantage. In the Old City portion of Philadelphia, a real estate company called "Historic Landmarks for Living" has renovated old factories and warehouses into cooperative apartments. The apartments are marketed emphasizing their unique character gained through this adaptive use.[16]

Another example of a company capitalizing on dramatic adaptive use is the Malmaison hotel chain, primarily in Europe. It deliberately concentrates on converting and adapting structures into hotels that were not originally designed as such.[17] One is a converted church, another a converted warehouse, and another a former seamen's mission. The juxtapositions have become part of the marketing strategy of the company. Economics factors may have contributed to the decisions to convert existing structures rather than build new ones. However, it appears that it has been led, at least in part, by an attempt to capitalize on the unique settings that such conversions can yield.

The unique experience of spending a few nights within a converted church or warehouse is part of the selling point for this hotel chain. It differentiates this hotel chain from the competition and becomes part of its corporate identity. Hotel reviews may mention the unique architectural aspects of the hotels. The marketing of the hotel itself uses the slogan: "In a world where everyone wants to be the same - an Hotel that dares to be different."[18]

Chapter Three

Packaging

Introduction

Sites and networks of sites may have their uniqueness and perceived distinctness from surrounding sites intentionally enhanced. Herbert depicts a "balance between conservation and enhancement of a site" that is constantly considered and adjusted in order to compete in the ever more competitive tourism market.[1] In the attempt to broaden the appeal and access for large segments of the population, there is a risk of sacrificing an area's uniqueness, especially if its distinctness from the surrounding area is emphasized with a formulaic approach.

Packaging is a method of gathering together objects to enhance their distinctness. The Oxford English Dictionary has several definitions for the term "package." The most relevant one in terms of describing the packaging of locations for tourist and other visitors is: "Any related group of objects that is viewed or organized as a unit."[2] In this discussion, the objects grouped together are sites within a single location or at multiple locations around an urban area or region.

Packaging is often an integral part of the marketing of a product. The product in this discussion is primarily "the tourist experience." A theme tying together one or more spaces can be used to package various sites. It is an act of simplifying, grouping and setting apart from the surroundings.

Packaging can be done physically, functionally, and/or through stories. For example, bringing a group of buildings "back" to a specific moment in time creates a distinct visual package. An area tied together with a functional cohesiveness like an arts district also creates a package. Tying together a series of discontinuous sites with stories, such as a guidebook listing sites of significance for certain ethnic groups is yet another method of packaging.

The creation of a package begins with the decision of the criteria for organizing and grouping it. The objects within that group either have already been, or need to be marked and named, set off from the surrounding objects. MacCannell describes a concept called sight sacralization. The first stage, naming, involves the marking of the object as distinct from other objects. The second stage, framing, puts the object(s) on display for both their protection and enhancement. [3] Though he discusses it primarily in terms of single sights or views of specific objects (sites), these concepts also hold with multiple, related groupings of objects.

Expanding on this, Stewart writes: "Without marking, all ancestors become abstractions, losing their proper names; all family trips become the same trip—the formal garden, the waterfall, the picnic site, and the undifferentiated sea become attributes of every country." [4]

Packaging also heightens the anticipation and desire of experiencing a location, as it might the opening of a smaller gift. Willis describes how "possession delivers a commodity's use value into the hands of the consumer. Packaging acts to separate the consumer from the realization of use value and heightens his or her anticipation of having and using a particular commodity." [5]

Stories read, heard or seen prior to visiting a site heightens the anticipation. Boniface and Fowler state that "advertising, and the brochure especially, are the cultural bait for a holiday package. Guidebooks may, themselves, provide cultural frameworks to travel." Urry feels that places are chosen in anticipation of pleasure. "Such anticipation is constructed and sustained through a variety of non-tourist practices, such as film, TV, literature, magazines, records and videos, which construct and reinforce that gaze." [6]

There is a distinct inside and outside of the package. What might be experienced inside the package is alluded to in the stories. On actually visiting the location, a photo or souvenir from inside this distinct package can be taken with you beyond its bounds. What is taken with you is both concrete and describable, enjoyed by the individual or shown to others. The experiences related about the visited environment can be recounted through these photos or souvenirs.

MacCannell suggests that "souvenirs are collected by individuals, by tourists, while sights are "collected" by entire societies." Urry offers that "tourism in general and photography in particular serve to organize one's experience of time and space."[7] Whether as an individual or a larger society then, the act of collecting becomes key. The collecting of sites as souvenirs, photos, and experiences becomes part of the game of anticipation and realization involved in tourism.

Marking as Distinct

A consistent visual style within an area will create a package. The look of Society Hill (Philadelphia), Nantucket, and Sante Fe are examples. Whether historical or contemporary, vernacular or contrived, these areas have distinct enough features compared to the areas that surround them that they are perceived as unified areas. This type of package has an internal, integral difference from the surrounding areas. It would likely be discernible standing within the considered area compared to standing in a position outside of it.

By the use of consistent street furniture, signage, canopies, paving, etc., a distinct district or grouping of sites may be created that does not have historical precedent. This method can also enhance the package and distinctness of a district with historical precedence defining it as a unit.

A package can also be formed by wrapping the exterior thereby creating boundaries surrounding it. The artist, Christo, takes the concept of packaging literally, when he wraps large physical spaces such as buildings in a fabric or other clearly visible media. His art involves a literal wrapping and packaging that marks sites and sets them off from the surroundings. They are framed by the boundary created around the object. Attention is brought to these wrapped locations and curiosity is created as to what special things lie within.

Waterfronts, groupings of sites near large bodies of water, have strong boundaries as well. The water's edge defines a clear boundary on one or more sides. That may be a contributing factor to the frequent theming and packaging of waterfronts. The area is inherently set off as different from surrounding areas since a distinct boundary already encircles a portion of the area.

Many inner city highways run either along the water's edge or a block or two inland of it. The boundary is sometimes permeable to the pedestrian, sometimes not. These highways and railroad tracks that now physically cut off many waterfront areas from the main portions of cities, act as boundaries that heighten the sense of separation. A Waterfront/Not Waterfront distinction is clearly made. The bounds of inside/outside of the waterfront package are defined.

Packaging does not need to focus on the visual, however. It can also deal with the functions an area is known for, such as art galleries, jewelry, or electronics stores. The district can be formed as part of a deliberate overall plan (Avenue of the Arts, Phila.), or can occur incrementally over time (Jewelers' Row, Phila.) as is often the case.

A physical cohesiveness can enhance a functional one. New street furniture (including lighting, signage, paving, etc.) has been added to portions of Philadelphia's Broad Street to create this new image of the Avenue of the Arts, since the sites along it are visually diverse. Jewelers' Row, in contrast, has a fairly consistent physical appearance inherent within the various sites. In New York City, Soho is now known functionally for its art galleries and boutiques, while visually is held together by the cast iron warehouses that comprise much of the area. This further enhances its distinctness.

Distinctive decorations may act as symbols for the larger package.[8] Whether a single landmark or distinctive detailing throughout the larger area, the package will be easily conceptualized. More depth and richness may lie within the package, but the distinctness will appear, at first glance anyway, to be fairly simple and obvious.

A series of warehouses along the waterfront may work in a similar manner. No longer needed for their original function, they may be adapted for use as restaurants and retail stores, fulfilling present day demands. Though the functional components tying these sites together is no longer that of storing goods, the new use of retail and restaurants might generate a certain internal functional and visual consistency. The consistency of physical forms will still bind the area together, regardless of the change of use. The visual distinctness of the warehouse, then comes to represent the use of retail shops and restaurants.

A landmark structure or view (e.g., Manhattan skyline, Baltimore Harborplace, Osaka aquarium) may serve as an icon, a marker that stands for the larger whole. The package is defined from the center out, rather than the boundaries that confine it. Landmarks of high imageability, rather than typical street scenes, are represented on postcards and other tourist memorabilia. These symbolic centers represent the larger areas for those newly viewing an area. "A strong trait," Tuan writes, "is made to stand for the whole personality."[9]

As was mentioned previously, just by defining an area as "the waterfront" sets up a distinction between that which is included and excluded from it. The included portions become a package, a bundle of related things, whether the relationships are fact or fiction. Labels and names serve to represent stories. Lippard suggests that "naming is, with mapping and photography, the way we image (and imagine) communal history and identity."[10]

An initial simplification is made by naming an area. By that act it is conceptually removed from the rest of the city or countryside. It may remain otherwise indistinguishable from the rest of the city physically, socially, economically and politically. Hough wrote that "the names people give to places imbue them with a symbolic significance that unnamed places lack."[11]

A single site may be marked with a plaque or sign indicating its significance in comparison to the surrounding sites. "The plaques on the sides of buildings are signifiers that otherwise mundane buildings are worthy of being gazed upon."[12] This conceptual marking continues with longer and more detailed stories, whether verbal or written.

Stewart discusses narratives generated by sets of objects and sets of objects generated by narratives.[13] Beyond sets of souvenirs, this concept can also include sets of visitor sites. Where academic interpretation may be led by the objects themselves, marketing stories may actually generate the sets of objects. These are not clear cut divisions, however. A narrative, whether done for marketing purposes or for more academic interpretations may be used to tie various sites into a coherent story or package.

Descriptions of areas by word of mouth, marketing brochures, or academic texts, influences people's perceptions of them. An area described as an artistic hotbed for example, may truly be so, or may just be packaged as such to attract certain groups of people. Form, function and description frequently do overlap however, to reinforce and strengthen various packages.

Packaged Networks

The stories, as well as the selection of objects chosen to have stories told about, have inherent biases. Simplifying is a natural way to introduce a space to individuals. It allows an easily grasped initial understanding of an area. Festival marketplaces do this when they clean up rough edges that do not conform to the simplified notion of a place they wish to present. Lippard feels that "because of our social ease with simulacra, we are more drawn to a created image of what we think a place "was like then" than to any accurate rendition of other times, with their bad smells and rough sights."[14]

Any location or series of locations that has been selected and interpreted has been simplified and packaged. Tunbridge and Ashworth declare that "selected resources are converted into products through "interpretation." This could be described as "packaging," as long as this is understood to mean not merely marginal enhancement but the selection, assembly and integration of the chosen resources in an appropriate mix with the aim of deliberately creating a particular product."[15]

The selection of sites deemed worthy of names and stories always has a degree of bias within it. Lowenthal put this succinctly when he said: "What heritage does not highlight it often hides."[16] The selection of sites considered worth naming and highlighting may be easily accepted as a given for many observers, ignoring the inherent biases embedded within those initial decisions.

Striking architecture and locations associated with famous names or patriotic associations are among the core group of tourist attractions. Shopping locations, which have always been a key element of urban life in one form or another, are also frequently selected as sites worth visiting in guidebooks and other tourist literature.[17]

In describing packaging in general, Willis notes that it "catches the consumer's eye, even though as a phenomenon of daily life, it is all but invisible."[18] In the same vein, the packaging of sites as tourist attractions and generally significant locations is also ubiquitous, and therefore possibly more difficult to see or notice.

The sites selected and classified as tourist attractions frequently become the baseline from which tourists choose sites to be visited. These pre-selected sites become part of the framework of a tourist experience. The attentions of tourists are then focused on the sites and their interpretation, and away from the framework.

Within any named and packaged site, certain decisions of its interpretation will be made. Boniface and Fowler write, "There is nearly always someone with claims of some sort on any piece of land and, as we are increasingly learning, interpreting that piece of land is increasingly a sensitive matter." Herbert questions if there is "a case for accurate, statutory statements to make clear what a site represents—almost an intellectual health warning." Possibly richer more complex packages, multiple tours and interpretations could address these issues that naturally result from the simplifying aspects of packaging.[19]

Sites exist in multiple networks. A restaurant in an old warehouse along the waterfront may in one context be part of a revitalized waterfront. In another context it may be listed in a restaurant guidebook for a particular type of food. In another guidebook it may be listed as being housed in an architecturally significant warehouse demonstrating a particular type of brickwork. This restaurant, as well as all other sites in the city, exists in overlapping networks of context.

Each of the contexts is true and each individually tends to simplify things by isolating them. In one context the restaurant is thought of and listed in a guidebook as one portion of waterfront warehouse district (adapted to new uses) distinct from the rest of the city. In another context, possibly another guidebook, it is part of a network of restaurants across the entire city. In the third part it is part of the architecturally significant sites of the city.

This categorization (and simplification) may be a necessary feature of modern day tourism, particularly for dealing with any type of short term or infrequent visitor that needs to make selections quickly. Slowly learning the intricacies of an area over time is not a realistic option for many visitors, so guidebooks and other methods of pre-selected locations and groupings are used.

Of first time visitors, Steele writes: "We seldom come to a setting completely cold, but acquire images from various sources. In the first few moments there, we have a sense of place that is formed from both the actual setting and our built-up images through which we "know" it in advance and at a distance."

These images may be acquired through guidebooks, mass media, literature, etc. The inherent risk is that we might be blind to "the richness of what is actually there. We are looking so hard for what we are supposed to see that we do not allow new unexpected features to emerge."[20]

By mapping only the highlights, a distinct network is created. This seems to pull specific buildings, shops, restaurants, etc., out of their natural context of the local setting of nearby stores, buildings and neighborhood and into a simplified almost pre-chosen set of elements comprising the tourist city. Willis suggests that "just as the path is posted with warnings— "Stay on Trail" —so too does the map function to reduce our experience of canyon, woods, or meadow to its designated reality."[21]

The packaging of a commodity is usually fairly clear cut, with distinct boundaries of inside and outside the package. For larger objects (i.e. sites), the boundaries do not necessarily have to be as hard edged. A large mall may have these distinct boundaries, when you first open the front door and encounter the air conditioned spaces. Festival marketplaces, such as South Street Seaport or Baltimore's Harborplace, may have less distinct boundaries, at least in terms of visibility to the user and passerby. The edges are more permeable, not as sharply defined.

Taking this idea of permeable boundaries of packages one step further is the packaging of networks of tourist attractions. These networks are sometimes contiguous, sometimes not. The packaging of sites in guidebooks, basically the locations that are mentioned as worth seeing, and what categories they are grouped by (e.g., functional, visual, historical time period), all create a conceptual package for the consumer, the visitor or tourist.

An example of an area packaged by function is "Museum Mile" in Manhattan. A functional theme, by the label "museum" is created in the minds of the users. It is not the most common building use in the rather large geographic area of that "mile" of Manhattan. The labeling however, creates a package. It remains a very permeable one since the bounds may not be strongly demarcated. When traveling from one museum to another, the permeability is further felt. Other sites functioning as residences, offices, boutiques and drug stores, are encountered along the way. There is an inherent wandering in and out of the conceptual package. The packaging is therefore permeable, and the richness (variety and choices) of the city come through.

When in a car, bus, or taxi between specific museums, the spaces in between are passed by quickly in transit. The sites experienced more fully are the museums themselves. The route is still permeable, but the network of attractions visited is more simplified and pulled apart from the complexities of the larger city. If the connections between various sites are made by walking, then the permeability is even more easily experienced.

Tourist destinations can also be packaged across an entire city or region. Boorstin writes that "the rise of the tourist was possible . . . when attractive items of travel were wrapped up and sold in packages (the "package tour")." There has been a shift over time from individual traveler to mass tourism which keeps the tourist in an insulated bubble.[22] The tour bus or similar concept of visiting sites, envelops and insulates a visitor as he or she travels from site to site, never experiencing the complexities of the city in an unsheltered environment. The city is experienced as a simplified network of tourist sites.

These non-contiguous sites can also be experienced by a visitor in a more self determined manner. On/off sightseeing buses in many cities allow the same sites to be linked, but more freedom of which shall be chosen and how long they will be experienced for. Though the simplified network of tourist attractions remains, the package of tourist sites in the city again becomes more permeable.

Within Philadelphia's Center City, the "Phlash" tourist vans are an example of packaging the tourist destinations of a city in such a manner. They are geared primarily for the tourist, and so stop at pre-defined tourist destinations. They connect the tourist sites of Philadelphia into a tight network of locations, and by doing so, simplify the city. The choices of which sites to see, and how long to see them are left open to the visitor.

The places between the designated tourist sites of Philadelphia are likely lost to the visitor, and only seen through the window of the van. This jitney service was designed to make Philadelphia more tourist friendly, and does so. Unfortunately, much of the complexity of the city, both good and bad, is sacrificed in the process. It is the compromise that packaging offers.

Walking or taking a city bus opens up the sites in between (non-designated as tourist attractions). The packaging of the city may then be unravelled and the complexities revealed, but possibly more complexity than most visitors' desire during a brief visit to the city.

Boston's longstanding Freedom Trail is a red line on the sidewalk that threads through the city and strings together a history package. Since 1995, markings (colored dots) on the sidewalks of lower Manhattan try to link together about 50 sites of interest under four different groupings, on trails totalling 4½ miles.[23] These self-guided walking tours sponsored by Heritage Trails New York are meant to encourage tourism and integrate it into the existing fabric of lower Manhattan.

They both connect visitor attractions of the city (generally historical ones) through physical markings on the city itself. They create long linearly connected packages that thread through portions of the city. Along these routes, individuals are also led past other portions of the city that do not necessarily fit the categorization of the themed, history packages. The wider contexts are therefore (albeit inadvertently) shown. In general, most any walking tour of a city will have a similar effect.

Whether using a tour guide, a guidebook, or an audio tour, a theme is set up and focused on. The points of interest are not necessarily isolated from the surrounding areas, however. You would likely pass by or see in the distance, locations outside of the theme or package even when you follow the prescribed path. It is permeable packaging that you can easily move in and out of. You can turn off the recorder, close the guidebook, leave the cab, and easily walk away on your own path.

Multiple interpretive tours of a given location, whether a single tourist attraction or larger portion of the city, are one way to retain the security of packaging, while revealing the richer complexities of a site. These interpretations may be encapsulated in guidebooks, offered in the form of audio tours (headphones and tape players) or given by tour guides.

The guidebook *Six Heritage Tours of Lower East Side*, covers six separate tours within the same bounded area. Each focuses on a different ethnic history.[24] This single guidebook attempts to acknowledge the complexities and multiple readings of sites within a single portion of Manhattan. It is an attempt to overcome the overt simplification that Alexander has described as inherent in the way people tend to structure the world. Single locations can and do have multiple histories and are part of multiple networks. As a guidebook, it still creates a very selective grouping of sites, but presents them as part of a lattice, rather than a simple tree.

The multiple interpretation method provides an attempt to serve the tourist with limited time by highlighting limited sights, yet provide him or her with less simplistic, more challenging interpretation of an area. Moscardo relates that interpretation of historical sites now try "to produce mindful visitors; visitors who are active, interested, questioning and capable of reassessing the way they view the world." To accomplish this, he suggests that "a structure underlying the content or organization of the exhibits, or cognitive orientation system, combined with novelty, surprise or conflict, will induce mindfulness and result in learning."[25]

This attempt at richer, more complex interpretations are meant to allow deeper understandings, insights and enjoyment for those who visit the sites, and open the packages. Furthermore, the underlying structure of a fixed physical site combined with a variety of interpretations are the same basic building blocks suggested in the previous chapter to create a rich physical environment. It is an interpretive combination of predictability and surprise.

Waterfront Districts

Predictability can include both order and variety. Surprise lies outside of predictability. There is a balance that is sought between predictability and surprise for people to feel attracted to a location. The lure may be of slight variety, a minor surprise, but not of total unpredictability. Boniface and Fowler feel that "difference has a place, but for many people the crucial element in a touristic experience is that it should not threaten, or allow them to feel uncomfortably deprived of the comforts of home." The authors discuss how tourist brochures promote exotic, distinctive locations, while at the same time offering the comforts of home, in nice new hotels, etc.[26]

When a visitor enters a city to sightsee and the waterfront is listed as an attraction, certain assumptions of what might be found there are typically made. In the U.S., these might include some type of walkway fronting the water and providing a view, seating and areas to relax in, restaurants or cafes, possibly maritime museums or aquariums, shopping areas, and frequently a historical ambience created in part by conserved or preserved structures. Though these areas may be distinct from their immediate surroundings in appearance, they may not be unique compared to other waterfronts.

Many different waterfront areas have certain historical similarities. These similarities of shipping histories, and early commercial and industrial uses may still exist either in function, stories, or in physical remnants. They frequently have influenced the new package being created for locals or visitors.

South Street Seaport for example is packaged using historical forms from structures that have been conserved or recreated in the area. A grouping of functions focusing on retail store shopping and eating are overlaid onto this. Finally seafaring stories are used to further package and enhance the area. These stories include the educational component based on the history of the port through the Seaport Museum, explanatory signs within the complex, and marketing literature capitalizing on the theme.

The same type of themed areas in different geographic locations can create a type of predictability for those individuals whose travels include many waterfront cities (regionally, nationally, or internationally). Sorkin believes that "the urbanism of Disneyland is precisely the urbanism of universal equivalence. In this new city, the idea of distinct places is dispersed into a sea of universal placelessness as everyplace becomes destination and any destination can be anyplace."[27]

There is an inherent contradiction in attempting to replicate or create a formula for executing successful urban design, when an element of that formula involves uniqueness. The similarity of a number of waterfronts that have tried to repeat successful festival marketplace formulas highlights the risks of losing the uniqueness of a site.[28] Examples include a number of sites developed (or influenced) by the Rouse Corporation, such as Boston's Fanueil Hall, Baltimore's Harborplace, New York City's South Street Seaport, and Osaka's Tempozan Village. There are attractions that many people enjoy at each of these sites, as well as differences in the treatment of each waterfront. Still, there is little surprise of what attractions may lie within, if any others of this set of international waterfronts have been visited.

Tunbridge and Ashworth describe this paradox:

> The very universality of this resource exploitation gives rise to stereotypical outcomes in the broad components utilised and new functions accommodated, so that underlying the detailed sense of place now so strongly promoted there is increasingly a certain sense of "deja vu". Whatever the dimensions of the post-modern city as a whole, the tourist-historic waterfront would seem to command a prominent position in this evolving identity.[29]

Finding a waterfront/entertainment district treated very similarly to another, though in a totally different city, can be somewhat disorienting. The identity of the waterfront district within its particular city is distinct, but in the larger view of multiple waterfront districts, its identity is less clear.

A certain minimum difference is useful between these waterfront locations. If no significant difference is discernible, why not just visit the aquarium and waterfront back home? How widely traveled a visitor is, may be the cue for how distinct a waterfront is found to be, and how much of a lure that distinctness is for the individual. In Osaka, though certain aspects such as the tall ship, the plaza and the aquarium have strong similarities to Baltimore, for those who have not been to Baltimore, Osaka remains a distinct, and even unique place.

Sites may be marked, grouped and packaged. The act of packaging simplifies and demonstrates biases in its nature. It also can serve to attract consumers, visitors to a site, building anticipation, creating the desire in people to collect (visit and experience) these sites. This commodification, using sites as objects in a collection, is not necessarily a flawed use of the physical environment. Referring more specifically to heritage sites, Herbert claims: "Whatever reason or chance brought them there, many sites seek to inform, to educate or to make the visit more interesting by conveying information in a variety of legible and easily assimilated ways."[30]

Chapter Four

Historical Ambience

Introduction

The concept of historical ambience will be described as a subset of the concepts of distinctness and uniqueness. Historical attributes are frequently highlighted to emphasize a location's distinctness from other locations. This is particularly evident in the world of tourism and attracting people in a world market. The importance of sites contributing to a historical ambience goes beyond that of attracting and satisfying exclusively tourists. People frequently enter a situation with a set of motives, such as business person, shopper, and tourist combined.[1]

Maccannell, in his book *The Tourist,* states that ""the tourist" is one of the best models available for modern-man-in-general." He goes on to say that "the progress of modernity ("modernization") depends on its very sense of instability and inauthenticity. For moderns, reality and authenticity are thought to be elsewhere: in other historical periods and other cultures, in purer, simpler lifestyles."[2] The lure of the historical, therefore, is relevant for a wide range of the population.

At one level the attraction of a building or environment may be functional, by what is actually offered at the site. At another level the attraction may be the result of its location in space. Is it located near or along a convenient route for people? The lure of a particular site may also be aesthetic.

An additional criterion, however, is that of the historical. Does it offer some level of continuity and familiarity to the user? Lowenthal writes, "Beleaguered by loss and change, we keep our bearings only by clinging to remnants of stability. . . . Mourning past neglect, we cherish islands of security in seas of change."[3]

These "islands of security" may include everyday structures and environments that have been designated as having historic value by the experts, or those left officially unacknowledged and unprotected but still clearly representative of the past.

Does the site evoke the past in a way to support some communal memories? Nuryanti describes each site as having unique attributes, "but heritage, although its meaning and significance may be contested, reinterpreted and even recreated, is shared by all."[4]

This essay will explore the concept of historical ambience, look at reasons why certain sites may serve as lures and discuss how they may be perceived by the public. It will also examine how the historical sites are displayed using either consonance or dissonance with the surroundings.

Concept of Historical Ambience

Ambience is defined in the Oxford English Dictionary as "Environment, surroundings; atmosphere. The Fr. Form ambience is used in Art for the arrangement of accessories to support the main effect of a piece." Merriam-Webster defines it as "a feeling or mood associated with a particular place, person, or thing: atmosphere."[5] The term ambience will be used within this essay as an atmosphere associated with a particular environment. It may be a single location or series of locations. Elements within the environment support the particular ambience being created.

The ambience discussed herein has an evolving life. It is not an objective state of a physical environment, but the subjective viewing of that environment over time by an individual. It may begin before a person ever physically visits a site, formed during an initial virtual visit through the descriptions of others. These initial impressions can be created from the images (words, sounds, or pictures) of what might be expected in this type of environment from marketing, documentary sources, comments of friends, etc.

As Steele points out, even if the individual may never have physically visited a particular site, still fantasies of what life might have been like in that setting are projected onto it. Tuan describes a similar sensation, "When the tourist steps into an old city he feels he has moved back in time."[6]

An ambience is felt strongly when visiting a location for the first time, as a first impression. It exists, though less powerfully, during multiple visits to the location, and remains as memory after those visits are complete. This ambience in the earliest stages of a persons consciousness may tend to dominate the perceptions and understanding of a location. As actual visits to a location occur over time and multiply, the ambience recedes to the background as the location takes on richer meanings based on experience. Once these visits are complete, the ambience takes on a larger significance again. The specific details of experiences may recede, but the general impressions of the area again come to the fore.

Urban ambience, waterfront ambience, rural ambience, historical ambience—these all might be considered initial perceptual cues for a person entering an area. It serves as a frame of reference for the viewer. This frame then relates back in the person's mind to previous experience in either that particular area or an area with seemingly similar characteristics drawn from personal memories.

The historical ambience referred to is an environment creating the effect of a historical atmosphere. The term "historical" is used rather than "historic" to connote that it is not necessarily tied to a specific recognized historic event, but still is clearly from the past. It is noticeable from the arrangements of historic structures, accents and landscape features. Historical in this context means non-contemporary in appearance, apparently from an earlier era. It is being focused on as a subconscious simple initial distinction that would be made in visiting an area. It can be perceived without expert knowledge. It is a basic first stage of understanding of an area.

Lowenthal distinguishes between history and heritage as follows: "History strives to know as much of the past as well as possible; heritage is helped by imprecise impression and sketchy surmise." He goes on to explain that "attachment to heritage depends on feeling and faith, as opposed to history's ascertained truths. Lack of hard evidence seldom distresses the public at large, who are mostly credulous, undemanding, accustomed to heritage mystique."[7]

Nasar describes how "historical content may be authentic or not. If observers consider a place historical, it has historical content to them."[8] This notion of heritage as a sketchy, possibly imprecise history meshes well with the notion of historical ambience, imprecise yet powerful.

Initial impressions do count with the environment around us. They may determine, as a visitor especially, if we make a first step into an area. Are we intrigued? Do we feel safe? Do our previous associations regarding an area (with a similar ambience) promote positive connotations and expectations?

There are many further classifications describing more subtle under-standings of an urban area to be made beyond the initial impression of historical or contemporary. Within either broad category might be further breakdowns such as gritty or urbane, rural or urban, monumental or quaint. Ambience is being used to describe a cohesive set of impressions. Basically there are a series of projections that a person places over an area to begin to form a series of expectations of what might be there: coffee shops or sidewalk cafes, small side streets or contemporary atriums, danger or safety.

Whether gritty or urbane is described as an ambience in itself in lieu of historical, or as descriptors within the larger umbrella of historical ambience, there is essentially a layering of meanings and understandings that is gained when experiencing a location. Tuan suggests that "what begins as undifferentiated space becomes place as we get to know it better and endow it with value."[9] An ambience may contribute to that transition.

Physical materials used, forms, scales and uses all may affect the initial distinction between contemporary or historical. As the under-standing of a viewer experiencing the space deepens, this initial ambience may gradually fall away to allow specific experiences and knowledge of individual locations to substitute for atmospheric qualities. Of this building up of understanding, Lynch writes, "Nothing is experienced by itself, but always in relation to its surroundings, the sequences of events leading up to it, the memory of past experiences."[10]

Imagine you are visiting Society Hill in Philadelphia for the first time using a guided tour. Possibly after one tour your understanding is focused on eighteenth century residences. It reconfirms the expectations from the tourist brochures that described in words and pictures a historical ambience reminiscent of the eighteenth century. On another tour you focused on the ethnic enclaves of the nineteenth century and a third tour on the twentieth century redevelopment plans. Finally you visit the home of a friend living in the area to see a newly renovated eighteenth century interior with a distinctly contemporary kitchen.

Even within the architectural focuses of these various visits, the viewer's understanding of the area builds and the simplicity and generalizations that the eighteenth century historical ambience first hinted at becomes confirmed or refuted. The imagined place becomes a real place with added meanings and associations. The frozen time period alluded to in the first images and impressions starts to fit within a larger architectural, social, political and economic context.

The most recent visit may update your understanding of the current situation of Society Hill as a residential area for the well to do. You may then realize that these buildings that look old on the outside may actually be new on the inside. The friend you visited may point out difficulties involved in maintaining an old building. The same geographic area is taking on new meanings. The historical ambience (whether you initially perceived it as eighteenth century or just generally historical) served as an initial lure, and still provides a cohesion and enjoyment while strolling the streets. The first impressions remain, but recede to the background.

The ambience of the area is gradually overlaid by a series of experiences and more distinct places within this historic area. Lippard proposes that "history known is a good thing, but history shared is far more satisfying and far reaching. The layered history of words and places is barely visible to the outsider, and less and less visible even to the insider."[11]

The first impression, a basic initial ambience, may tap into shared cultural memories, a shared sense of the past. It is not shared by all, but by many who view the same scene. The more first hand knowledge and direct experience, the more personal an individual's judgment of a place may become. The ambience of the area is gradually overlaid by a series of experiences and an understanding of finer distinctions within this historic area.

It is as if a scene is being looked at from the test lenses used in eye exams. The first view is initially out of focus so only general impressions of an area can be discerned. The scene is gradually pulled into focus, with every visit serving as a new lens. Eventually details are perceived and more subtle distinctions between different areas of the scene are revealed.

This ambience is from the viewpoint of the person experiencing the environment. Therefore, the concept of ambience does not initially distinguish between actual age of structures, but rather perceived age. Does it appear historical, encompassing whatever qualities the viewer associates with that particular ambience?

With any type of preservation (deliberate or not) certain selections are made of what to keep and what to remove, what era to "bring a building back to" and what era to ignore. Historical ambience points to the fact that it does not appear contemporary, no more, no less. The particularly decisions made in attaining this ambience may be made through preservation done of entire structures, or of exteriors and not interiors or through retaining an original function at a location though the structure may be new. These all retain only slices of a fuller history, pointers to prior times. Lynch suggests that "it is the sense of depth in an old city that is so intriguing. The remains uncovered imply the layers still hidden."[12]

Historical ambience describes both the intentional and unintentional preservation of environments, whereby a sense of age can be perceived by the average user of this environment. This notion of ambience differs from the more formal definitions of preservation as defined by guidelines created by experts. More formal definitions of sites worthy of historic preservation typically dwell on the history of the site rather than the memories the site evokes. Criteria used to judge the value of a site or series of sites includes rarity of form, fame of the designer, or significance of an event that occurred at that location. For example, the National Register's criteria for evaluating significance include properties:

> A. That are associated with events that have made a significant contribution to the broad patterns of our history; or
> B. That are associated with the lives of significant persons in our past; or
> C. That embody the distinctive characteristics of a type, period, or method of construction, or that represent the work of a master, or that possess high artistic values, or that represent a significant and distinguishable entity whose components may lack individual distinction; or
> D. That have yielded or may be likely to yield, information important in history or prehistory.[13]

Intentional preservation through the creation of official landmark designations and historic districts are one way of laying the groundwork for a historical ambience to be perceived. Unintentional preservation by minimal intervention over the years without any formal designations may also form an area perceived to have a historical ambience.

There would likely be noticeable differences between these, yet both may be considered historical. Deliberately preserved areas tend to have a higher level of repair. Areas not deliberately preserved may contain certain signs of age, but also may contain more stylistic variations and a less cohesive look. It may not be visually frozen in time and therefore its distinctness from the surroundings may not be as apparent. It may, however, have a stronger visual continuity over time allowing a range of different styles and moments in history to be represented.

There are always some indications of age in an environment that are visible to the observer. Sometimes it looks old, sometime new. Sometimes the true age is revealed by certain objects, sometimes it misleads. Old can look newer by restoration that may remove any patina of age. New can be designed to look old, through style and occasionally through the application of an artificial patina.

Ambience deals with physical indicators and expectations that the particular set of indicators suggests to people. The expectations that you may have associated with a particular ambience may be proved or disproved, enhanced or diminished as your understanding increases. The power of the initial ambience may gradually become just a subtle aura, but some of those initial impressions remain.

Perceptions of Age

What are the perceptual cues that allow people to distinguish a contemporary area from a historic one? Though it may be a case of "you know it when you see it," this section will try to break it down into a series of possible indicators.

Some possible indicators for a historical ambience are: styles associated with distinctly earlier eras (including scales of overall massing); detailing of the visible facades; building materials reflective of another era (such as brick or wood). This includes unevenness of color or texture (indicative of minimal reliance on machinery in production and construction); signs of weathering (such as staining and deterioration due to runoff or pollution); mature vegetation in the landscape (such as a full grown oak trees rather than a spindly sapling).

The style of the exterior may show the age of the building. The degree of accuracy with which this can be read is heavily dependent on the background knowledge of how experienced the observer is in reading building styles.

The scale of the building also may serve as a clue, with larger structures and larger building footprints frequently a sign of more recent construction. A first clue to an observer, as to the existence of a holdout from an earlier era, may be the scale. For example, a two-story building in a sea of high rises may suggest the relative disparity in ages.

The knowledge of the observer lets him or her differentiate between different building styles. An architect or other trained observer might be able to date many international style high rises (possibly by the decade, if not the year) through slight changes in building materials or window and facade detailing. An untrained observer might not discern these subtleties when looking at a building, and consequently might not interpret an older international style building as being from a significantly different time period as a contemporary structure.

The differences in styles before the modern movement (international style) and after, forms a more easily perceived dividing line for much of the public between sites considered "historical" and those more contemporary. A style clearly understood as new is needed to be able to mentally place another style as historical.

Certain building details, combining building materials in a way that may contribute to a recognizable style, may hint at building age as well. Large portions of flat continuous surfaces may appear more modern than more highly articulated facades.

A brick wall that is flat, with minimal indentations or projections, as is frequently done on curtain walls today, may not age as gracefully (with what is commonly perceived as a "patina") as an old style wall with a greater complexity of patterns, projections and indentations. This surface complexity helps allow the weathering over time to become but one more level of complexity on top of the existing forms. In the case of a large flat surface of a homogeneous material (frequently of recent vintage), the weathering may appear more as signs of dirt, lack of maintenance and neglect.[14]

Details of the joining of different building elements or details visible within the finishes and forming of the materials themselves may indicate a measure of crafting by hand or by machine. Indications of being crafted by hand often may be read as a sign of age. Indications of being assembled or finished with machine-like precision and consistency may be read as having a more recent construction date. Jackson felt that "the handmade article was therefore doubly satisfying: it indicated that the iniquitous factory system had been bypassed, and it offered visible evidence of the process of creation in the mark of the tool."[15]

Certain materials, such as stone and brick, concrete or vinyl, small or large expanses of glass or exposed stainless steel, are frequently hints as to the age of a building. Knowledge of the use of these materials may tighten the estimation on the time period of construction. Knowing a material such as concrete was not used in Philadelphia prior to a certain date, or brick was not used in Yokohama after a certain date may provide clues to an observer if aware of these facts.

The use of a particular material does not necessarily restrict the assumption of the age of a structure to a specific time period. For example, the use of glass block has gone in and out of fashion since its inception. Therefore, knowledge of stylistic trends may also provide clues as to construction dates.

Brick and mortar bonds may be perceived as indicative of different time periods as well. Flemish bond brick is indicative of colonial construction in the USA. Within an area such as Society Hill, Flemish bond may now be used in contemporary construction to evoke the historical and relate to older surrounding examples.

Materials themselves age differently over time. As a material becomes more processed and highly manufactured, it frequently loses internal natural variations and become more homogeneous. The uniformity of many recent, highly processed materials means that a change over time such as weathering, will be accentuated as a break in that uniformity.

Natural or only slightly processed materials show remains of their previous state. Unpainted wood shows it had an earlier history as a tree. You look at one object and you see a previous one in it—dual states. Painted wood that still reveals the uneven surface graining patterns displays this as well. The more natural their state, the more built-in unevenness and imperfections are inherent in the material itself. Therefore, materials such as wood and stone can add a certain visual complexity and richness to a structure or product in and of itself.

Alexander declares that a quality building "must be made, at least in part, of those materials which age and crumble."[16] More complex massing, shaping and detailing may also be done, but the material itself offers an inherent richness.

A narrow definition of weathering involves the wearing away and reduction of the surface of a material by wind, water, and the elements in general over time. I will use the term weathering more broadly, to incorporate the concepts of patina or accumulated dirt or pollution within its definition.

The Oxford English Dictionary defines "patina" as "a film or incrustation produced by oxidation on the surface of old bronze, usually of a green colour and esteemed as an ornament. Hence extended to a similar alteration of the surface of marble, flint, or other substances."[17] Patina is a natural, gradual alteration of the surface of a material by the elements in what is commonly perceived of in a positive sense.

Dirt, pollution, or other layers of material may cover (slightly or dramatically) the surface of a material. There is no single reading, however, of the same site. For example a recent cleaning of the ceiling of the Sistine Chapel raised controversy. The patina of age was removed during the cleaning, making it appear newer than it had in centuries. This lack of patina on a historic artwork by Michaelangelo initially surprised many who saw it. It may be read as a positive patina of age or as a sign of lack of maintenance on a surface. It may reflect the interpretations of the individual, which will partially be derived from his or her cultural background as well.

Many natural materials upon aging, gradually get dirtier, but they already show variations within the material so it is not as noticeable. Wear and weathering possibly even enhances and highlights some aspect of natural materials. Copper (bronze) oxidizes into what is frequently considered an improved finish over its original shiny appearance. Stone walls can look more permanent (and historical) and less "brand new" with some signs of weathering showing on its surfaces.

At the level of smaller objects, a wood table can become burnished with the oils of people touching it enhancing the grain. Leather jackets may look better to many eyes with distress marks from age. More processed materials may also have some of these qualities. Waxed canvas is an example of a processed material that may look better to many with age and use. One or two creases in the fabric may look unintentional, but many combine to form a pattern. These signs of age overlaid on top of original surfaces may be read as signs of a historical ambience, a positive appearance of age.

The result of time and the elements on a material is usually a softening of edges of the material and a more "natural" appearance. Whether the eventual appearance is preferred or not, the surrounding environment has begun to integrate a man-made object into its domain. Mostafavi and Leatherbarrow propose that "in the process of subtracting the "finish" of a construction, weathering adds the "finish" of the environment." They explain more fully, "In the time after construction, buildings take on the qualities of the place wherein they are sited, their colors and surface textures being modified by and in turn modifying those of the surrounding landscape."[18]

Nature, therefore, is related to the age of appearance of a structure or a scene. In his early study, Lynch noted that in "the landscape features of the city: the vegetation or the water, were often noted with care and pleasure." Nasar discusses a consistent preference shown for nature in a number of studies. He states that it might be due to the forms themselves or the uses that people associate with these forms.[19]

Possibly, structures look more historic when they are more integrated with nature. Whether nature has surrounded its base (suburban house) or climbed its walls (ivy covered walls) or surrounds and frames a built form (large trees in foreground or background). Possibly the sea acts in a similar manner to a mature grove of trees in this sense. A view of the water evokes a feeling of age, permanence and natural cycles of time.

Trees may provide a compelling clue to age. The age of the tree can be read through size and shape: the taller, the thicker, the more gnarled, the older the tree. The tree can then reflect back onto the surroundings. An initial assumption may be made that certain trees may have been planted during construction of the adjacent structures. For example, the age of a suburban community may be easier to initially judge for the typical observer, by the size of the trees and plantings than by the styles of the houses.

There can be extremes in weathering or lack of it, that may affect people's judgements. Too clean and perfect may lead to a sense of disbelief in the historical validity of the structures by the experts. For the general public the perceptions could be different however. Possibly the initial disbelief when confronted with areas looking pristine is not as much of an issue. A historical ambience may have been created that they enjoy without the secondary distinction of believable or not.

The opposite level of repair—that of appearing dirty or un-kempt—may exclude an area from having perceived value as a historical ambience for the general public. As the appearance crosses over from minimally maintained to more dramatically abused, showing signs of abandonment, neglect, and possible danger, it would be on the other side of the threshold of acceptability.

The overriding perception of a street may rely more on perceptions of state of repair than on judgments of historical or contemporary. These may be read as cues to safety by people. Judgments of safety, related to self-preservation, must first be met. Once the safety threshold has been crossed and it is felt safe by the viewer, then other evaluations such as historical or contemporary ambience can follow.

The more ambiguous category is that of safe, but not well cared for. This lack of maintenance may sway an individual's opinions as to the historical value of the place. The perception might be that if the local residents and owners do not care about maintaining their physical environment, maybe it is not really an important location. There does seem to be some precondition of importance to locations considered to have a historical ambience. It does not have to be monumentally important, but at least must appear a somewhat valued environment.

Tuan believes that "culture and experience strongly influence the interpretation of environment."[20] Whether a person grew up in the city or the suburbs or the country may be a factor in judging whether a site is judged as well maintained or neglected. National backgrounds may also be a strong factor. The level of cleanliness and repair of streets and public spaces is higher in Japan than much of the USA. The expectations of street cleanliness and repair for Japanese, therefore, may be different than for Americans. Possibly a Japanese may rate a space as shabby and unacceptable, while an American might read it as historic. The threshold between well maintained and neglected, does not necessarily lie at a single point for each culture, but also varies according to the individual.

Lure of Historical Elements

This research stems from my initial interests in understanding the attraction that certain urban environments, frequently not contemporary in design, had and have as destinations for travel and for places of residence. The historic preservation movement has gone from minor to mainstream in the last 30 years in the USA. Tourist destinations in the historic cores of European cities such as Prague, Paris, Florence, London, and Venice have been flourishing for years (and centuries in some cases).

In the USA, Boston has been luring visitors for years by emphasizing its historical roots and rich traditional architecture, as have cities and neighborhoods throughout the country. Flipping through a guidebook of Boston, historical attractions from old churches to reenactments of the Boston Tea Party to the rowhouses of the Back Bay fill many of the pages trying to lure the average visitor. Jackson wrote that part of the lure is nostalgic, idealizing the time before our individual memories. Part of the lure is seeing these historical sites and what they represent as a reinterpretation of history.[21]

Other examples include Savannah, Charleston, Philadelphia, Providence and New York City. In some case the historical is a prime attraction.

Most often, however, the history and architecture are supplemental contributors to the identity and attraction of an area. Appearance and use combine in different proportions to determine the identity and attraction of an area for different individuals.

Tunbridge and Ashworth observe that "monuments, objects and past events and personalities, together with their interpretive markers, are one, often the principal, means through which places create a separate distinctive identity. New towns or districts lack identity precisely because they are silent in this respect."[22]

The historical can also serve to provide a level of continuity and possibly some sense of comfort for an individual in an area. Though all people will not equate comfort with continuity, knowing some sense of the history of an area is an integral part of many of our interactions with the physical environment around us. New structures inherently lack this history. This continuity may be more of an attraction for those that already know an area, or even live in the area, rather than for first time visitors.[23]

Within historical preservation, the exteriors of structures are often preserved to evoke the past, rather than the interiors or the functions within them. Even the exteriors of the structures alone can be meaningful artifacts that serve as useful conceptual entrees into their origins. In different guises, it can be viewed as a sculptural object or a functional container. It can be stepped back from and seen in its physical context or approached and examined in detail. It can also be viewed in its political, economic, or social context as well as its historic context. It can have an original shell and still be used for its original function (e.g., Fisher Fine Arts Library) or it can be adapted to a new function (e.g., Hard Rock Cafe in Reading Terminal Headhouse), or it can continue a previous function in a new shell (e.g., Reading Terminal Market).

These remains can evoke just so much of the past, more for the trained observer or resident aware of the local history, less for the layman or visitor. Boniface and Fowler comment that: "standing structures, whatever their social or architectural status, are only the tip of the cultural iceberg in urban circumstances. The other none-tenths of the archaeological cake, to change the metaphor, lie buried in layers below the icing of the visible, but only superficial, streetscapes and buildings."[24]

Still, understanding can be made easier by holding a physical object that links to that concept literally or metaphorically. It becomes a visual anchor for the point being made, or using Tuan's phrase, "Objects anchor time."

Lowenthal suggests that "however depleted by time and use, relics remain essential bridges between then and now. . . . We respond to relics as objects of interest or beauty, as evidence of past events, and as talismans of continuity."[25]

Objects can become storytelling props, though the prop should have a meaningful link with its physical location for it to have historical relevance to the site. It will not be a foreign object placed in an arbitrary location, but will rather carry some meaning in the object's own history related to that particular location. Hough offers that "the basic purpose of maintaining old parts of town is to link us with the past—to enhance one's knowledge of a place's cultural roots."[26]

I will take an example in Yamashita Park in Yokohama to illustrate how specific historical objects (whether or not the larger ambience is considered historical) can begin to educate and anchor a place geographically and historically. The ability to create a distinct look can serve as a visual landmark. This distinct look can be historical and thereby serve as a clue that it deals with something from the past, though the exact historical time period need not be indicated on the surface.

Within Yamashita Park is a series of small landmarks, sites that are clearly identifiable, some of which clearly point back to history. They may attract the attention of the viewer more than the park as a whole. The park itself is not generally inward looking, but rather outward looking towards the bay. There are some focal points within the park, like the India Memorial (see *Appendix: Yokohama*). This unique object attracts attention to itself by its difference from the surroundings. It appears exotic and historical. At this level it may evoke a historical ambience. It may reassure a visitor that the area has a rich past, without specifically defining it.

Whether an explanatory plaque tells a story or the structure itself serves as a physical clue to a story to be told, the site still can act as a historical reminder. The object itself has the ability to have people admire it aesthetically as an ornately decorated canopy, functionally as a seat in a shaded area, spiritually as a space for contemplation, or to serve as a physical clue for questioning and delving into the history of the area. Why is this object here? Why does it look different then everything else around it? Why is it located in Yamashita Park?

Hayden observes that "places trigger memories for insiders, who have shared a common past, and at the same time places often can represent shared pasts to outsiders who might be interested in knowing about them in the present."

She later proposes that "networks of such places begin to reconnect social memory on an urban scale."[27]

Questions like this allow people to historically and geographically anchor these locations and possibly themselves within them. If they did not already know, they could learn some of the history of the area from either a plaque or brochure. They also might learn from a companion who is familiar with the monument's history. In that sense it serves a similar function as that of certain trees or natural locations for the Apache Indians. Basso recounts how these sites become physical reminders for stories. The stories are metaphors embodying the shared history of the tribe, the values of their culture, and their communal memories.[28]

Through understanding the India Memorial, people might also learn of the Great Kanto Earthquake of 1923. They would learn that there were many foreign residents from India living in this area during the earthquake. These residents donated this structure in memory of all the assistance they received in rebuilding. People could also learn that Yamashita Park itself was built from the rubble of the earthquake which was then dumped on the water's edge as part of the rebuilding plan.[29]

Light suggests that informal education is "at the heart of interpretation. . . . Interpretation is designed to communicate the significance of heritage places, in a manner appropriate to visitors engaged in leisure activities during their leisure time."[30] Several empirical studies have pointed to an interest shown for historical structures by the general public. Taylor and Konrad in a 1980 study, found people had a preference for historical sites. A study done in Vicoria, B.C. in 1992 by Murphy indicated the tourist appeal of heritage resources in the area.[31]

Nasar summarizes a number of other studies focusing on heritage resources. He suggests that historical significance creates greater imageability of a structure, and thereby may serve as an aid to wayfinding.[32]

A separate study by Teo and Huang, revealed the attraction of restored historical structures (old colonial buildings) for visitors to Singapore. However, it also pointed out that local "Singaporeans attach a great deal more to activities and lifestyles within the district that have since been removed or have disappeared because of conservation."[33] This highlights differences that may exist in the attraction of historical structures relative to the background or intent of the individuals experiencing the area.

Consonance, Dissonance, and Identity

Though planners and architects often speak about contextual design, all design is actually contextual when time is considered. Some structures appear old, some new. Some try to fit comfortably together, some play off of each other. Some structures are designed to ignore the surroundings, but even in the act of ignoring surrounding sites, the political, social and economic context of the time period shaping the choices is being acceded to. The temporal dimension is the context that all environments fit within.

Lynch states, "The arguments of planning all come down to the management of change."[34] An initial question of new development is which structures to keep and which to remove to allow room to build upon. A subsequent decision involves how the new should fit with the old.

Alexander observes that "the features which you remember in a place are not so much peculiarities, but rather the typical, the recurrent, the characteristic features: the canals of Venice, the flat roofs of a Moroccan town, the even spacing of the fruit trees in an orchard, the slope of a beach towards the sea, the umbrellas of an Italian beach, the wide sidewalks, sidewalk cafes."[35]

Individual new structures can be designed to either reinforce or react against the existing structures. The larger relationship that is created is one of consonance or dissonance. Consonant if the new buildings reinforce the existing buildings stylistically and spatially, dissonant if the new designs ignore or react against the existing. If they are consonant, then the new and the existing "reinforce" a singular identity of the overall area against the surrounding areas. If the new "reacts" against the existing, the resulting dissonant relationship will set off the existing building(s) from the new and the new from the existing.

The effect of a historical ambience is strongest when it is evoked by something with an identity distinct from its surroundings. This may be a singular distinct object, a series of objects that together create a network with a distinct identity, or an overall area with an identity set off from the surrounding area.

Lowenthal points out that "whether museumized or readapted, the preserved past is strongly differentiated from the everyday milieu."[36] The preserved past does not have to be strongly differentiated from the everyday. However, a site may not be noticed unless it is somehow differentiated from its surroundings. The distinctness of a historical ambience can be attained by the contrast of an object with a historical appearance from its surroundings by shape, function, style, or material. Markers explaining the significance of the object also may set it off from its surroundings.

It is the concept of object and field that creates the perception of identity. Differences between an object and its surroundings bring attention and heighten those differences. Contrasts between sites may be between scales of objects. Contrasts may also lie between entities of the same scale, such as detail to surrounding details, building to surrounding buildings, or district to surrounding districts.

Within the set of areas judged to have historical ambience will be those containing a wide range of historical styles. Areas with a variety of historical periods represented within them may encompass a landscape of greater depth than one encompassing only a single time period.[37] However, the narrower the range of styles in a single area, the stronger the visual identity.

An occasional contemporary object within surroundings with a historical ambience will not necessarily destroy the ambience of either contemporary object or the historical surroundings. The historical surroundings may simply be accentuated by the newness of the contemporary object.

The reverse scenario of an object with historical ambience within a predominantly contemporary appearing setting can also potentially enhance both object and setting. More even proportions of contemporary and historical, or situations with less dominant segments of styles may serve to confuse and blur rather than enhance the respective identities.

The two surveys used within this essay will be located along waterfronts in the USA and Japan. Though the locations vary geographically, they are both urban waterfronts, and offer some basic levels of comparison. Most large American and Japanese cities have grown up along waterfronts. Industry and shipping initially thrived in these areas. More recently these concerns moved away from the city centers due to changes in industry and shipping requirements. These waterfront areas then became available for new types of development.

The use of the waterfront in many central city locations have shifted from commercial and industrial to that of public amenity. The visible open space of these waterfronts, whether people actually take a boat out on the water or merely look out over it from a dock, still provides apparent relief from the denser, more compressed spaces of the cities. Tuan suggests that "a healthy being welcomes constraint and freedom, the boundedness of place and the exposure of space."[38]

The water as an amenity provides a lure for both local residents and visitors to enter, use and enjoy these areas. Within these waterfront areas are developments that in many cases try to attract people to the area and frequently try to take advantage of some aspect of the waterfront location. Though some start from scratch, many developments try to build from the historical fabric already in place.

The following surveys analyze a number of different configurations of elements in waterfront settings that evoke some degree of historical ambience. Within the particular case studies chosen, dissonance seems more heavily used in Japan than the USA. There is the possibility that this split may occur over the larger set of Japanese and American waterfronts as well, but this is still untested. It is also possible that smaller areas of historical ambience can take on greater relative significance to the viewers of these areas in Japan because of their infrequency.

Appearance of age is a major element used in the analysis of these sites. Whether the historical ambience is judged strong or weak is not meant to equate with inherently good or bad. It is just meant to rethink the way areas may be perceived by the public.

One of the larger goals of historic preservation is to protect built resources that significant amounts of the general public perceive as valuable, so they may continue to enjoy and learn from them into the future. Though experts may prefer original structures over adaptations or reproductions, the general public may not be as concerned about these distinctions.[39] Trying to understand the attraction certain places hold for portions of the general public should be useful in rethinking what resources to protect for the future.

Possible implications also lie in new developments adjacent to and surrounding the protected resources. Design decisions in these new developments will effect the perceptions of identity of the existing structures, as well as that of the larger area. I hope the concepts of historical ambience, consonance, dissonance and identity will contribute to this reexamination.

Historical ambience is not crystal clear in its bounds, but hopefully with these explanations, a general groundwork has been laid out. Dealing with historical ambience, judged from the impressions of the lay viewer, can hopefully expand the traditional definitions of historic preservation initially derived from expert opinion and a different set of criteria.

The concepts of consonance, dissonance, and identity all tie into that of historical ambience. In describing a perception of historical ambience, I have described a number of contributing factors. In the empirical analysis of the next sections, I have taken four large descriptors relating to the age of appearance of structures in urban waterfronts, "restored," "pseudo-historical," "adaptive use," and "modern." The analysis then looks at group preferences for these four descriptors (and others) within the surveyed populations of Philadelphia and Yokohama.

Chapter Five

Survey Background

User Surveys for Urban Design

Two exploratory photo surveys have been completed, one in Philadelphia (USA) and the other in Yokohama (Japan). They were designed to gather, quickly and efficiently, user knowledge of an area. This section will briefly frame the research methods. The photo survey technique used has a number of potential uses, all related to supplementing expert knowledge by gaining responses from a larger cross section of an area's users.

The method I have been working with is a simple, low-tech way of gaining a wide variety of opinions in a short amount of time. A number of rolls of photographs are initially taken and printed as a standard 3½"x5" photo. Each displays a different view taken within the study area. Of those, 36 are eventually selected to be representative of the set of sites that are to be analyzed. These photos are then reduced 50% using a color copier (to keep expenses down) and assembled on a single photo board. All 36 photos can then be scanned at a single glance by the respondent. Each photo was numbered and keyed to an attached map of the area. Admittedly not a breakthrough technology, but that is part of its appeal. It is relatively easy to assemble the photos, and the photos themselves act as a lure for potential respondents. For the respondent it is not a dry academic survey dealing with abstract concepts. It is an interesting way to spend a few minutes, looking at some local photos and reacting to them.

Each surveyed individual was asked to "pick out 6 photos that show what you like most or think interesting about this area." I did not specifically ask about "significant sites" to the respondents because I did not want to overly formalize or intellectualize their selections. If "significant sites" were asked of them, people might default to the more established standards of significance which have been established by others. After selecting these photos, follow-up questions were asked about reasons they chose those particular images. Finally some background data on each participant was obtained.

There are many levels of subjectivity imbedded within this process. The selection of the bounds of the study area is a subjective decision of inclusion and exclusion. The selection of sites to be photographed within this geographic area similarly eliminates many choices prior to ever being seen by a respondent.

The photos themselves also potentially "lead" the viewer. The composition, time of day, lighting of the photo, and cropping of the image, all may potentially affect the "likability" or "interest" of the site being looked at. The inclusion or exclusion of people within the images and the apparent level of enjoyment of these people might affect perceptions of those viewing the photos. The locations of the actual survey and the potential preference for that site might also create a skewed sample and must be taken into account.

It sometimes appears that an almost infinite number of potential biases must be watched for in the survey. Since this is a field study, not a laboratory experiment, it is inherently messier, with more variables that are difficult to control. The survey results should state these potential biases up front and try to minimize their effects where possible.

In a 1985 article, Kaplan describes a number of surveys of user preferences for various landscape scenes. It challenges the validity of categorizations based on expert viewpoints, used for the management of visual resources. A main objective was to demonstrate the usefulness of preference measurement as a tool to explore landscape perceptions.

The preference rating approach Kaplan uses, has participants look at photographs or slides. Most are black and white photos printed eight to a page. Each participant then rates how much each image is preferred on a 5-point scale. Kaplan emphasizes that "while direct questioning regarding environmental perception is unlikely to be fruitful, it has been shown that the use of preference reactions to photographic material is a highly effective procedure for deriving salient perceptual categories."[1]

Stamps meta-analysis of a number of different photo studies supports the implicit assumption of using photos to simulate the environment. He found that the use of photographs to elicit preferences correlates highly to preferences yielded directly within those environments.[2]

Nasar writes that "in contrast to the conventional wisdom that beauty is in the eye of the beholder, research shows strong consistencies in what people like and dislike in the environment." Still, these "public" tastes will likely not be of a singular mind, but rather encompass a variety of diverse opinions. Within these possible consistencies of public opinions, various subgroups of opinions may emerge based on common use, demographics or cultural backgrounds. Hayden notes that certain sites may be found to have special significance for one or more of these subgroups.[3]

Many have already tried to identify criteria that influence people's preferences. Using empirical methods, Nasar has defined five criteria for "likable features" including naturalness, upkeep, openness, order, and historical significance. His methods included phone interviews, and oral and written responses to mapping.[4]

My surveys and analysis have similarities to both Kaplan and Nasar. My approach differs in several respects, however. It consists of intercept interviews on site, using 36 color photos on a single photo board. Each individual photo is not rated using a 5-point scale, but rather 6 of the 36 photos available are simply selected as "preferred." My study also has a particular focus regarding historical ambience as perceived in urban waterfronts.

Study areas do not need to be limited to waterfront areas. Urban waterfronts are useful to this research because of the core historical properties that lie in many of these areas along with the mix of visitors and locals they attract. With minor adjustments this survey method can just as easily be applied to edge cities, small towns, or new urbanism developments.

Though the data gained in these particular surveys are quantifiable, their importance lies predominantly in the focus on public preferences for the built environment. The specific numbers are not as important as the indications of shared preferences.

Waterfront Surveys

The exploratory surveys have been designed to serve multiple purposes, both to test the waters for certain tendencies in public preferences, as well as to refine this particular photo survey technique. The Philadelphia Waterfront Survey has been done as both a complement to the Yokohama Waterfront Survey and as a next step of refinement.

The survey in Yokohama was conducted in December 1997. It was followed by an initial analysis of the data. The Philadelphia Survey was executed in November 1998, and analyzed using a slightly more refined method. This more refined analysis technique was then applied to the initial data set of Yokohama as well. Within the following pages, the Philadelphia Survey will be presented first, the Yokohama Survey, second.

The particular questions asked of the survey data relate to the preceding essays dealing with the distinct and the unique, predictability and surprise, packaging, and historical ambience. The survey begins to empirically test out certain theoretical arguments made in these essays. The driving force behind both the theoretical and empirical analysis is to better understand and access public preferences for urban design.

The Yokohama Survey had primarily Japanese respondents commenting on a Japanese waterfront area. This area was developed over the past one hundred years, with a large portion of it developed over the last decade. The Philadelphia Survey had primarily American respondents commenting on an American waterfront area. This portion of Philadelphia was developed continuously over the past three hundred years and includes a mix of eighteenth, nineteenth, and twentieth century structures.

Both locations are in waterfront areas that include public amenities such as promenades, plazas and seating overlooking the water, as well as maritime museums and historical ships used as tourist attractions. Both have elements consciously designed to attract visitors, and include restaurants, retail shops, and hotels. Yokohama includes a higher concentration of office space, a convention center, and a small amusement park, while Philadelphia includes a higher proportion of residences within its survey bounds. Both have a mix of old and new structures. Both exist as second cities, located close to more dominant ones (Tokyo or New York).

Direct comparisons are difficult however, because the structures differed in each city along with the culture of the survey populations. I have tried to remove the barriers of the different physical locations being evaluated by categorizing and grouping those locations (through their images) according to more general evaluative criteria. The categories include "Age of Appearance," "Historical Ambience Tests 1-3," "Greenery in View," "Water in View," "Expected in an Urban Waterfront," and "Labelled on a Tourist Map." Using categories rather than specific sites, will allow some cross cultural comparisons between Japanese and American preferences to be made.

Each of the next two chapters are laid out in a similar format. They begin with some background about the survey area, along with specifics about the methodology. The evaluative criteria will be described in the Philadelpha chapter only.

The analysis of the data collected in this survey has been divided into the next three sections. The first focuses on findings based on those surveyed as a whole. Overall preferences are ascertained in a number of evaluative areas. The overall demographics of the surveyed group is also discussed.

The next focuses on demographic breakdowns. The same evaluative criteria analyzed in the overall preferences, are reexamined using the preferences of demographic subgroups. An analysis of findings is described in the final section of each chapter.

An additional section looks at a series of internal comparisons between related pairings of photographs. Since this is not the prime focus of this survey, it has been placed in the Appendix. Supplemental material used in these surveys and their analysis have also been added to the Appendix.

Chapter Six

The Philadelphia Survey

Waterfront Background

The city of Philadelphia was first laid out in 1682 by Thomas Holme and William Penn. Though eventually filling out the area between the Delaware and Schuylkill Rivers over the years, settlement began along the Delaware River. This original waterfront is that of the survey area. The areas alongside this waterfront have kept evolving over the years, but examples from many different eras remain. The prime districts included in this Philadelphia study include portions of Old City and Society Hill. Smaller areas include Penn's Landing, Headhouse Square and South Street.

A residential area dating from the city's founding, Old City became known as a commercial area by the nineteenth century. Commercial buildings replaced most of the residential structures. More recently, many of these commercial structures have been converted to condominiums, art galleries and related shops. The area is presently known as the arts district of Philadelphia.[1]

Society Hill is another early area of the city. Mostly residential, it contains the highest concentration of original eighteenth century structures in the country. Gradually becoming dilapidated, it was the center of an urban renewal program begun in the 1950s. Buildings originally from the eighteenth century have been restored. It is now known as an affluent residential area.[2]

Penn's Landing was originally the prime port area of the city. It was lined with docks for commercial shipping. Over the years shipping declined, and what remained shifted outside of this central area. In 1967, the redevelopment of this area fronting the Delaware River was begun. It was converted primarily into a recreational area.[3]

Headhouse Square is focused around a restored early nineteenth century headhouse (firehouse) and market shed.[4] It is surrounded by both restored nineteenth century and contemporary structures, housing many retail shops and restaurants.

South Street is a primarily commercial area at this point in time. Still containing eighteenth and nineteenth century structures, many have been adapted to house contemporary shops and restaurants. The area is eclectic, with a prime focus on attracting the young.

Survey Specifics

This survey follows a similar format to the Yokohama Survey. Thirty six photos were shown to respondents, each a different view taken within the study area. These photos are presented as a "photogrid," in a manner that allows all 36 to be viewed simultaneously. A map was also displayed that showed the bounds of the survey area and keyed the locations of where each photograph was taken from.

Survey takers were spread out over 13 locations within the study area. Each team (consisting of two to three survey takers) had a display board showing the photographs and map. Each also had a list of questions to ask each respondent. Respondents were selected at random from people walking by the street corners where the survey takers were located.

The survey takers were students at the University of Pennsylvania. They had been briefed as to proper survey techniques, and practiced giving the survey to each other, before going out into the field for the actual survey. The survey itself was given primarily between 1:00 P.M. and 2:00 P.M. on Thursday, November 5, 1998. Some additional surveys were given on the following day at approximately the same time. This allowed the survey to include many people working in the area during their lunch hours, as well as visitors to the area. On average, one of every three people who were asked to take the survey, agreed to take it. A total of 127 respondents took this survey. The average time per survey was about 6½ minutes for each respondent.

The 127 individuals surveyed are not intended as a representative slice of the U.S. or Philadelphia population. It is more a localized snapshot of the city. It also is limited to those who were willing to stop for five to ten minutes and take this survey. So the busiest people likely did not stop and are not part of those surveyed. It is, however, intended as fairly representative of people in the public portions of the study area at the time and dates of the survey.

When the survey population was broken down using demographic criteria, those in the subgroups decreased accordingly. The findings became less convincing at very small numbers of a demographic subgroup. At the most extreme level in this particular survey, where only two individuals were classified as age 14 or under, the subgroup was removed from the relevant analysis.

The Philadelphia photos were chosen using a more simplified system than the Yokohama Survey. Photos included in this survey are more closely focused towards specific sites. In most cases there are two different photos of each site.

It was unknown going into the study if different photos of the same site would reveal different levels of preference between them. This then might indicate a bias for or against a photographic image, rather than a site. The exploratory Philadelphia Survey attempts to acknowledge this possibility and explore it, as well as simultaneously trying to offset any biases related specifically to the photograph, by including two photos of most sites.

Of the 18 photo pairs chosen in this study, 11 showed images of the same structure from different angles. The remaining 7 photo pairs showed different sites within the same pairing category (e.g. views of opposite sides of the street in a Society Hill residential area, or views of the Walnut and South St. Pedestrian Walkway).

The following pages display an entire survey instrument including photos, key map and questionnaire. The original photos and key map were displayed on a 17"x22" board. They have been rearranged and reduced slightly to fit these pages.

1 2 3

4 5 6

7 8 9

10 11 12

Figure 6.1. Philadelphia: Photos #1-12

13

14

15

16

17

18

19

20

21

22

23

24

Figure 6.2. Philadelphia: Photos #13-24

25

26

27

28

29

30

31

32

33

34

35

36

Figure 6.3. Philadelphia: Photos #25-36

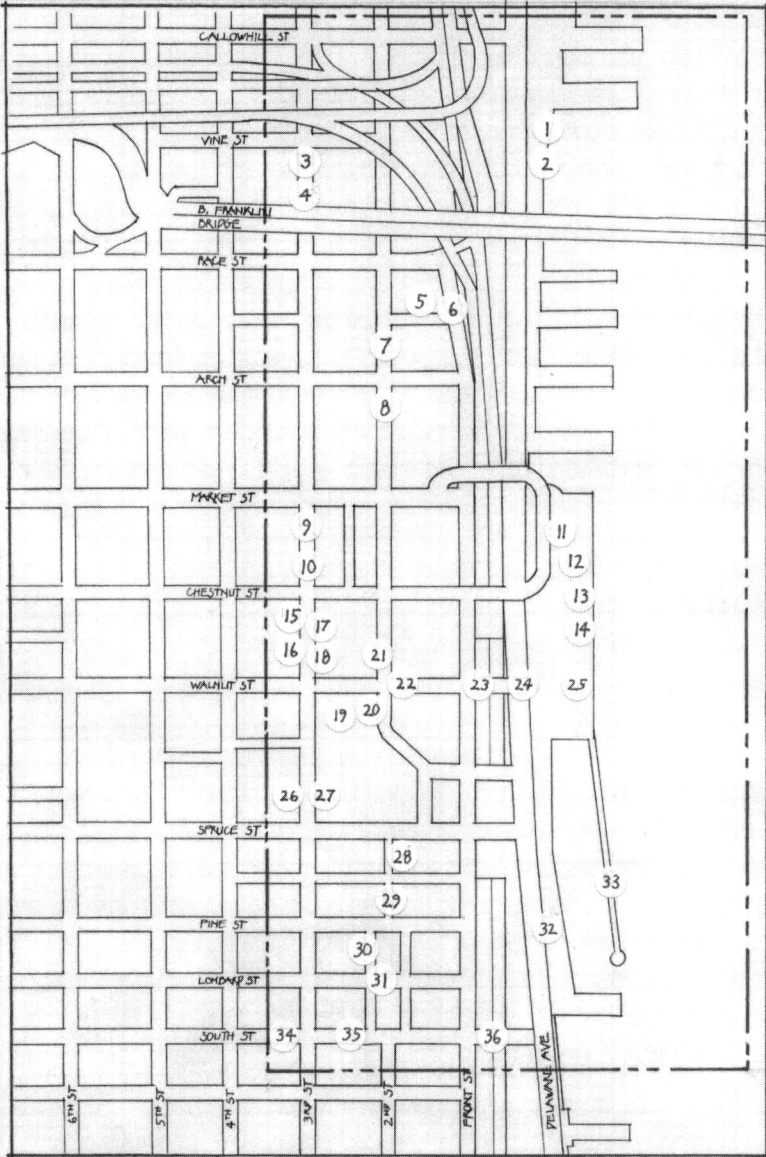

Figure 6.4. Philadelphia: Key Map

Evaluative Criteria

The survey results have been set into a matrix associating each photo with its accompanying evaluative criteria. Though many different criteria were initially tested out, for the purposes of this study, only a small number were ultimately selected that had particularly meaningful results within the context of this work.

Evaluative category breakdowns are designed to test out possible factors affecting preference. The categories are artificial constructions in that each tries to take a photograph (and the site it represents) and divides it into two, three, or four discrete characteristics.

Each category however, attempts to use a clearly definable criteria matching a particular photograph (and its underlying site), to a particular description of it. For example, in the category "Water," photo #13 (Penn's Landing) is listed as having a "View of Water," while photo #14 (South St.) is listed as "No View."

There may be some ambiguity in the dividing lines, such as what constitutes Minimal Greenery and Moderate Greenery. Not all categories can be as clear cut, but the definitions are always stated. There has been an attempt to provide fairly consistent selections. Other variations and interpretations could always be tried in the future as clearer distinctions are made in these and other categories. Infinite category variations are possible.

The number of photos is only 36. Though all evaluative categories exist in more than a single photo, they may only occur in a handful. It is somewhat difficult to distinguish between a photo being chosen for one particular characteristic rather than another in this circumstance. "Pseudo Historical" for example, is associated with only three photographs.

Another common characteristic of the chosen photos may actually be the lure, since there is also substantial overlap between several categories. They exist between Restored and Moderate Greenery, as well as between Adaptive Use, Unexpected, and Not on Map. The likelihood for being misled decreases as more photos with more permutations of characteristics are available in the original photoset.

The pages following this section describe the evaluative category matrix. The first chart lists the photo number, photo pair and location that it is linked with. The next lists the evaluative categories of "Age of Appearance" and "Historical Ambience." "Age of Appearance" is defined by four separate characteristics. "Historical Ambience" has three test definitions, each regrouping these four characteristics into two.

The concept of "historical ambience" is based on user perceptions rather than historical facts which the typical user may or may not be aware of. Each test tries regrouping the characteristics to yield the strongest preferences between those with "historical ambience" and those without it. The strength of the groupings may confirm or reject possible definitions of "historical ambience." These may then serve to supplement or revise the understanding of the concept as described in the previous essay.

The next chart includes four other evaluative categories. "Greenery in the Image" and "Water in the Image" describe what is found in the frame of the photograph itself, but it alludes to what can be seen at the site itself. "On Tourist Map" and "Expected in Urban Waterfront" describe the photographed site in relation concepts to outside of the image.

The final chart lists several additional categories that have been added as a stability analysis for this survey. This consists of creating several possible categories related to the photographs that could be influencing decision making of the respondents unintentionally. Two categories relate to the qualities of the photograph itself, rather than those of the site. Another deals with the location of the photographs chosen compared to the location where the survey was taken. These tests help insure that a characteristic of the medium itself are not unintentionally influencing the selections of those surveyed to a significant degree.

The following definitions should clarify these categories further:

Age of Appearance

This category divides photos into four characteristics based on the perception of age of the photographed site or structure. These are defined (for this analysis) as follows:

Adaptive Use - Historical structure with external signs of a new use occurring within it. Designed prior to the influence of the International Style.

Modern - Style loosely based on International Style of the twentieth century.

Pseudo - Structure designed in the mid to late portions of the twentieth century, with strong stylistic debts to surrounding historic structures. Often it is described as contextual.

Restored - Historic structure (pre-International Style) that appears to continue its earlier use. There are no obvious external signs of a new use occurring within it.

Historical Ambience: Test 1

Historical Ambience is defined (for this analysis) as follows:
Historical Ambience - "Restored."
Not Historical Ambience - "Pseudo" or "Adaptive" or "Modern."

Historical Ambience: Test 2

Historical Ambience is defined (for this analysis) as follows:
Historical Ambience - "Restored" or "Pseudo."
Not Historical Ambience - "Adaptive" or "Modern."

Historical Ambience: Test 3

Historical Ambience is defined (for this analysis) as follows:
Historical Ambience - "Restored" or "Pseudo" or "Adaptive."
Not Historical Ambience - "Modern."

Greenery in Image

Expanse of greenery, which was analyzed for Yokohama (and found not significant), was not a category in the Philadelphia sites photographed. Images with open expanses of greenery were not part of the Philadelphia photos. However, greenery did exist in these images in the forms of shrubs, trees and small patches of grass.

This category divides photos into three characteristics based on levels of greenery found within the image. Greenery encompasses any visible plant life including lawns, trees (with or without leaves), flowers, and shrubs. This is defined (for this analysis) as follows:

Moderate Greenery - A significant amount of greenery is visible in the scene. It occupies a substantial, though not dominant portion of the scene.

Minimal Greenery - Some greenery is visible, but it only occupies a small portion of the scene.

No Greenery - No visible greenery in the scene.

Water in Image

This category divides photos into two characteristics based on levels of water found within the image. This is defined (for this analysis) as follows:

Water - Any water visible in the scene.

No Water - No water visible in the scene.

On Tourist Map

"On Tourist Map" touches on the concept of packaging from an earlier chapter. It deals with labelling a site as special and worthy of attention. It also, however, may be defining a site as predictable. A certain level of predictability and conformity can be expected in a standard visitor's map issued by the Chamber of Commerce or other official visitor's bureau.

A basic map of Philadelphia's Center City distributed at no cost by the Philadelphia Convention & Visitor's Bureau. This is the map that the following definitions are based on (see Appendix: Philadelphia).

On Map - Labelled on standard Visitor's Bureau Map.

Not on Map - Not labelled on standard Visitor's Bureau Map.

Expected in Urban Waterfront

"Expected in Urban Waterfront" alludes to earlier chapters on Predict-ability/Surprise, Consonance/Dissonance, and the Distinct. Context is crucial for creating the baseline of what is felt to be Predictable or Consonant. Only from this baseline can Surprise, Dissonance, and Distinctness be expressed.

Photographs offer only the limited context of what is in the frame of the picture. Therefore, the framework of Predictability developed to judge Surprise or Distinctness in this survey is expanded beyond the frame of the picture. It is based on general expectations of what might be found in an urban waterfront in the U.S.

The context for this analysis is urban revitalization of waterfront areas in the U.S. Tourism is included as an integral part of the revitalization of these areas, as are building on the existing historical roots of the areas. Several projects by the developer, the Rouse Corporation, seem to capture much of what people have come to expect in an urban waterfront. The particular developments in mind for choosing the criteria for this category were Baltimore's Harborplace and Manhattan's South Street Seaport.

Expected sites include cultural institutions related to the water such as maritime museums or aquariums, large public open spaces fronting the water, and buildings and ships that appear historical. This is defined (for this analysis) as follows:

Expected - Expected within a Tourist-Historic Waterfront.
Unexpected - Not expected within a Tourist-Historic Waterfront.

Photo Orientation

This category divides photos into two characteristics based on the orientation of the photograph on the presentation board. This is defined (for this analysis) as follows:

Horizontal - Longer horizontally than vertically, as if printing an image in landscape mode.
Vertical - Longer vertically than horizontally, as if printing an image in portrait mode.

Photo Exposure

This category tested if photos that were slightly underdeveloped (with large dark area within them) substantially differed in times chosen than photos that were more balanced in exposure. This is defined (for this analysis) as follows:

Dark - Large portions of the image were very dark (underexposed).
Normal - Image did not have large dark areas within it.

Photo Location

This category tested if the location where the survey was given, influenced the photos that were selected. It is intended to see if people were simply favoring sites that were closest to them during the time of the actual survey. These areas are defined (for this analysis) as follows:

Waterfront
Old City
Society Hill
Headhouse Square
South Street

PHOTO#	PHOTO DESCRIPTION	PHOTO PAIR
1	Dave & Buster's	Delaware Ave
2	Rock Lobster	Delaware Ave
3	Doorway	Painted Bride
4	Full Building	Painted Bride
5	Hidden Alcove	Elfreth's Alley
6	Main Alleyway	Elfreth's Alley
7	Front Elevation	Old City Galleries
8	Sidewalk	Old City Galleries
9	Front Elevation	Greek Revival (lunch)
10	Full Building	Greek Revival (lunch)
11	Plaza & Canopies	Penns Landing (plaza)
12	Promenade	Penns Landing (plaza)
13	Boat on Water	Penn's Landing (river)
14	Couple Looking Out	Penn's Landing (river)
15	Full Building	Greek Revival (Bank)
16	Front Facade	Greek Revival (Bank)
17	Tower	Visitors Center
18	Reflective Glass	Visitors Center
19	Sidewalk	Ritz 5
20	Front Elevation	Ritz 5
21	Sidewalk	City Tavern
22	Full Building	City Tavern
23	Walnut St.	Pedestrian Walkway
24	Overlooking Water	Seaport Museum
25	Front Facade	Seaport Museum
26	Older Rowhouses	Society Hill (residential)
27	New Rowhouses	Society Hill (residential)
28	Tree & Tower	Society Hill Towers
29	Full Buildings	Society Hill Towers
30	Sidewalk	Headhouse Square
31	Cobblestone St	Headhouse Square
32	Steamship	Ship & Skyline
33	Sailboat	Ship & Skyline
34	Colorful Facades	South St
35	Controlled Signage	South St
36	South St	Pedestrian Walkway

Table 6.1. Philadelphia: Photo Criteria—Photo Pairs

PHOTO#	AGE OF APPEARANCE	HISTORICAL AMBIANCE Test 1	HISTORICAL AMBIANCE Test 2	HISTORICAL AMBIANCE Test 3
1	Adaptive	Not	Not	Ambiance
2	Adaptive	Not	Not	Ambiance
3	Adaptive	Not	Not	Ambiance
4	Adaptive	Not	Not	Ambiance
5	Restored	Ambiance	Ambiance	Ambiance
6	Restored	Ambiance	Ambiance	Ambiance
7	Adaptive	Not	Not	Ambiance
8	Adaptive	Not	Not	Ambiance
9	' Adaptive	Not	Not	Ambiance
10	Adaptive	Not	Not	Ambiance
11	Modern	Not	Not	Not
12	Modern	Not	Not	Not
13	Modern	Not	Not	Not
14	Modern	Not	Not	Not
15	Restored	Ambiance	Ambiance	Ambiance
16	Restored	Ambiance	Ambiance	Ambiance
17	Modern	Not	Not	Not
18	Modern	Not	Not	Not
19	Modern	Not	Not	Not
20	Modern	Not	Not	Not
21	Restored	Ambiance	Ambiance	Ambiance
22	Restored	Ambiance	Ambiance	Ambiance
23	Pseudo	Not	Ambiance	Ambiance
24	Modern	Not	Not	Not
25	Modern	Not	Not	Not
26	Restored	Ambiance	Ambiance	Ambiance
27	Pseudo	Not	Ambiance	Ambiance
28	Modern	Not	Not	Not
29	Modern	Not	Not	Not
30	Restored	Ambiance	Ambiance	Ambiance
31	Restored	Ambiance	Ambiance	Ambiance
32	Adaptive	Not	Not	Ambiance
33	Adaptive	Not	Not	Ambiance
34	Adaptive	Not	Not	Ambiance
35	Adaptive	Not	Not	Ambiance
36	Pseudo	Not	Ambiance	Ambiance

Table 6.2. Philadelphia: Photo Criteria—ambience

PHOTO#	GREENERY IN VIEW	WATER IN VIEW	ON TOURIST MAP	EXPECTED IN URBAN WATERFRONT
1	minimum	WATER	no	UNexpected
2	none	none	no	UNexpected
3	none	none	YES	UNexpected
4	MODERATE	none	YES	UNexpected
5	MODERATE	none	YES	UNexpected
6	MODERATE	none	YES	expected
7	none	none	no	expected
8	minimum	none	YES	expected
9	none	none	no	UNexpected
10	none	none	no	UNexpected
11	none	WATER	YES	expected
12	none	WATER	YES	expected
13	none	WATER	YES	expected
14	none	WATER	YES	expected
15	minimum	none	YES	expected
16	MODERATE	none	YES	expected
17	none	none	YES	expected
18	minimum	none	YES	expected
19	minimum	none	no	UNexpected
20	none	none	no	UNexpected
21	MODERATE	none	YES	expected
22	MODERATE	none	YES	expected
23	minimum	none	YES	expected
24	none	WATER	YES	expected
25	none	none	YES	expected
26	MODERATE	none	YES	expected
27	MODERATE	none	YES	expected
28	MODERATE	none	no	UNexpected
29	minimum	none	no	UNexpected
30	MODERATE	none	YES	expected
31	MODERATE	none	YES	expected
32	none	WATER	no	expected
33	minimum	WATER	YES	expected
34	minimum	none	YES	UNexpected
35	minimum	none	YES	expected
36	none	none	YES	expected

Table 6.3. Philadelphia: Photo Criteria—other

PHOTO#	PHOTO ORIENTATION	PHOTO EXPOSURE	PHOTO LOCATION
1	Horiz	normal	Waterfront
2	Horiz	normal	Waterfront
3	Horiz	normal	Old City
4	Horiz	Dark	Old City
5	Vert	Dark	Old City
6	Horiz	normal	Old City
7	Horiz	normal	Old City
8	Horiz	normal	Old City
9	Vert	normal	Society Hill
10	Horiz	normal	Society Hill
11	Horiz	normal	Waterfront
12	Horiz	normal	Waterfront
13	Horiz	normal	Waterfront
14	Horiz	normal	Waterfront
15	Horiz	normal	Society Hill
16	Vert	Dark	Society Hill
17	Vert	Dark	Society Hill
18	Horiz	Dark	Society Hill
19	Horiz	normal	Society Hill
20	Horiz	normal	Society Hill
21	Vert	normal	Society Hill
22	Horiz	normal	Society Hill
23	Horiz	normal	Waterfront
24	Horiz	Dark	Waterfront
25	Vert	Dark	Waterfront
26	Horiz	normal	Society Hill
27	Horiz	normal	Society Hill
28	Vert	normal	Society Hill
29	Horiz	normal	Society Hill
30	Vert	normal	Headhouse
31	Horiz	normal	Headhouse
32	Horiz	Dark	Waterfront
33	Vert	normal	Waterfront
34	Horiz	normal	South St
35	Horiz	normal	South St
36	Horiz	Dark	South St

Table 6.4. Philadelphia: Photo Criteria—stability

Selections Overall

Within the findings of each evaluative category, there is a small chart comparing the overall number of times a photo with that characteristic was selected to the number of times that characteristic appears in the photogrid. The selected photos (each associated with a single characteristic) always totals 762. This is due to 127 respondents choosing 6 selections each. The photoset (the set of photos comprising the photogrid) always totals 36.

Comparisons, therefore, need to be done according to percentages. The more extreme the difference between the percentage listed in the "selected" and that in the "photoset," the stronger the indication of preference (or lack of preference) for that characteristic within the overall surveyed population.

A 10% difference is being used as large enough to indicate a strong preference or lack of it. It could, however, have been set higher (to highlight more potential patterns of preference) or lower (to increase confidence).

At the end of this section are a chart and images that have been reordered in terms of most to least frequently chosen photograph overall. The demographic breakdown of the survey population is the final chart of the set.

Age of Appearance	- Selected -		- Photoset -	
	(N)	**Prob.**	**(N)**	**Prob.**
Restored	(297)	39 %	(9)	25 %
Pseudo	(81)	11 %	(3)	8 %
Adaptive	(171)	22 %	(12)	33 %
Modern	(213)	28 %	(12)	33 %
Total	**(762)**	**100 %**	**(36)**	**100 %**

Table 6.5. Philadelphia: Age of Appearance

In "Age of Appearance" a strong preference is shown for structures that are "Restored." They are selected 14% more frequently than they occur in the photoset. Also of note is the strong lack of preference shown for "Adaptive" structures. Images with this characteristic are chosen 11% less frequently than they occur in the photoset.

Historical Ambience: Test 1	- Selected -		- Photoset -	
	(N)	Prob.	(N)	Prob.
Historical Ambience	(297)	39 %	(9)	25 %
No Historical Ambience	(465)	61 %	(27)	75 %
Total	(762)	100 %	(36)	100 %

Table 6.6. Philadelphia: Historical Ambience Test 1

In Test 1, "Restored" becomes the embodiment of "Historical Ambience." Therefore it captures the same strong preferences. Photos with the characteristic "Historical Ambience" are selected 14% more frequently than they occur in the photoset. A comparable lack of preference is shown for those with "No Historical Ambience."

Historical Ambience: Test 2	- Selected -		- Photoset -	
	(N)	Prob.	(N)	Prob.
Historical Ambience	(378)	50 %	(12)	33 %
No Historical Ambience	(384)	50 %	(24)	67 %
Total	(762)	100 %	(36)	100 %

Table 6.7. Philadelphia: Historical Ambience Test 2

In Test 2, "Restored" and "Pseudo" combine to describe "Historical Ambience." In this definition, "Historical Ambience" is preferred even more convincingly. Photos with the characteristic are selected 17% more frequently than they occur in the photoset. A comparable lack of preference is shown for those with "No Historical Ambience."

Historical Ambience: Test 3	- Selected -		- Photoset -	
	(N)	Prob.	(N)	Prob.
Historical Ambience	(549)	72 %	(24)	67 %
No Historical Ambience	(213)	28 %	(12)	33 %
Total	(762)	100 %	(36)	100 %

Table 6.8. Philadelphia: Historical Ambience Test 3

In Test 3, "Restored," "Pseudo," and "Adaptive" are combined to describe "Historical Ambience." In this definition, the characteristic "Historical Ambience" does not reveal a strong preference either way.

Greenery in Image	- Selected -		- Photoset -	
	(N)	Prob.	(N)	Prob.
Moderate	(316)	41 %	(11)	31 %
Minimum	(189)	25 %	(10)	28 %
None	(257)	34 %	(15)	42 %
Total	(762)	100 %	(36)	100 %

Table 6.9. Philadelphia: Greenery in Image

In "Greenery in Image" a noticeable preference is shown for structures that have "Moderate Greenery." They are selected 10% more frequently than they occur in the photoset.

Water in Image	- Selected -		- Photoset -	
	(N)	Prob.	(N)	Prob.
Yes	(207)	27 %	(8)	22 %
No	(555)	73 %	(28)	78 %
Total	(762)	100 %	(36)	100 %

Table 6.10. Philadelphia: Water in Image

No strong preference is revealed either way for "Water in Image."

On Tourist Map	- Selected -		- Photoset -	
	(N)	Prob.	(N)	Prob.
Yes	(647)	85 %	(26)	72 %
No	(115)	15 %	(10)	28 %
Total	(762)	100 %	(36)	100 %

Table 6.11. Philadelphia: On Tourist Map

In "On Tourist Map" a strong preference is shown for structures that are "On the Map." They are selected 13% more frequently than they occur in the photoset. A comparable lack of preference is shown for those "Not on Map."

Expected in Urban Waterfront	- Selected -		- Photoset -	
	(N)	Prob.	(N)	Prob.
Yes	(152)	20 %	(12)	33 %
No	(610)	80 %	(24)	67 %
Total	(762)	100 %	(36)	100 %

Table 6.12. Philadelphia: Expected in Urban Waterfront

In "Expected in Urban Waterfront" a strong preference is shown for structures that are "Expected." They are selected 13% more frequently than they occur in the photoset. A comparable lack of preference is shown for those "Not Expected."

Photo Orientation	- Selected -		- Photoset -	
	(N)	Prob.	(N)	Prob.
Horizontal	(600)	79 %	(27)	75 %
Vertical	(162)	21 %	(9)	25 %
Total	(762)	100 %	(36)	100 %

Table 6.13. Philadelphia: Photo Orientation

Photo Exposure	- Selected -		- Photoset -	
	(N)	Prob.	(N)	Prob.
Normal	(630)	83 %	(27)	75%
Dark	(132)	17 %	(9)	25 %
Total	(762)	100 %	(36)	100 %

Table 6.14. Philadelphia: Photo Exposure

In the stability tests, "Photo Orientation" and "Photo Exposure," no strong preferences are revealed either way. A test was also done to see if sites in the vicinity of the location where the survey was taken were strongly favored. This was initially considered a possible flaw of the survey technique, but was not found to be the case in this survey.

Summary of Selections Overall

Three categories have shown a statistically significant difference between the expected probabilities from the photoset and the estimated probabilities from people's selections. These are "Historical Ambience: Test 2," "On Tourist Map," and "Expected in an Urban Waterfront."

Within these categories, a number of these evaluative characteristics stand out as preferred over the percentage that they occur in the photoset. These include "Restored," "Pseudo," and two definitions of "Historical Ambience" (test 1 and 2). The preferred images also include views with "Moderate Greenery," "On the Map" and "Expected" in an Urban Waterfront.

Evaluative characteristics that stand out as least preferred include "Adaptive Use" and "No Historical Ambience (test 1 and 2)." Others are "Not of Map" and "Unexpected" in an Urban Waterfront.

The analysis did not reveal any significant correlations in the stability analysis, comprised of the categories of "Photo Orientation" and "Photo Exposure." Nor was a strong correlation found between location that a survey was given at and the photographs chosen. This helps support the underlying concept that the view or site is determining people's preferences, rather than (these particular) aspects of the medium or survey methodology. Further tests can always be done to increase confidence in this analysis method in the future.

Survey Demographics

The demographics of the overall group that has made the selections summarized in the previous few pages now follows. Its importance also lies as a rough snapshot of people in the survey area at the time of the survey. As will be shown in the section after this one, many preferences follow demographic patterns.

The preferences of the overall survey group are inherently the preferences of the demographics that comprise this surveyed group. Therefore, these overall survey group preferences are not necessarily proof of a more universal preference for a characteristic.

The chart on the following page breaks down the survey population into a number of demographic categories. As the chart shows, a broad mix of ages were surveyed. It appears to be a fairly normal distribution, with the 35-44 year olds likely being the largest portion of respondents in a 10 year span. The 45-64 category includes more respondents, but covers a twenty year span. If broken into two groups of roughly equal proportions, they would average about 16% apiece, substantially less than the 27% at 35-44 years old. The age group 14 years and under contained only two respondents. This small number limited the usefulness of this group for age related portions of the analysis.

The education breakdown shows most respondents describing their highest education level as having graduated college (35%). Next highest was those having some college (25%) followed by post graduate education (20%). This sample group was generally well educated, with 55% having at least a college diploma, and 80% having at least some college.

Gender within the surveyed population was fairly evenly divided. Only slightly more males (54%) took the survey than females. The breakdown of Philadelphia local residents, local workers, and visitors included a mix that included a high proportion of individuals both residing and working within Philadelphia (52%). Of all those surveyed, 76% either lived, worked or both in Philadelphia, while 24% were visitors (both lived and worked outside of the city of Philadelphia).

OVERALL DEMOGRAPHICS of Survey

AGE (6 groups)	<=14	15-24	25-34	35-44	45-64	65+	unknown	Total
(n)	2	19	23	34	41	7	1	127
%	2%	15%	18%	27%	32%	6%	1%	100%

EDUCATION (5 groups)	Some HS	Grad HS	Some Col	Grad Col	Post Grad		unknown	Total
(n)	6	17	32	45	26		1	127
%	5%	13%	25%	35%	20%		1%	100%

GENDER				Female	Male		unknown	Total
(n)				57	68		2	127
%				45%	54%		2%	100%

LOCAL / VISITOR (4 groups)	Resident & Worker	Phila. Resident	Phila. Worker	Visitor		unknown	Total
(n)	66	14	17	30		0	127
%	52%	11%	13%	24%		0%	100%

Note:
Percentages may not total to 100% due to rounding errors.
Percentage rows are highlighted.

Table 6.15. Philadelphia: Overall Survey Demographics

Selections by Demographics

The following explanations and charts focus on the previously mentioned evaluative categories. Each demographic category is tested against each evaluative category.

A Rank Sums test is used because of the non parametric nature of the data. This test essentially assigns a rank to each individual of the survey in terms of number of times the six photos he or she selected encompass the evaluative quality being tested for. This is then summarized for the entire survey population.

The level of preference (based on times selected) for that evaluative characteristic is determined for each demographic subgroup. A p-value (Prob>ChiSq) is then calculated to determine the significance of the difference between subgroups. A p-value of 0.05 is used as the baseline for statistical significance. The smaller the p-value, the greater the confidence that a meaningful difference exists between the subgroups.

When the p-value is not determined as significant, only the number is entered into the summary sheet. When the p-value is determined as significant, the row is highlighted and positive and negative correlations are noted.

The results of each evaluative category is summarized with a chart that breaks down preferences for that quality by demographics. These include age, education level, gender, and whether the individual resides in, works in, or is just visiting Philadelphia.

The pages following the summary sheet include the detailed evaluation of this rank sum test for those with significant differences. Also included (above each test) is a means diamonds graph. This allows a quick visual analysis of how each demographic subgroup compares to each other.

Each diamond describes a subgroup. The location on the Y-Axis relates to the number of times the evaluative characteristic was chosen by individuals. The width of the diamond relates to the number of people tested within the demographic subgroup, the wider the diamond, the more people, and the more confidence in the results.

The mean is represented by the center, horizontal line of the diamond. The top and bottom of each diamond represents a 95% confidence interval. When diamonds do not overlap, the represented groups are significantly different. However, this does not mean that the reverse is necessarily true.[5]

Age of Appearance

In the category "Age of Appearance," there were significant differences between age groups, education levels, local/visitor status.

There is a strong and generally positive correlation between increasing age and increasing preference for "Restored." The lowest preference is within the 15-24 age group, the highest in the 45-64 group. Only in the 65+ group does the preference drop back down.

Education demonstrates an equally strong and positive correlation between increasing education level and increasing preference for "Restored." Those with post-graduate education chose sites with this characteristic with noticeably higher frequency than any other education level.

The highest preference for "Modern" was in the 15-24 age group, the lowest in the 45-64 group. The means of preference for the age groups in between did not decrease steadily, but rather were staggered. Those in the 65+ group raised back up over the level of the 45-64 group.

Education level showed a strong negative correlation between preference for "Modern" and increasing education. Only those with some high school did not fit this pattern. Those who graduated high school chose sites with this characteristic with the highest frequency. This frequency decreased steadily as education level increased. Those with a post-graduate education chose these sites with the lowest frequency.

Local/visitor status showed a significant correlation. Four characteristics arranged in a rough continuum have been created for this category. They range between those who spend most of their time in the city of Philadelphia (both reside and work in the city) to those who have likely spent the least time in the city (visitors, who reside and work outside of the city). The two center groups are those who only reside in the city and those who only work in the city.

Those who both reside and work in the city of Philadelphia selected "Modern" with a significantly higher frequency than those just visiting. Those who just reside or just work within Philadelphia selected these sites at a level somewhere between these two extremes.

Historical Ambience: Test 1

In the category "Age of Appearance: Test 1," "Historical Ambience" is defined as containing only "Restored." As was the case for "Restored" in "Age of Appearance," there were significant differences between age groups and between education levels.

There is a strong and generally positive correlation between increasing age and increasing preference for "Historical Ambience." The lowest preference is within the 15-24 age group, the highest in the 45-64 group. In the 65+ group the preference drops back down again.

Education level demonstrates an equally strong and positive correlation between increasing education level and increasing preference for "Historical Ambience." Those with post-graduate education chose sites with this characteristic with noticeably higher frequency than any other education level.

"No Historical Ambience" is defined in this case as containing "Pseudo Historical" or "Adaptive Use" or "Modern." "No Historical Ambience" shows the reverse correlation of "Historical Ambience." There is a strong and generally negative correlation between increasing age and increasing preference for "No Historical Ambience." The highest preference is within the 15-24 age group, the lowest in the 45-64 group. In the 65+ group the preference raises back up again.

Education demonstrates an equally strong and negative correlation between increasing education level and increasing preference for "No Historical Ambience." Those with post-graduate education chose sites with this characteristic with noticeably lower frequency than any other education level.

Historical Ambience: Test 2

In the case of "Historical Ambience: Test 2," "Historical Ambience" is defined as containing "Restored" or "Pseudo-Historical." "No Historical Ambience" is defined as containing "Adaptive Use" or "Modern." There were no significant differences found between the demographic subgroups tested for these categories.

Historical Ambience: Test 3

In the case of "Historical Ambience: Test 3," "Historical Ambience" is defined as "Restored" or "Pseudo-Historical" or "Adaptive Use." There were significant differences between age groups, education levels and visitor/local status.

There is an uneven correlation between age and preference for "Historical Ambience." The lowest preference is within the 15-24 age group, the highest in the 45-64 age group. The means of preference for the age groups in between did not increase steadily, but rather were staggered. Those in the 65+ group also dropped back down beneath the level of the 45-64 group.

Education level demonstrates a strong and positive correlation for "Historical Ambience" and increasing education. Only those with some high school did not fit this pattern. Those who graduated high school chose sites with this characteristic with the lowest frequency. This frequency increased steadily as education levels increased. Those with a post-graduate education chose these sites with the highest frequency.

Local/visitor status showed a significant correlation. Those who both reside and work in the city of Philadelphia selected "Historical Ambience" with a significantly lower frequency than those just visiting. Those who just reside or just work within Philadelphia selected these sites at a level somewhere between these two extremes.

"No Historical Ambience" shows the reverse correlations found in "Historical Ambience." There is an uneven correlation between age and preference for "No Historical Ambience." The highest preference is within the 15-24 age group, the lowest in the 45-64 age group. The means of preference for the age groups in between did not decrease steadily, but rather were staggered. Those in the 65+ group also raised back up above the level of the 45-64 group.

Education level demonstrates a strong and negative correlation for "No Historical Ambience" and increasing education. Only those with some high school did not fit this pattern. Those who graduated high school chose sites with this characteristic with the highest frequency. This frequency decreased steadily as education level increased. Those with a post-graduate education chose these sites with the lowest frequency.

Local/visitor status showed a significant correlation. Those who both reside and work in the city of Philadelphia selected "No Historical Ambience" with a significantly higher frequency than those just visiting. Those who just reside or just work within Philadelphia selected these sites at a level somewhere between these two extremes.

AGE OF APPEARANCE

AGE (5 groups)	p-value		15-24	25-34	35-44	45-64	65+
	0.01	Restored	(--)	(-)	(-)	(++)	(+)
	0.11	Pseudo					
	0.33	Adaptive					
	0.01	Modern	(++)	(-)	(+)	(--)	(+)

EDUCATION (5 groups)			Some HS	Grad HS	Some Col	Grad Col	Post Grad
	0.01	Restored	(--)	(-)	(-)	(+)	(++)
	0.29	Pseudo					
	0.06	Adaptive					
	0.05	Modern	(+)	(++)	(+)	(-)	(--)

GENDER			Female	Male
	0.48	Restored		
	0.09	Pseudo		
	0.33	Adaptive		
	0.45	Modern		

LOCAL / VISITOR (4 groups)			Resident & Worker	Phila. Resident	Phila. Worker	Visitor
	0.40	Restored				
	0.84	Pseudo				
	0.61	Adaptive				
	0.03	Modern	(++)	(-)	(-)	(--)

Legend: (++) Most Positive Correlation   (-) Negative Correlation
(+) Positive Correlation   (--) Most Negative Correlation

Note: There were a small number of missing demographic responses on the actual surveys.
These respondents have been temporarily removed from the relevant analysis
Age =<14 contained only 2 respondents.
This group has been removed from the Age analysis because of its small size.
P-values =<0.05 are highlighted, and further analyzed on the following pages.

Table 6.16. Philadelphia: Age of Appearance—overview

Age

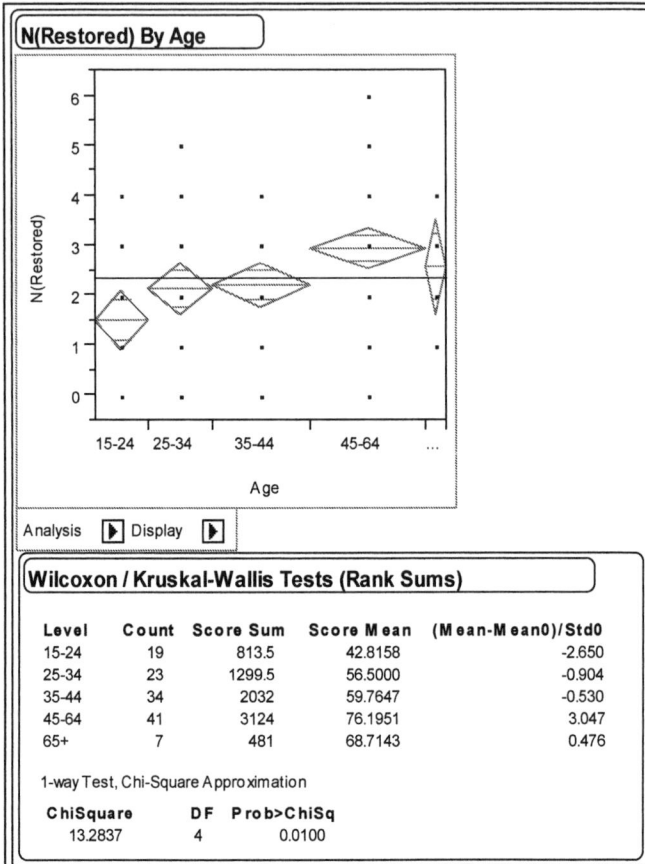

N(Restored) By Age

Wilcoxon / Kruskal-Wallis Tests (Rank Sums)

Level	Count	Score Sum	Score Mean	(Mean-Mean0)/Std0
15-24	19	813.5	42.8158	-2.650
25-34	23	1299.5	56.5000	-0.904
35-44	34	2032	59.7647	-0.530
45-64	41	3124	76.1951	3.047
65+	7	481	68.7143	0.476

1-way Test, Chi-Square Approximation

ChiSquare	DF	Prob>ChiSq
13.2837	4	0.0100

Figure 6.5. Philadelphia: Age of Appearance—restored by age

Education

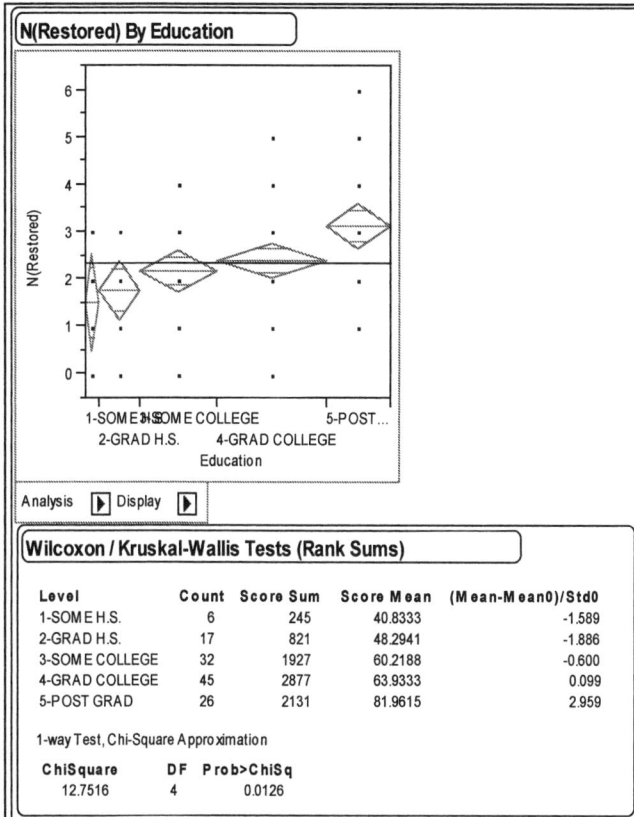

N(Restored) By Education

Analysis ▶ Display ▶

Wilcoxon / Kruskal-Wallis Tests (Rank Sums)

Level	Count	Score Sum	Score Mean	(Mean-Mean0)/Std0
1-SOME H.S.	6	245	40.8333	-1.589
2-GRAD H.S.	17	821	48.2941	-1.886
3-SOME COLLEGE	32	1927	60.2188	-0.600
4-GRAD COLLEGE	45	2877	63.9333	0.099
5-POST GRAD	26	2131	81.9615	2.959

1-way Test, Chi-Square Approximation

ChiSquare	DF	Prob>ChiSq
12.7516	4	0.0126

Figure 6.6. Philadelphia: Age of Appearance—restored by education

Age

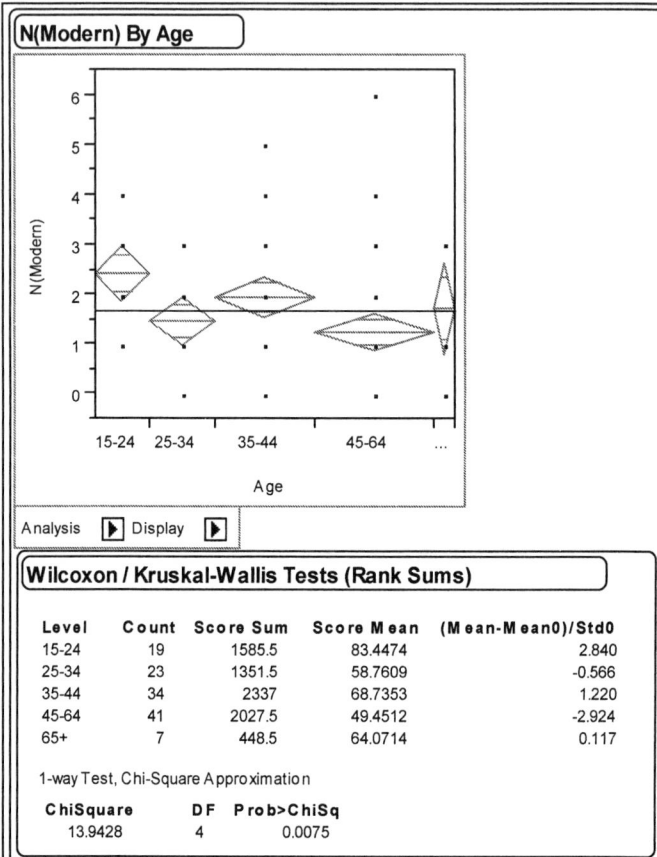

N(Modern) By Age

Level	Count	Score Sum	Score Mean	(Mean-Mean0)/Std0
15-24	19	1585.5	83.4474	2.840
25-34	23	1351.5	58.7609	-0.566
35-44	34	2337	68.7353	1.220
45-64	41	2027.5	49.4512	-2.924
65+	7	448.5	64.0714	0.117

1-way Test, Chi-Square Approximation

ChiSquare	DF	Prob>ChiSq
13.9428	4	0.0075

Figure 6.7. Philadelphia: Age of Appearance—modern by age

Education

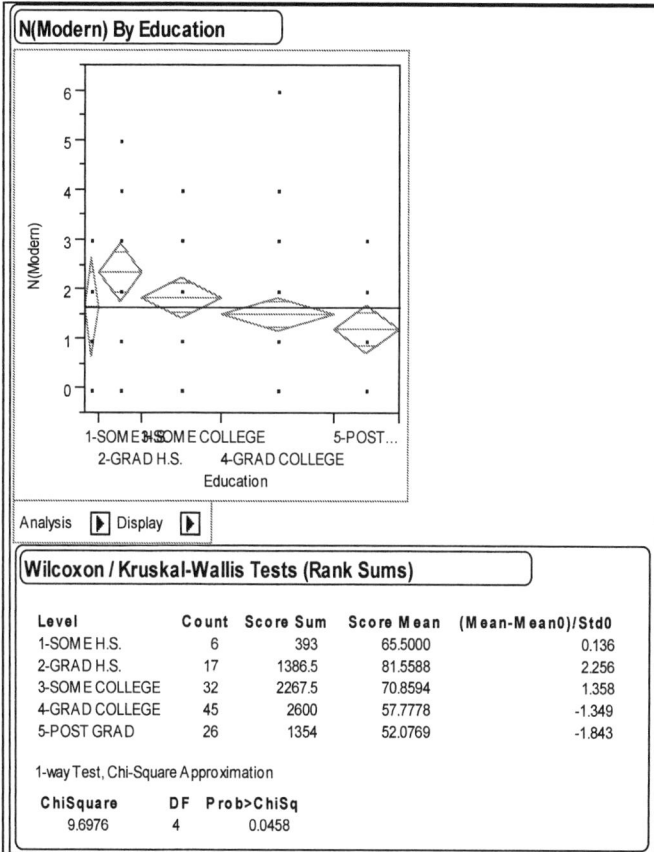

N(Modern) By Education

Analysis ▶ Display ▶

Wilcoxon / Kruskal-Wallis Tests (Rank Sums)

Level	Count	Score Sum	Score Mean	(Mean-Mean0)/Std0
1-SOME H.S.	6	393	65.5000	0.136
2-GRAD H.S.	17	1386.5	81.5588	2.256
3-SOME COLLEGE	32	2267.5	70.8594	1.358
4-GRAD COLLEGE	45	2600	57.7778	-1.349
5-POST GRAD	26	1354	52.0769	-1.843

1-way Test, Chi-Square Approximation

ChiSquare	DF	Prob>ChiSq
9.6976	4	0.0458

Figure 6.8. Philadelphia: Age of Appearance—modern by education

Local / Visitor

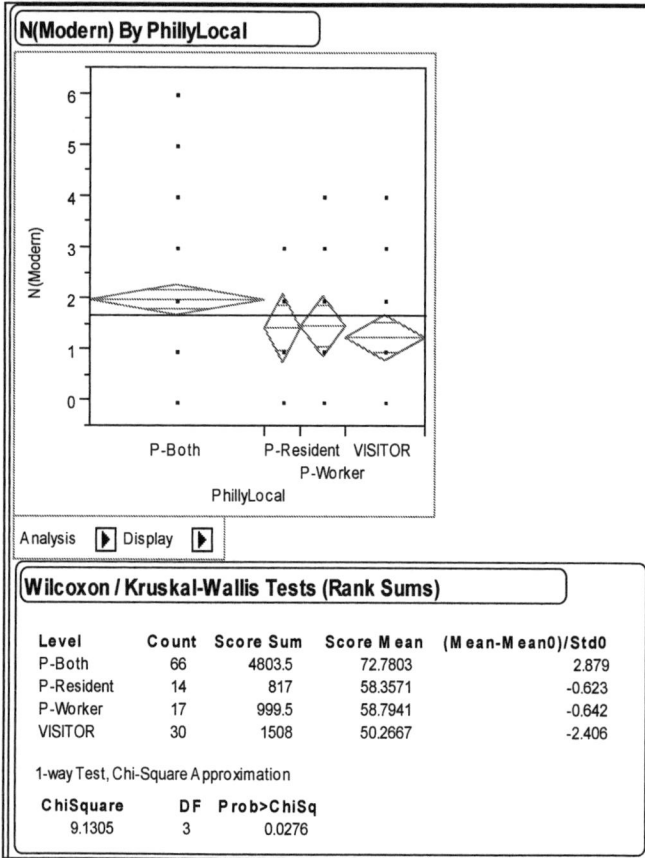

N(Modern) By PhillyLocal

Wilcoxon / Kruskal-Wallis Tests (Rank Sums)

Level	Count	Score Sum	Score Mean	(Mean-Mean0)/Std0
P-Both	66	4803.5	72.7803	2.879
P-Resident	14	817	58.3571	-0.623
P-Worker	17	999.5	58.7941	-0.642
VISITOR	30	1508	50.2667	-2.406

1-way Test, Chi-Square Approximation

ChiSquare	DF	Prob>ChiSq
9.1305	3	0.0276

Figure 6.9. Philadelphia: Age of Appearance—modern by local

HIST AMBIANCE: Test 1

	p-value						
AGE (5 groups)			**15-24**	**25-34**	**35-44**	**45-64**	**65+**
	0.01	**HIST AMB (Restored)**	(--)	(-)	(-)	(++)	(+)
	0.01	**NO (Pseud/Adap/Mod)**	(++)	(+)	(+)	(--)	(-)

			Some HS	Grad HS	Some Col	Grad Col	Post Grad
EDUCATION (5 groups)			**Some HS**	**Grad HS**	**Some Col**	**Grad Col**	**Post Grad**
	0.01	**HIST AMB (Restored)**	(--)	(-)	(-)	(+)	(++)
	0.01	**NO (Pseud/Adap/Mod)**	(++)	(+)	(+)	(-)	(--)

			Female	Male
GENDER			**Female**	**Male**
	0.48	HIST AMB (Restored)		
	0.48	NO (Pseud/Adap/Mod)		

			Resident & Worker	Phila. Resident	Phila. Worker	Visitor
LOCAL / VISITOR (4 groups)			**Resident & Worker**	**Phila. Resident**	**Phila. Worker**	**Visitor**
	0.40	HIST AMB (Restored)				
	0.40	NO (Pseud/Adap/Mod)				

Legend: (++) Most Positive Correlation   (-) Negative Correlation
           (+) Positive Correlation   (--) Most Negative Correlation

Note: There were a small number of missing demographic responses on the actual surveys.
These respondents have been temporarily removed from the relevant analysis
Age =<14 contained only 2 respondents.
This group has been removed from the Age analysis because of its small size.
P-values =<0.05 are highlighted, and further analyzed on the following pages.

Table 6.17. Philadelphia: Ambience Test 1—overview

Age

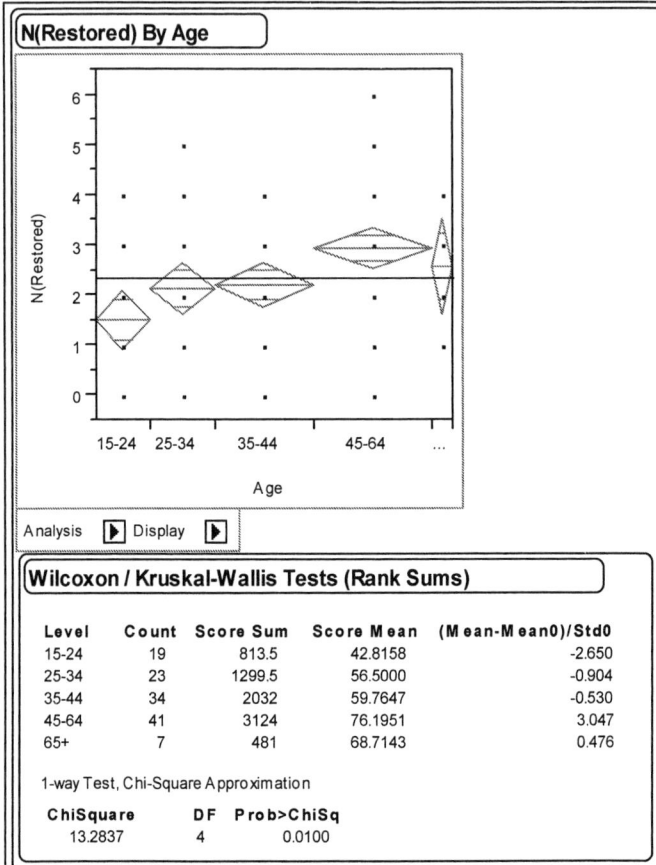

Figure 6.10. Philadelphia: Ambience Test 1—ambience by age

Education

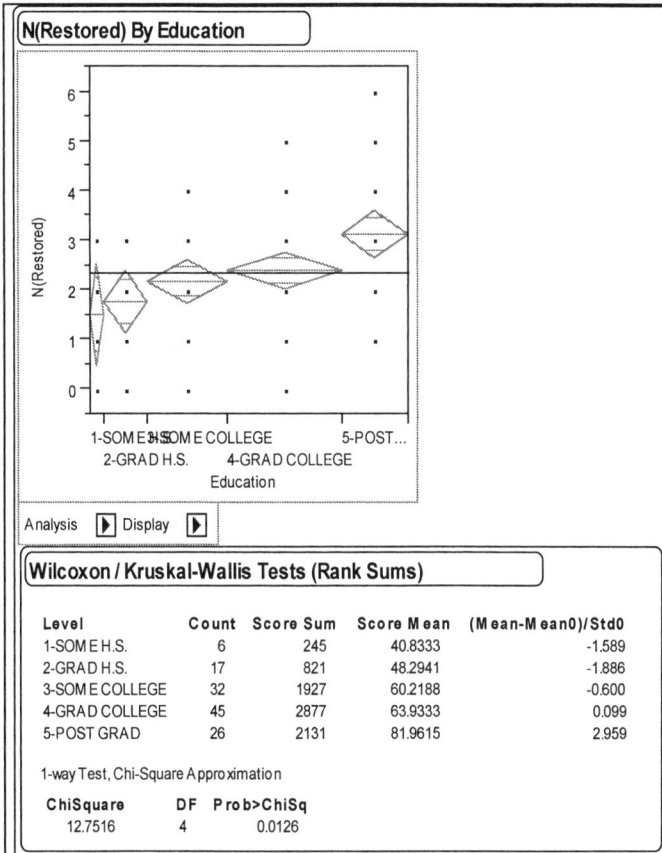

N(Restored) By Education

Analysis ▶ Display ▶

Wilcoxon / Kruskal-Wallis Tests (Rank Sums)

Level	Count	Score Sum	Score Mean	(Mean-Mean0)/Std0
1-SOME H.S.	6	245	40.8333	-1.589
2-GRAD H.S.	17	821	48.2941	-1.886
3-SOME COLLEGE	32	1927	60.2188	-0.600
4-GRAD COLLEGE	45	2877	63.9333	0.099
5-POST GRAD	26	2131	81.9615	2.959

1-way Test, Chi-Square Approximation

ChiSquare	DF	Prob>ChiSq
12.7516	4	0.0126

Figure 6.11. Philadelphia: Ambience Test 1—ambience by education

Age

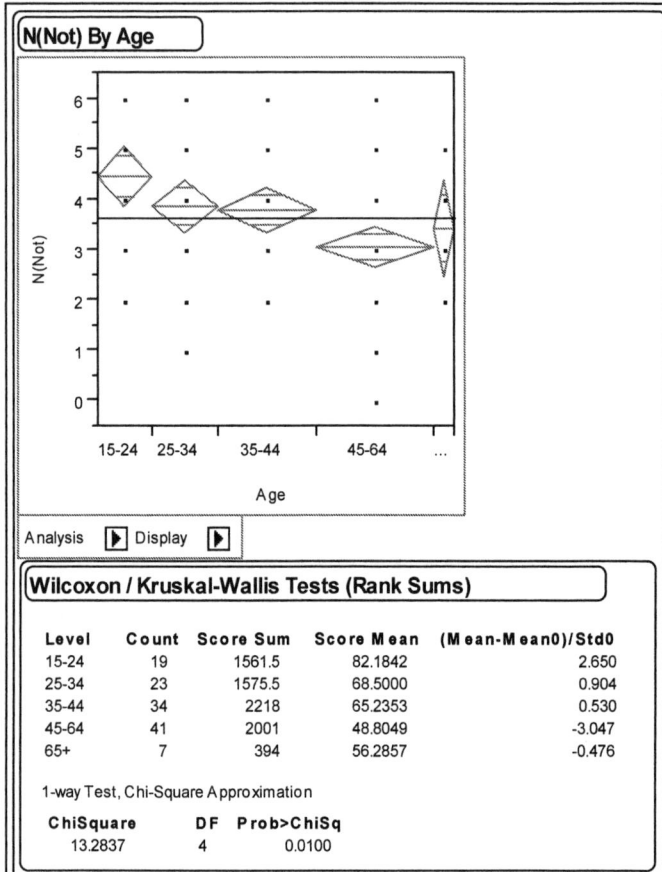

N(Not) By Age

Wilcoxon / Kruskal-Wallis Tests (Rank Sums)

Level	Count	Score Sum	Score Mean	(Mean-Mean0)/Std0
15-24	19	1561.5	82.1842	2.650
25-34	23	1575.5	68.5000	0.904
35-44	34	2218	65.2353	0.530
45-64	41	2001	48.8049	-3.047
65+	7	394	56.2857	-0.476

1-way Test, Chi-Square Approximation

ChiSquare	DF	Prob>ChiSq
13.2837	4	0.0100

NOTE: (not)=not restored

Figure 6.12. Philadelphia: Ambience Test 1—no by age

Education

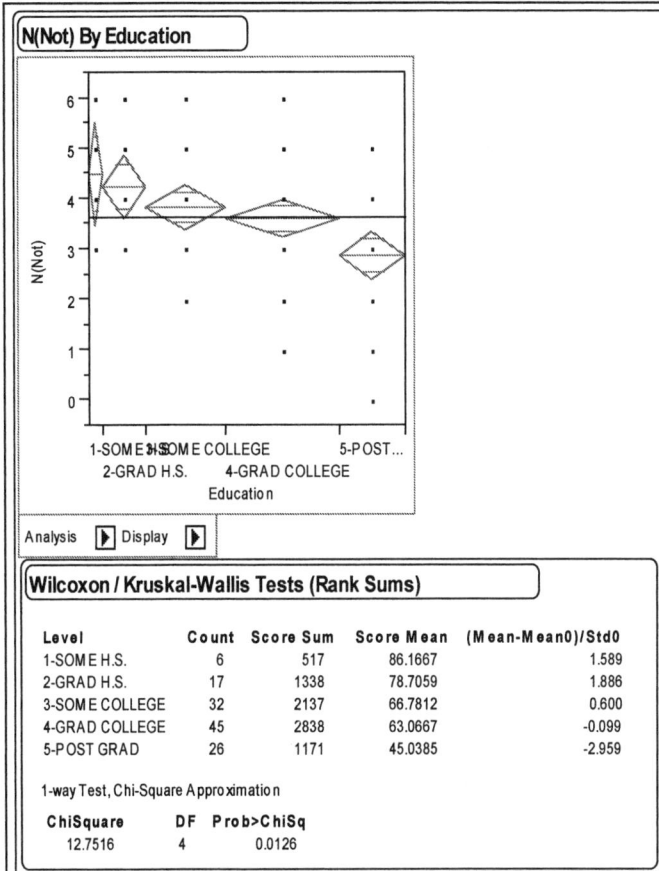

N(Not) By Education

Analysis ▶ Display ▶

Wilcoxon / Kruskal-Wallis Tests (Rank Sums)

Level	Count	Score Sum	Score Mean	(Mean-Mean0)/Std0
1-SOME H.S.	6	517	86.1667	1.589
2-GRAD H.S.	17	1338	78.7059	1.886
3-SOME COLLEGE	32	2137	66.7812	0.600
4-GRAD COLLEGE	45	2838	63.0667	-0.099
5-POST GRAD	26	1171	45.0385	-2.959

1-way Test, Chi-Square Approximation

ChiSquare	DF	Prob>ChiSq
12.7516	4	0.0126

NOTE: (not)=not restored

Figure 6.13. Philadelphia: Ambience Test 1—no by education

HIST AMBIANCE: Test 2

	p-value		15-24	25-34	35-44	45-64	65+
AGE (5 groups)							
	0.13	HIST AMB (Restored/Pseudo)					
	0.13	NO (Adaptive/Modern)					

			Some HS	Grad HS	Some Col	Grad Col	Post Grad
EDUCATION (5 groups)							
	0.06	HIST AMB (Restored/Pseudo)					
	0.06	NO (Adaptive/Modern)					

			Female	Male
GENDER				
	0.10	HIST AMB (Restored/Pseudo)		
	0.10	NO (Adaptive/Modern)		

			Resident & Worker	Phila. Resident	Phila. Worker	Visitor
LOCAL / VISITOR (4 groups)						
	0.62	HIST AMB (Restored/Pseudo)				
	0.62	NO (Adaptive/Modern)				

Legend: **(++) Most Positive Correlation**   **(-) Negative Correlation**
                (+) Positive Correlation   **(--) Most Negative Correlation**

Note: There were a small number of missing demographic responses on the actual surveys. These respondents have been temporarily removed from the relevant analysis
Age =<14 contained only 2 respondents.
This group has been removed from the Age analysis because of its small size.
P-values =<0.05 are highlighted, and further analyzed on the following pages.

Table 6.18. Philadelphia: Ambience Test 2—overview

HIST AMBIANCE: Test 3

AGE (5 groups)	p-value		15-24	25-34	35-44	45-64	65+
	0.01	HIST AMB (Rest/Pseud/Adap)	(--)	(+)	(-)	(++)	(-)
	0.01	NO (Modern)	(++)	(-)	(+)	(--)	(+)

EDUCATION (5 groups)			Some HS	Grad HS	Some Col	Grad Col	Post Grad
	0.05	HIST AMB (Rest/Pseud/Adap)	(-)	(--)	(-)	(+)	(++)
	0.04	NO (Modern)	(+)	(++)	(+)	(-)	(--)

GENDER			Female	Male
	0.45	HIST AMB (Rest/Pseud/Adap)		
	0.45	NO (Modern)		

LOCAL / VISITOR (4 groups)			Resident & Worker	Phila. Resident	Phila. Worker	Visitor
	0.03	HIST AMB (Rest/Pseud/Adap)	(--)	(+)	(+)	(++)
	0.03	NO (Modern)	(++)	(-)	(-)	(--)

Legend: (++) Most Positive Correlation   (-) Negative Correlation
(+) Positive Correlation   (--) Most Negative Correlation

Note: There were a small number of missing demographic responses on the actual surveys. These respondents have been temporarily removed from the relevant analysis Age =<14 contained only 2 respondents. This group has been removed from the Age analysis because of its small size. P-values =<0.05 are highlighted, and further analyzed on the following pages.

Table 6.19. Philadelphia: Ambience Test 3—overview

Age

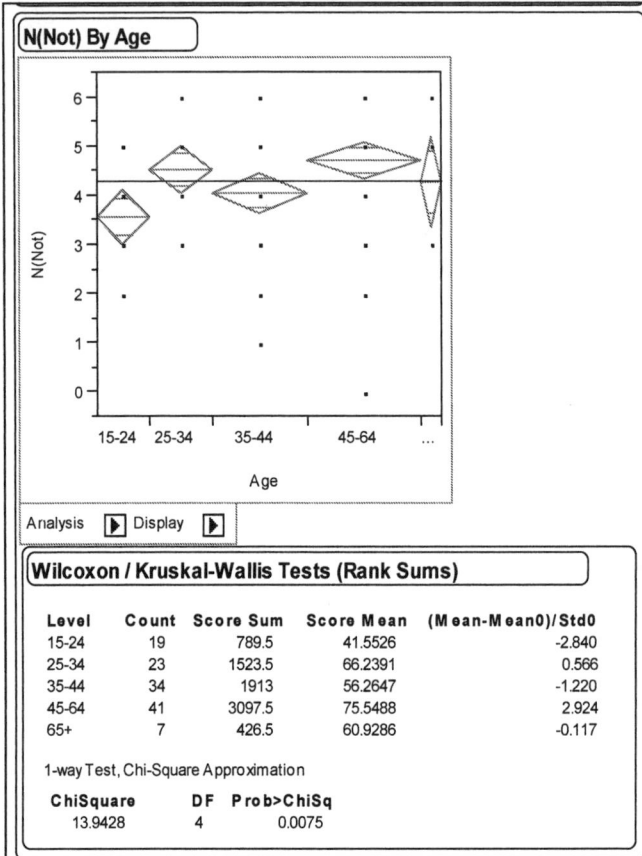

N(Not) By Age

Analysis ▶ Display ▶

Wilcoxon / Kruskal-Wallis Tests (Rank Sums)

Level	Count	Score Sum	Score Mean	(Mean-Mean0)/Std0
15-24	19	789.5	41.5526	-2.840
25-34	23	1523.5	66.2391	0.566
35-44	34	1913	56.2647	-1.220
45-64	41	3097.5	75.5488	2.924
65+	7	426.5	60.9286	-0.117

1-way Test, Chi-Square Approximation

ChiSquare	DF	Prob>ChiSq
13.9428	4	0.0075

NOTE: (not)=not modern

Figure 6.14. Philadelphia: Ambience Test 3—ambience by age

Education

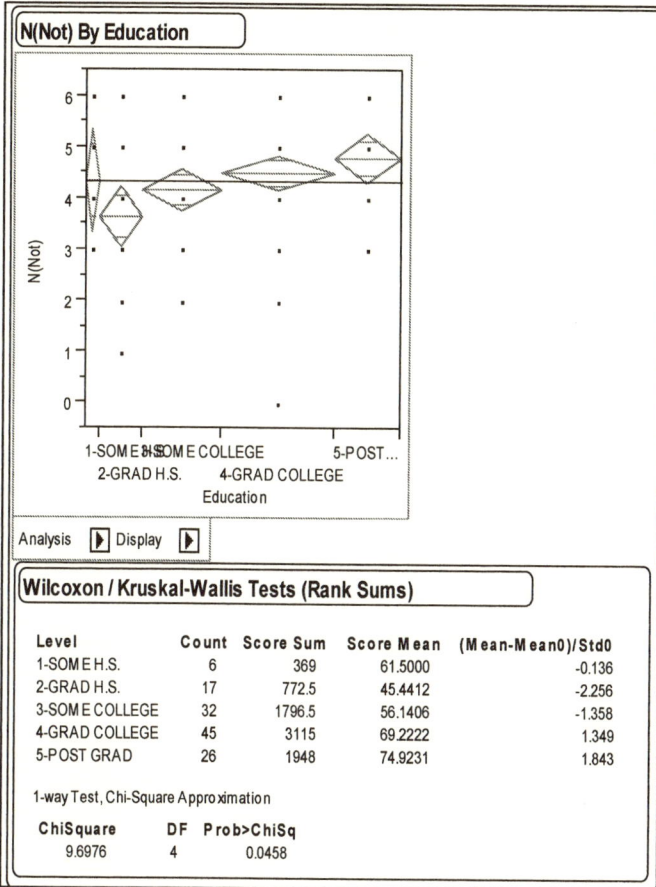

N(Not) By Education

Analysis ▶ Display ▶

Wilcoxon / Kruskal-Wallis Tests (Rank Sums)

Level	Count	Score Sum	Score Mean	(Mean-Mean0)/Std0
1-SOME H.S.	6	369	61.5000	-0.136
2-GRAD H.S.	17	772.5	45.4412	-2.256
3-SOME COLLEGE	32	1796.5	56.1406	-1.358
4-GRAD COLLEGE	45	3115	69.2222	1.349
5-POST GRAD	26	1948	74.9231	1.843

1-way Test, Chi-Square Approximation

ChiSquare	DF	Prob>ChiSq
9.6976	4	0.0458

NOTE: (not)=not modern

Figure 6.15. Philadelphia: Ambience Test 3—ambience by education

Local / Visitor

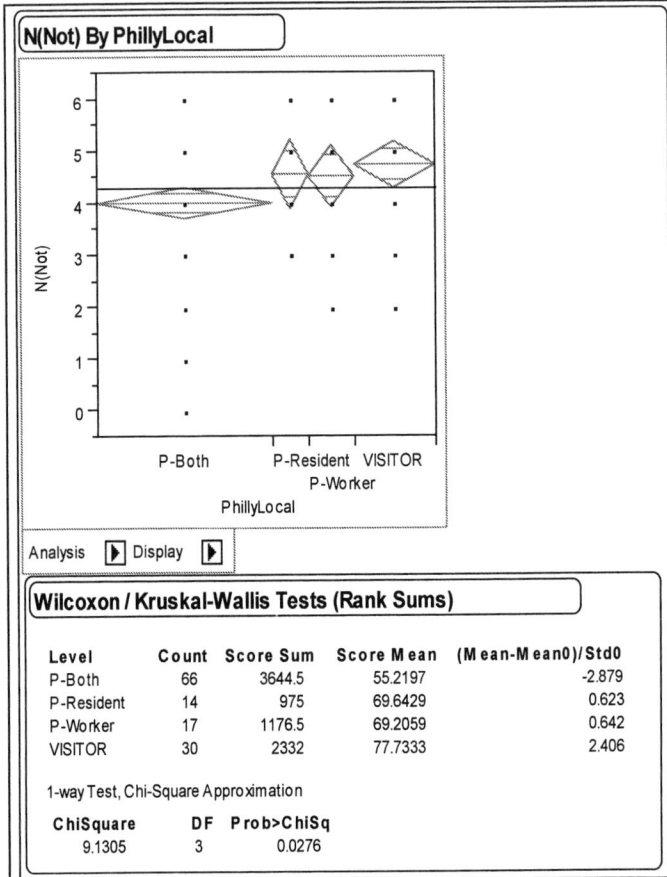

N(Not) By PhillyLocal

Analysis ▶ Display ▶

Wilcoxon / Kruskal-Wallis Tests (Rank Sums)

Level	Count	Score Sum	Score Mean	(Mean-Mean0)/Std0
P-Both	66	3644.5	55.2197	-2.879
P-Resident	14	975	69.6429	0.623
P-Worker	17	1176.5	69.2059	0.642
VISITOR	30	2332	77.7333	2.406

1-way Test, Chi-Square Approximation

ChiSquare	DF	Prob>ChiSq
9.1305	3	0.0276

NOTE: (not)=not modern

Figure 6.16. Philadelphia: Ambience Test 3—ambience by local

Age

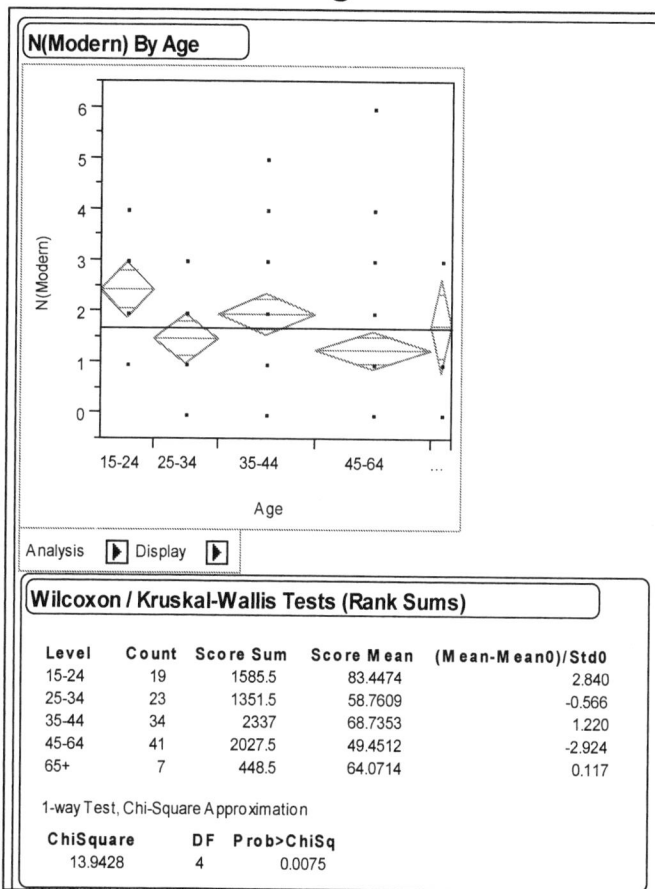

N(Modern) By Age

Analysis ▶ Display ▶

Wilcoxon / Kruskal-Wallis Tests (Rank Sums)

Level	Count	Score Sum	Score Mean	(Mean-Mean0)/Std0
15-24	19	1585.5	83.4474	2.840
25-34	23	1351.5	58.7609	-0.566
35-44	34	2337	68.7353	1.220
45-64	41	2027.5	49.4512	-2.924
65+	7	448.5	64.0714	0.117

1-way Test, Chi-Square Approximation

ChiSquare	DF	Prob>ChiSq
13.9428	4	0.0075

Figure 6.17. Philadelphia: Ambience Test 3—no by age

Education

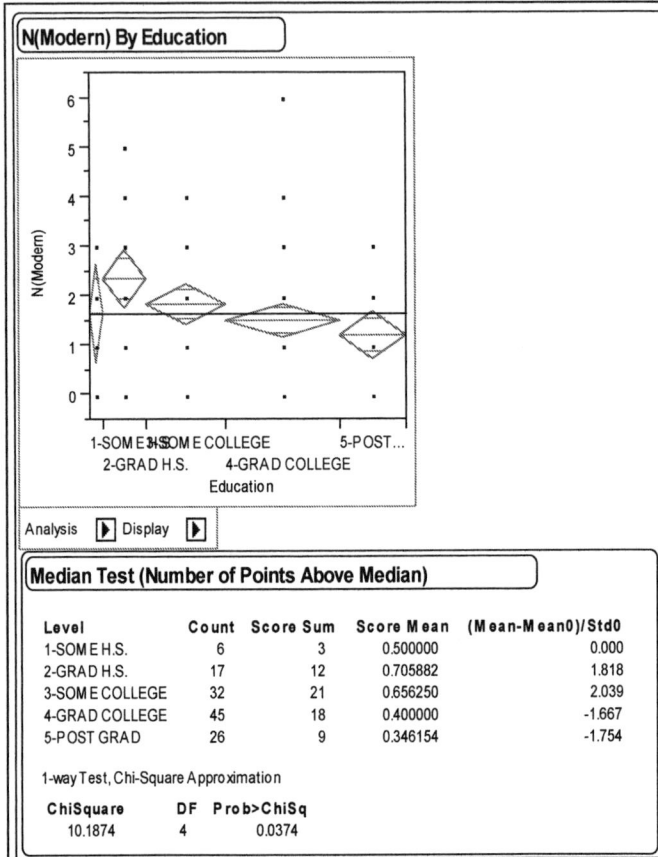

Level	Count	Score Sum	Score Mean	(Mean-Mean0)/Std0
1-SOME H.S.	6	3	0.500000	0.000
2-GRAD H.S.	17	12	0.705882	1.818
3-SOME COLLEGE	32	21	0.656250	2.039
4-GRAD COLLEGE	45	18	0.400000	-1.667
5-POST GRAD	26	9	0.346154	-1.754

1-way Test, Chi-Square Approximation

ChiSquare	DF	Prob>ChiSq
10.1874	4	0.0374

Figure 6.18. Philadelphia: Ambience Test 3—no by education

Local / Visitor

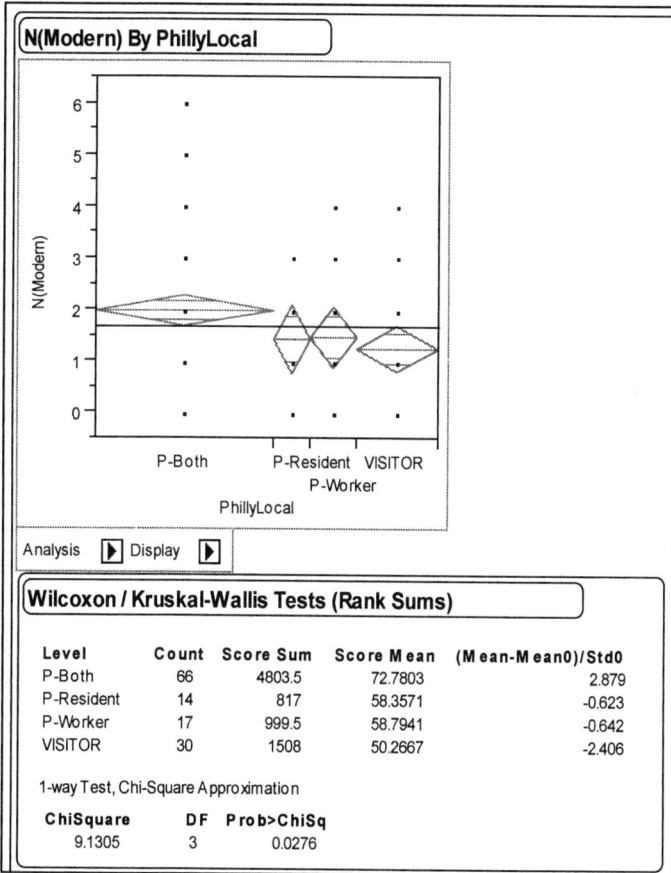

N(Modern) By PhillyLocal

Wilcoxon / Kruskal-Wallis Tests (Rank Sums)

Level	Count	Score Sum	Score Mean	(Mean-Mean0)/Std0
P-Both	66	4803.5	72.7803	2.879
P-Resident	14	817	58.3571	-0.623
P-Worker	17	999.5	58.7941	-0.642
VISITOR	30	1508	50.2667	-2.406

1-way Test, Chi-Square Approximation

ChiSquare	DF	Prob>ChiSq
9.1305	3	0.0276

Figure 6.19. Philadelphia: Ambience Test 3—no by local

Greenery in Image

In the category of "Greenery in Image," there were significant differences between education levels. Education level demonstrates a negative correlation to preference for "No Greenery." Those with post-graduate education chose sites with "No Greenery" significantly less frequently than any other education level.

Water in Image

In the category of "Water in Image," no significant differences were noted between the demographic subgroups that were analyzed.

On Tourist Map

In the category "On Tourist Map," there were significant differences between age groups and local/visitor status.

By aggregating the age groups into one group under age 35, and one 35 and over, significant differences were found that were hinted at, but not revealed with age as five separate groups. Local/visitor has been aggregated into two groups, locals (all those who reside, work or both in Philadelphia), and visitors. Significant differences were found in this demographic group as well, that were only hinted at when it was analyzed as four separate categories.

Those under 35 chose sites that were labelled "On the Tourist Map" with a significantly lower frequency than those over 35. Those who either reside, work or both in the city of Philadelphia chose sites "On the Tourist Map" with significantly lower frequency than visitors.

Conversely, those under 35 chose sites that were "Not on Tourist Map" with a significantly higher frequency than those over 35. Locals also chose sites "Not on the Tourist Map" with significantly higher frequency than visitors.

Expected in Urban Waterfront

In the category "Expected in Urban Waterfront," there were significant differences between age groups.

There is a strong and generally positive correlation between increasing age and increasing preference for "Expected." The preferences aggregate in two basic groupings, those under 35 and those 35 and over. Those under 35 chose sites that were "Expected" in an urban waterfront with significantly less frequency than those 35 and over.

Conversely there is a strong and generally negative correlation between increasing age and increasing preference for "Unexpected." Those under 35 chose sites that were "Unexpected" in an urban waterfront with significantly higher frequency than those over 35.

Summary of Demographic Analysis

The demographic category of age has a significant correlation to a number of different evaluative characteristics analyzed in this survey. Increasing age with 15-24 as the low point and 45-64 as the high, corresponds to increasing preference for "Restored," and "Expected" in an Urban Waterfront. Increasing age also corresponds to decreasing preference for "Modern," and for "Unexpected." Those under 35 showed a preference for sites "Not on the Tourist Map," compared to those 35 and over. Conversely those under 35 showed less preference for sites "On the Tourist Map" than those 35 and over.

The demographic category of education also has a significant correlation to a number of different evaluative characteristics analyzed in this survey. Increasing education corresponds to increasing preference for "Restored." It also corresponds to decreasing preference for "Modern." Only a small group of individuals surveyed for whom some high school was the highest education level attained, does not follow this trend for preference for "Modern."

Those groups with anything less than a post graduate education showed a greater preference for sites with "No Greenery" in them, than those with a post graduate education.

The demographic category of gender has shown no significant correlation with any of the evaluative categories analyzed in this survey.

The demographic category of local/visitor status has shown significant correlation between two evaluative categories, "Age of Appearance" and "On Tourist Map." Those who both reside and work in the city of Philadelphia showed a preference for "Modern" over those who are just visitors. Those who just reside or just work within Philadelphia showed a preference somewhere between the two.

The preference for sites that are labelled "On the Tourist Map" is greater for visitors than for locals. Conversely these visitors preferred sites "Not on the Tourist Map" less frequently than the other groups. It can not be known, however, if it was the labelling on the map that increased the attraction for visitors, or it was something inherent in the site itself that encouraged its placement on the map. Likely it was some combination of the two.

This breakdown of the younger age groups having a preference for sites off the tourist map (compared to older age groups), corresponds to the same younger age groups preference for the unexpected. Whether a site is expected in a waterfront area appears somewhat more significant than if the site is labelled on the tourist map for affecting preference. There was, however, much overlap between those photos that were on the tourist map and those that included expected sites along an urban waterfront with tourism, therefore, distinguishing which feature has a stronger effect on preference is difficult.

Additionally, those who are visitors to Philadelphia indicate a higher preference for sites "On the Tourist Map." This likely is due to the combination of the influence of the map and other tourist literature that highlights these particular sites, as well as the sites themselves. Those who created the map, pre-selected sites they felt were worth seeing for the visitor. This can become a default core package that becomes a tourist's Philadelphia. Those who reside, work or both in Philadelphia are less attracted to these sites. They are also less dependent on the tourist map for guidance.

GREENERY IN IMAGE

	p-value						
AGE (5 groups)			**15-24**	**25-34**	**35-44**	**45-64**	**65+**
	0.13	Moderate Greenery					
	0.55	Minimal Greenery					
	0.11	No Greenery					
EDUCATION (5 groups)			**Some HS**	**Grad HS**	**Some Col**	**Grad Col**	**Post Grad**
	0.07	Moderate Greenery					
	0.87	Minimal Greenery					
	0.04	**No Greenery**	(++)	(+)	(+)	(+)	(--)
GENDER			**Female**	**Male**			
	0.39	Moderate Greenery					
	0.23	Minimal Greenery					
	0.83	No Greenery					
LOCAL / VISITOR (4 groups)			**Resident & Worker**	**Phila. Resident**	**Phila. Worker**	**Visitor**	
	0.45	Moderate Greenery					
	0.64	Minimal Greenery					
	0.11	No Greenery					

Legend: Positive Correlation
(+) Positive Correlation
(-) Negative Correlation
(--) Most Negative Correlation

Note: There were a small number of missing demographic responses on the actual surveys. These respondents have been temporarily removed from the relevant analysis
Age =<14 contained only 2 respondents. This group has been removed from the Age analysis because of its small size.
P-values =<0.05 are highlighted, and further analyzed on the following pages.

Table 6.20. Philadelphia: Greenery—overview

Education

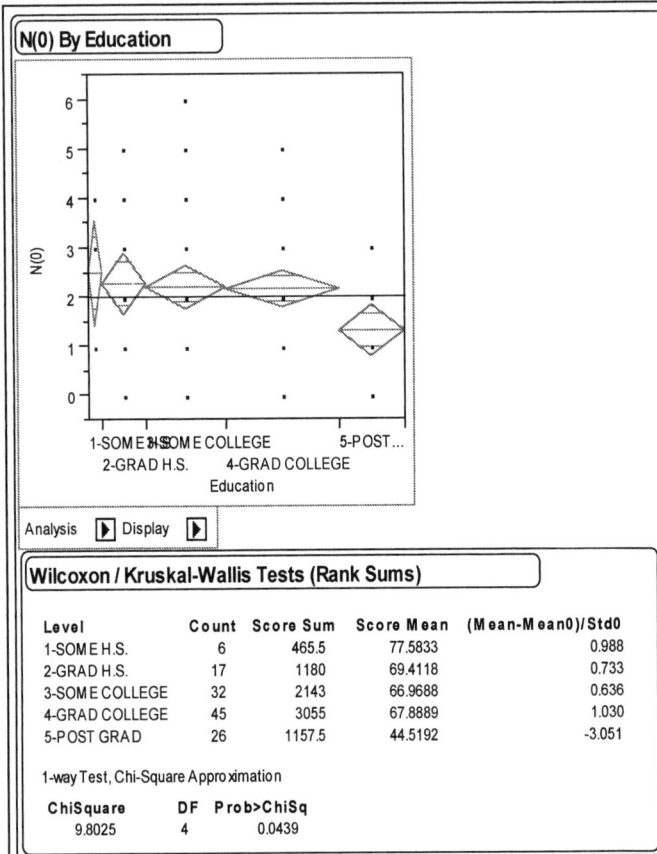

Figure 6.20. Philadelphia: Greenery—none by education

WATER IN IMAGE

	p-value		15-24	25-34	35-44	45-64	65+
AGE (5 groups)							
	0.61	Water					
	0.61	No Water					

			Some HS	Grad HS	Some Col	Grad Col	Post Grad
EDUCATION (5 groups)							
	0.63	Water					
	0.63	No Water					

			Female	Male
GENDER				
	0.73	Water		
	0.73	No Water		

			Resident & Worker	Phila. Resident	Phila. Worker	Visitor
LOCAL / VISITOR (4 groups)						
	0.17	Water				
	0.17	No Water				

Legend: Positive Correlation   (-) Negative Correlation
(+) Positive Correlation   (--) Most Negative Correlation

Note: There were a small number of missing demographic responses on the actual surveys. These respondents have been temporarily removed from the relevant analysis Age =<14 contained only 2 respondents. This group has been removed from the Age analysis because of its small size. P-values =<0.05 are highlighted, and further analyzed on the following pages.

Table 6.21. Philadelphia: Water—overview

ON TOURIST MAP

p-value		15-24	25-34	35-44	45-64	65+
AGE (5 groups)						
0.11	On Map					
0.11	Not on Map					

		<=34	35+
AGE (2 groups)			
0.01	**On Map**	**(--)**	**(++)**
0.01	**Not on Map**	**(++)**	**(--)**

		Some HS	Grad HS	Some Col	Grad Col	Post Grad
EDUCATION (5 groups)						
0.11	On Map					
0.11	Not on Map					

		Female	Male
GENDER			
0.76	On Map		
0.76	Not on Map		

		Resident & Worker	Phila. Resident	Phila. Worker	Visitor
LOCAL / VISITOR (4 groups)					
0.06	On Map				
0.06	Not on Map				

		Phila. Local	Visitor
LOCAL / VISITOR (2 groups)			
0.01	**On Map**	**(--)**	**(++)**
0.01	**Not on Map**	**(++)**	**(--)**

Legend: Positive Correlation   (-) Negative Correlation
        (+) Positive Correlation   (--) Most Negative Correlation

Note: There were a small number of missing demographic responses on the actual surveys. These respondents have been temporarily removed from the relevant analysis Age =<14 contained only 2 respondents. This group has been removed from the Age analysis because of its small size. P-values =<0.05 are highlighted, and further analyzed on the following pages.

Table 6.22. Philadelphia: On Tourist Map—overview

Age

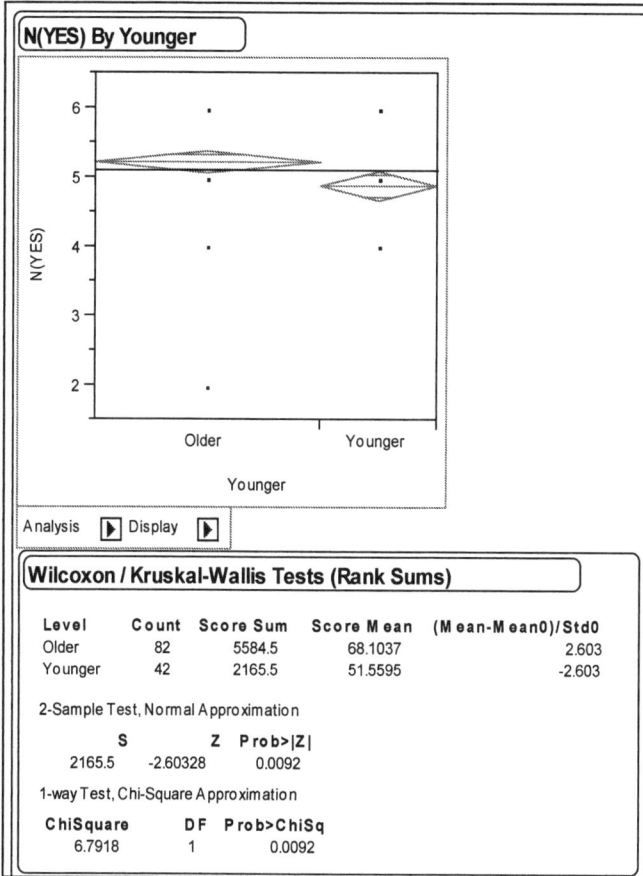

N(YES) By Younger

Wilcoxon / Kruskal-Wallis Tests (Rank Sums)

Level	Count	Score Sum	Score Mean	(Mean-Mean0)/Std0
Older	82	5584.5	68.1037	2.603
Younger	42	2165.5	51.5595	-2.603

2-Sample Test, Normal Approximation

S	Z	Prob>|Z|
2165.5	-2.60328	0.0092

1-way Test, Chi-Square Approximation

ChiSquare	DF	Prob>ChiSq
6.7918	1	0.0092

Figure 6.21. Philadelphia: On Tourist Map—yes by age

Local / Visitor

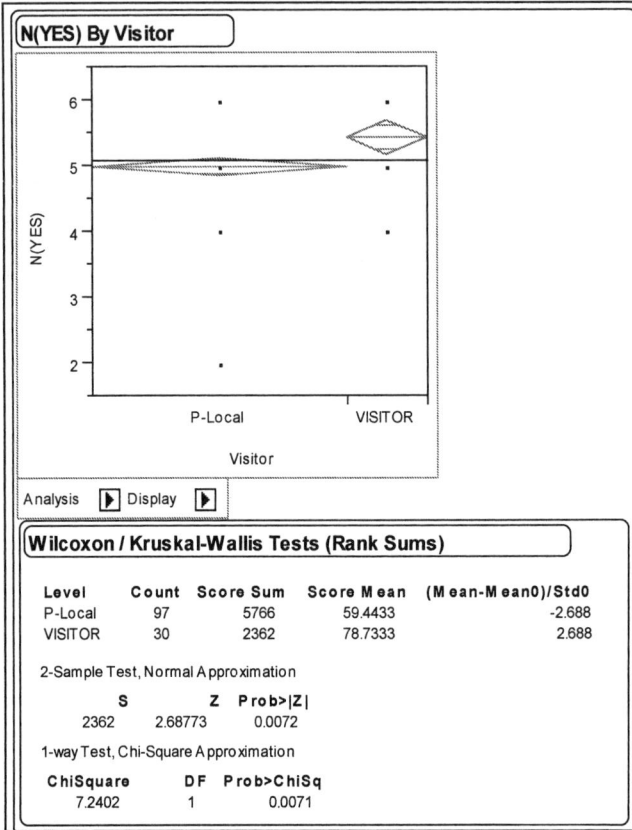

| N(YES) By Visitor |

P-Local   VISITOR

Visitor

Analysis ▶ Display ▶

Wilcoxon / Kruskal-Wallis Tests (Rank Sums)

Level	Count	Score Sum	Score Mean	(Mean-Mean0)/Std0
P-Local	97	5766	59.4433	-2.688
VISITOR	30	2362	78.7333	2.688

2-Sample Test, Normal Approximation

S	Z	Prob>|Z|
2362	2.68773	0.0072

1-way Test, Chi-Square Approximation

ChiSquare	DF	Prob>ChiSq
7.2402	1	0.0071

Figure 6.22. Philadelphia: On Tourist Map—yes by local

Age

N(no) By Younger

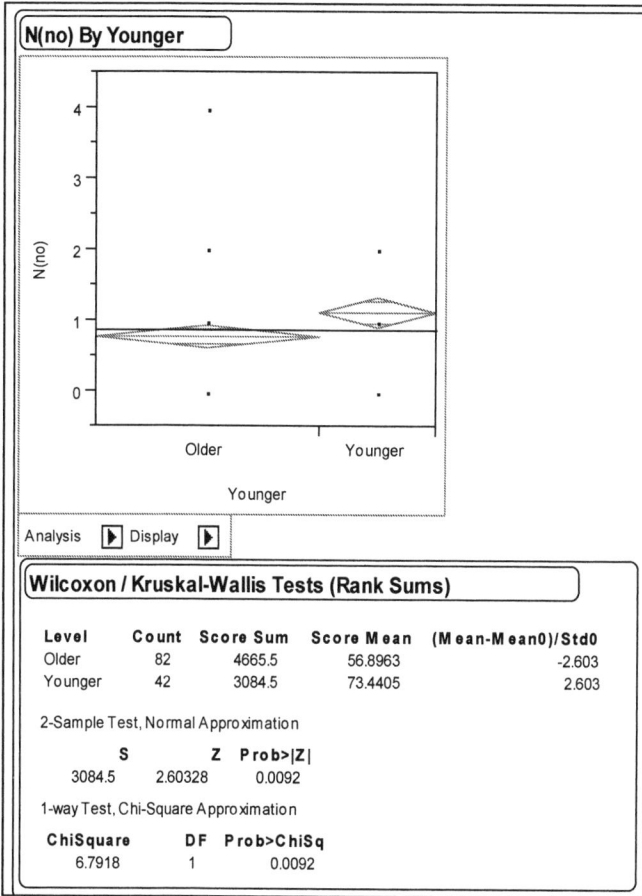

N(no)

Older   Younger

Younger

Analysis ▶ Display ▶

Wilcoxon / Kruskal-Wallis Tests (Rank Sums)

Level	Count	Score Sum	Score Mean	(Mean-Mean0)/Std0
Older	82	4665.5	56.8963	-2.603
Younger	42	3084.5	73.4405	2.603

2-Sample Test, Normal Approximation

S	Z	Prob>|Z|
3084.5	2.60328	0.0092

1-way Test, Chi-Square Approximation

ChiSquare	DF	Prob>ChiSq
6.7918	1	0.0092

Figure 6.23. Philadelphia: On Tourist Map—no by age

Local / Visitor

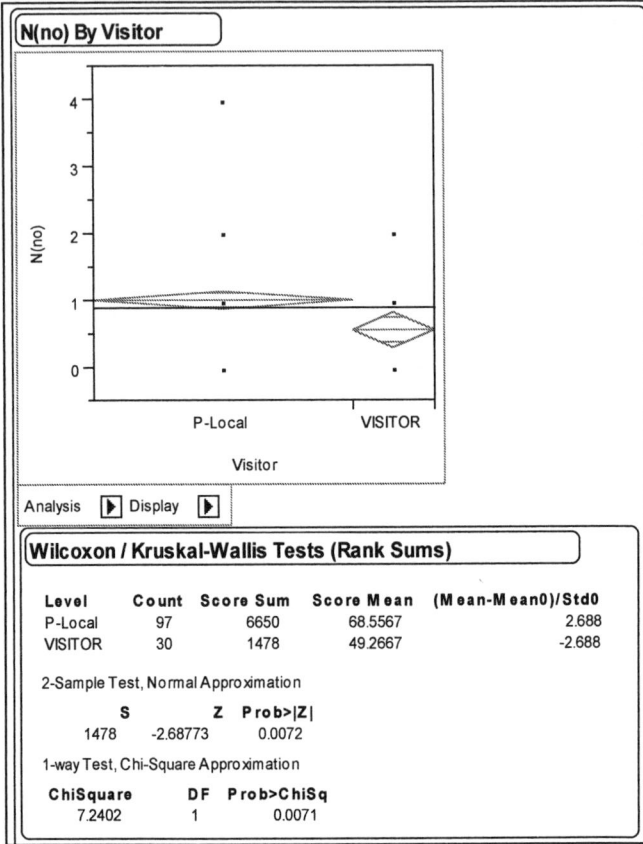

N(no) By Visitor

Analysis ▶ Display ▶

Wilcoxon / Kruskal-Wallis Tests (Rank Sums)

Level	Count	Score Sum	Score Mean	(Mean-Mean0)/Std0
P-Local	97	6650	68.5567	2.688
VISITOR	30	1478	49.2667	-2.688

2-Sample Test, Normal Approximation

S	Z	Prob>|Z|
1478	-2.68773	0.0072

1-way Test, Chi-Square Approximation

ChiSquare	DF	Prob>ChiSq
7.2402	1	0.0071

Figure 6.24. Philadelphia: On Tourist Map—no by local

EXPECTED IN URBAN WATERFRONT

AGE (5 groups)	p-value		15-24	25-34	35-44	45-64	65+
	0.03	Expected	(--)	(-)	(+)	(++)	(+)
	0.03	Unexpected	(++)	(+)	(-)	(--)	(-)

EDUCATION (5 groups)			Some HS	Grad HS	Some Col	Grad Col	Post Grad
	0.48	Expected					
	0.48	Unexpected					

GENDER			Female	Male
	0.48	Expected		
	0.48	Unexpected		

LOCAL / VISITOR (4 groups)			Resident & Worker	Phila. Resident	Phila. Worker	Visitor
	0.38	Expected				
	0.38	Unexpected				

Legend: Positive Correlation   (-) Negative Correlation
(+) Positive Correlation   (--) Most Negative Correlation

Note: There were a small number of missing demographic responses on the actual surveys.
These respondents have been temporarily removed from the relevant analysis
Age =<14 contained only 2 respondents.
This group has been removed from the Age analysis because of its small size.
P-values =<0.05 are highlighted, and further analyzed on the following pages.

Table 6.23. Philadelphia: Expected—overview

Age

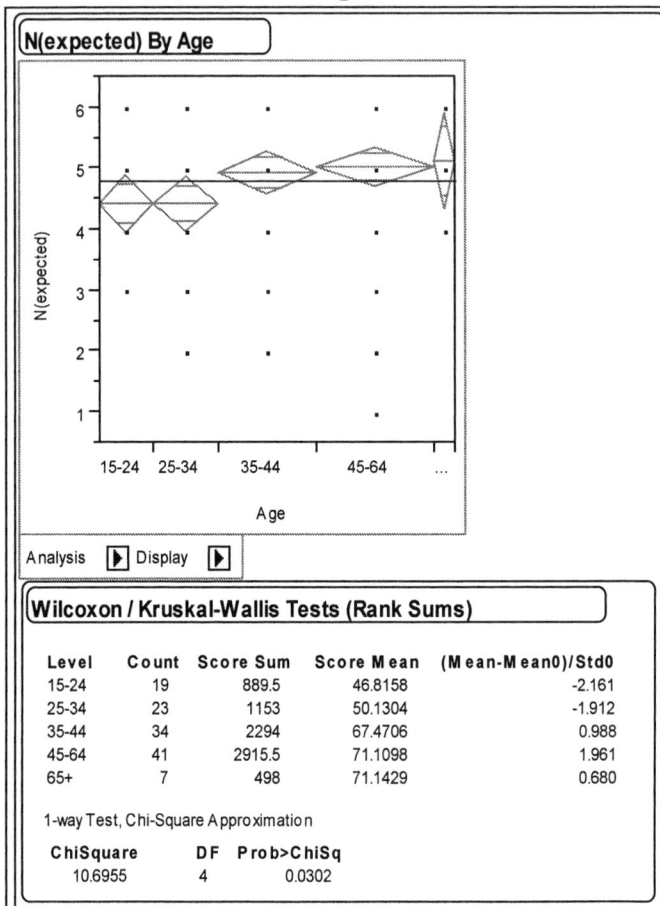

N(expected) By Age

Level	Count	Score Sum	Score Mean	(Mean-Mean0)/Std0
15-24	19	889.5	46.8158	-2.161
25-34	23	1153	50.1304	-1.912
35-44	34	2294	67.4706	0.988
45-64	41	2915.5	71.1098	1.961
65+	7	498	71.1429	0.680

1-way Test, Chi-Square Approximation

ChiSquare	DF	Prob>ChiSq
10.6955	4	0.0302

Figure 6.25. Philadelphia: Expected—expected by age

Age

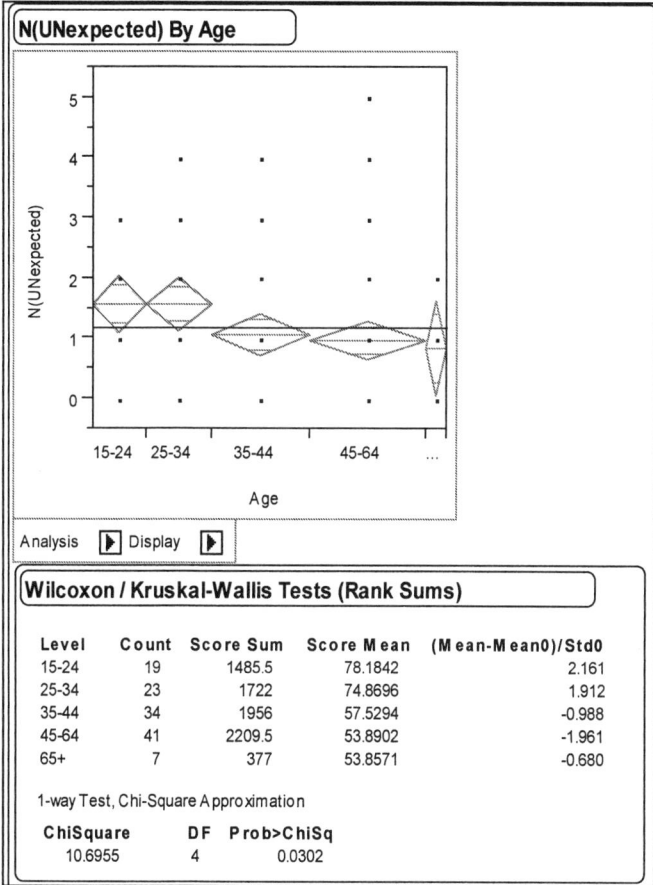

N(UNexpected) By Age

Analysis ▶ Display ▶

Wilcoxon / Kruskal-Wallis Tests (Rank Sums)

Level	Count	Score Sum	Score Mean	(Mean-Mean0)/Std0
15-24	19	1485.5	78.1842	2.161
25-34	23	1722	74.8696	1.912
35-44	34	1956	57.5294	-0.988
45-64	41	2209.5	53.8902	-1.961
65+	7	377	53.8571	-0.680

1-way Test, Chi-Square Approximation

ChiSquare	DF	Prob>ChiSq
10.6955	4	0.0302

Figure 6.26. Philadelphia: Expected—not by age

Analysis of Findings

The overall survey group preferences are useful in understanding the general preferences of those who are already in the Philadelphia waterfront area, whether residing, working, or visiting. From a single, or even double study, it is extremely difficult to claim an understanding of universal preferences for the qualities analyzed. The demographics of this surveyed population is not necessarily normal for the entire U.S., the State of Pennsylvania or even the City of Philadelphia. The overall survey group preferences, only describe a cross section of the population at the Philadelphia waterfront during the time of the survey.

The overall survey group preferences on their own, cannot be assumed to cross demographic lines. If a preference for a particular evaluative characteristic aligns closely with a demographic category, then the distribution of that demographic in the survey population may affect the results.

The categories of "On the Tourist Map" and "Expected in an Urban Waterfront" demonstrate a significant preference for the overall survey population. However, they also demonstrate significant differences in preferences along demographic lines. Age, in particular, is significant in both cases.

The age distribution of the overall population surveyed reveals that a large portion (65%) is 35 or over. Those 35 and over were found to favor sites labelled "On the Tourist Map" significantly more than those younger. The overall survey population preferences for "On the Tourist Map," therefore, reflects its demographics and cannot assume to represent a more universal preference.

Those 35 and over also favor sites "Expected in an Urban Waterfront" significantly more than those younger. Additionally, those visiting the area tend to favor these sites more than Philadelphia locals. Where the overall population surveyed showed a high percentage 35 and over, it simultaneously showed less visitors (25%) than locals.

In this case these overlapping demographic group preferences become contradictory. The effects on the overall survey population preferences, therefore, become more ambiguous. It is possible that a more universal preference is being demonstrated here, though this cannot be confirmed on the basis of this survey alone.

There is also a circular quality about the particular evaluative characteristic, "On the Tourist Map." Sites deemed worth noting on the map are more preferred by the overall survey population, as well as for those 35 and over and visitors, but their likeability by the public might be why they were listed on the map to begin with. This category therefore, does not provide very convincing results.

There is a problem of interpretation also occurring in sites "Expected in an Urban Waterfront." There is a logic in the results suggesting those 35 and over would prefer expected sites, while those younger might prefer more surprises. However there also is much overlap in the images that were described as "On the Tourist Map" and "Expected in an Urban Waterfront." This makes interpretation more difficult since the particular characteristic the preference should be attributed to cannot clearly be assigned.

The overall survey population also shows a significant preference for sites with "Historical Ambience" as defined in Test 2. This evaluative category does not reveal significant differences within the demographics analyzed. It might be that though these demographic factors individually did not reveal significant differences, compounded they do. It also might be that other demographic factors, not considered in this analysis, may be contributing to this overall preference. Here again, it is possible that a more universal preference is being revealed, though it cannot be proven with this survey alone.

The evaluative categories of "Historical Ambience: Test 2" and "Expected in an Urban Waterfront," both indicate a possible larger significance that crosses beyond the particular group of individuals surveyed on the Philadelphia waterfront. These categories, in particular should be tested in future studies in other locations to determine if these same preferences are shown elsewhere.

This study has shown gender not to be a significant factor in relation to preferences of the particular evaluative categories analyzed. However, significant correlation with age, education, and local/visitor status have been found. Other demographic factors (ethnic background, etc.) may prove equally or more important in determining preferences. These should also be examined in future studies to determine their level of influence over preferences.

SUMMARY OF SIGNIFICANCE - Philadelphia

Overall Survey Population   **Demographic Groups Within**

	Age	Educ	Gend	Visitor
Age of Appearance				
Restored (+) / **Restored**	Age	Educ		
Pseudo-Hist / Pseudo-Hist				
Adaptive Use (-) / Adaptive Use				
Modern / **Modern**	Age	Educ		Visitor
Hist Ambiance (Test 1)				
Hist Ambiance (+) / **Hist Ambiance**	Age	Educ		
Not (+) / **Not**	Age	Educ		
Hist Ambiance (Test 2)				
Hist Ambiance (+) / Hist Ambiance				
Not (-) / Not				
Hist Ambiance (Test 3)				
Hist Ambiance / **Hist Ambiance**	Age	Educ		Visitor
Not / **Not**	Age	Educ		Visitor
Greenery in Image				
Moderate Greenery / Moderate Greenery				
Minimal Greenery / Minimal Greenery				
No Greenery / **No Greenery**		Educ		
Water in Image				
Water / Water				
No Water / No Water				
On Tourist Map				
On Map (+) / **On Map**	Age			Visitor
Not on Map (-) / **Not on Map**	Age			Visitor
Expected in Urban Waterfront				
Expected (+) / **Expected**	Age			
Unexpected (-) / **Unexpected**	Age			

Note: P-values =<0.05 are highlighted.
(+) or (-) indicates a strong pos. or neg. relationship with a difference greater or equal to 10%

Table 6.24. Philadelphia: Summary of Significance

Chapter Seven

The Yokohama Survey

Waterfront Background

Yokohama is a relatively young city. It was nothing more than a small fishing village until the middle of the nineteenth century. But then it quickly grew, as did its importance in recent Japanese history. In 1923, the Great Kanto Earthquake of 1923 caused the destruction and burning of 80% of the city. The rebuilding began immediately after. Yokohama's history also includes being bombed heavily in WWII. Yokohama is currently the largest international trading port in Japan. In 1978, it became the second largest city in Japan with its population exceeding that of Osaka.[1]

Two areas that comprise many new commercial and recreational sites of interest along the waterfront in central Yokohama are Minato Mirai 21 (MM21) and Yamashita Park. The sites selected for this survey are located on or very near these areas. They consist of urban design elements visible to the general public.

Yamashita Park is outside the bounds of MM21 and predates it by 70 years. It is located in the Kannai district. This park was completed in 1930 using construction material gathered from the rubble of the Great Kanto Earthquake.[2] It serves as an interesting counterpoint to the newly developed recreational sites developed within MM21.

MM21 is the major new development on the waterfront of Yokohama. It is a third sector project in Japan, meaning it includes both private and public sector investment. Partially built on former industrial sites, partially built on new landfill, it includes commercial, residential, cultural, and recreational facilities.

An official brochure describes the intended image of MM21. It states that "preserving the red brick warehouses and stone docks evoking Yokohama's historical heritage, Minato Mirai 21 will form a spacious city environment framed by the sea and attractive greenery and steeped in *historical ambience*" (italics mine).[3] The phrase "historical ambience" has been borrowed from this brochure and expanded on in the research herein.

Survey Specifics

A series of intercept interviews were then taken outside of the Yokohama Maritime Museum. The questionnaire was written in both Japanese and English and was generally read by the interviewer to the subject in Japanese.

As an incentive and reward for participating, a souvenir telephone card from the Maritime Museum worth approximately 800 yen (about 6 dollars) was given upon completion of the ten to fifteen minute survey. The approximately one hundred interviews were administered over a two day period from 10:00 A.M. to 5:00 P.M. on Wednesday, December 10 and Thursday, December 11, 1997. I was supported in this entire process by a bilingual team of Japanese colleagues from WAVE, the Waterfront Vitalization and Environmental Research Center.

The survey in Yokohama was originally administered one year prior to the survey in Philadelphia, and served as a rough model. The Philadelphia Survey then used slightly more refined definitions of "Age of Appearance" and "Historical Ambience" in its analysis. This section will briefly describe a subsequent analysis of the Yokohama data incorporating these same refinements.

The category definitions remain constant in both for comparative purposes. The Yokohama analysis includes the categories of "Age of Appearance," "Historical Ambience: Test 1-3," "Greenery in View," "Water in View," and for stability analysis, "Photo Orientation," "Photo Exposure," and "Photo Location." The Yokohama analysis does not include the categories of "On Tourist Map" and "Expected in Urban Waterfront" because those categories were found slightly problematic in the Philadelphia Survey.

The two surveys do have slight methodological differences. The photogrid in the Yokohama Survey was chosen with a tiered system that tried to quantify the amount of times a structure was the focus of the photo, a split focus of the photo, or in the background of a photo. By assigning a weight to each category and summing the times in each photo, each major site was allowed a total number within a certain range. In this manner, I attempted to represent each site relatively equally in the overall mix of photos, and give an equal chance for each site to be selected by the respondent. The Philadelphia Survey used a simpler system.

Certain data relating to education was not gathered in the Yokohama Survey. Therefore, the category of education is removed from cross-cultural comparisons. However, because of the apparent strong correlation to evaluative categories demonstrated in the Philadelphia Survey, all future surveys should try to gather the education level of each survey participant as background data.

The local/visitor demographic was defined as one of four possibilities in the Philadelphia Survey. They are "local resident," "local worker," "both" (local resident and local worker), and "visitor" (not local resident or local worker). Upon further examination, those individuals who reside locally, but do not work a formal job (such as a parent providing full time care for a child) are not clearly classified. They might fall under "local resident" or "both." The category has, therefore, been reclassified into a clearer two choice definition, local or visitor, which will eliminate this ambiguity.

The mix of structures in the analyzed waterfront area of Yokohama is weighted towards stylistically modern construction. The Philadelphia areas analyzed contain more historic structures, both restored, adapted and pseudo-historical. There are some examples of each type of construction as defined in the "Age of Appearance" category within each analyzed area.

The photographs of the Yokohama Survey include greater mixes of sites within single photos. They also include some large indoor spaces used as shopping malls. These indoor urban spaces and other images which do not clearly fit the tighter categories of the Philadelphia Survey, were removed from this analysis. These adjustments, however, were ultimately not found to significantly alter the findings.

The locations of the respondent interviews in Yokohama were restricted to two areas, both close to the water's edge. They were within a section of the waterfront used mostly for passive recreation. These areas were generally reached by intentionally walking about a block off the main traffic corridor towards them. The surveys were conducted over two weekdays.

The demographic mix of the survey population of each city varies accordingly. The overall statistics provide a sample of the mix of people in those particular areas where the surveys were conducted and their overall preferences. Cross-cultural comparisons may be attempted within demographic groups. Comparisons within a demographic segment is informative since the overall survey group composition is not affecting the comparison.

1

2

3

4

5

6

7

8

9

10

11

12

Figure 7.1. Yokohama: Photos #1-12

13

14

15

16

17

18

19

20

21

22

23

24

Figure 7.2. Yokohama: Photos #13-24

25

26

27

28

29

30

31

32

33

34

35

36

Figure 7.3. Yokohama: Photos #25-36

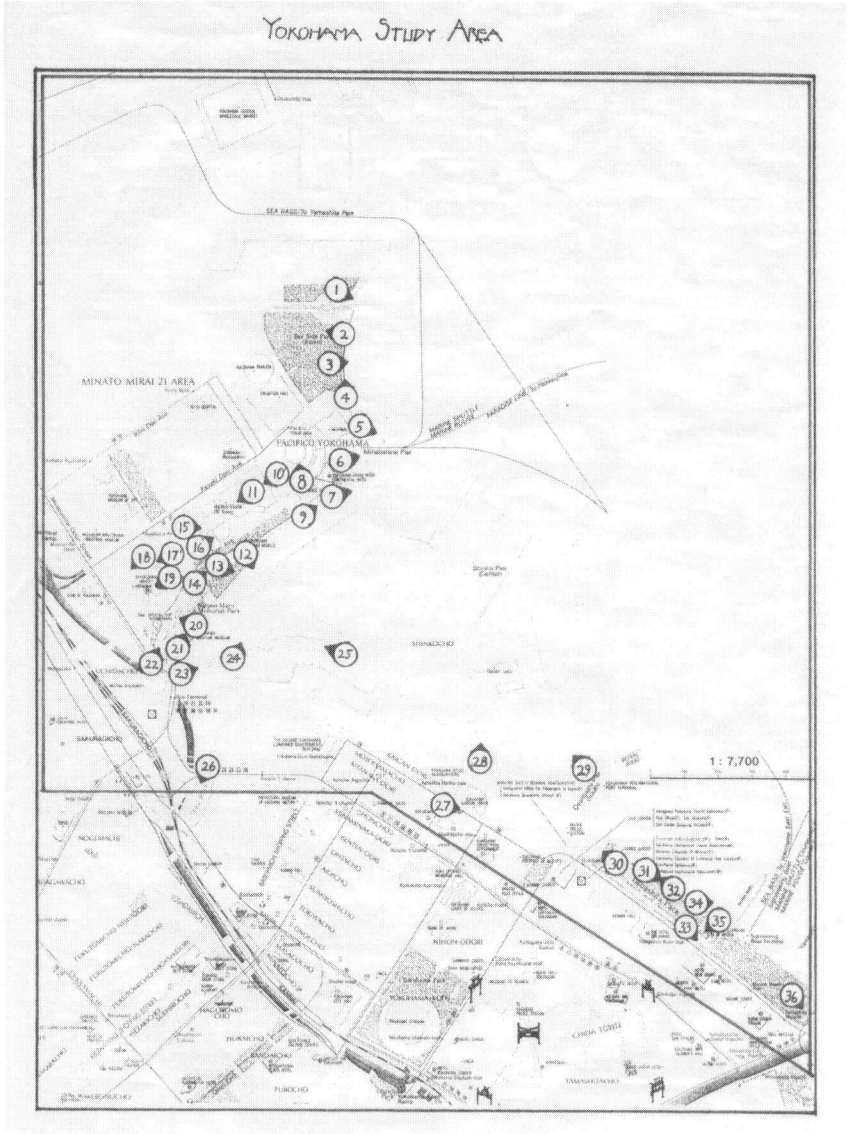

Figure 7.4. Yokohama: Key Map

PHOTO#	PHOTO DESCRIPTION	PHOTO PAIR
1	pedestrian bridge	Rinko Park
2	open field	Rinko Park
3	anchor monument	Rinko Park
4	walkway	Rinko Park
5	men on mast	Training Vessel
6	marine terminal	Pukari Sanbashi Pier
7	men fishing	Waterfront Promenade
8	festival	Pacifico Yokohama
9	walkers	Waterfront Promenade
10	outdoor entry	Queen's Square
11	indoor arcade	Queen's Square
12	bridge in distance	Kishamichi/Highrise
13	old warehouse	Cosmo World
14	ferris wheel	Pacifico Yokohama
15	performance	entryway amphitheatre
16	performance	entryway amphitheatre
17	looking down	DryDock2 / Tower
18	mall atrium	Landmark Plaza
19	view from base	DryDock2 / Tower
20	ship & skyscraper	NipponMaru / Tower
21	berm & skyline	Maritime Museum
22	water & ship	NipponMaru / DryDock1
23	view along bridge	kishamichi
24	sleek & old	Pacifico Yoko. / Old Warehouse
25	bridge & tower	Kishamichi / Tower
26	river reflections	River lined with buildings
27	street view	Customs House
28	field foreground	Red Brick Warehouses
29	water foreground	Red Brick Warehouses
30	monu. & walkers	India Monument
31	man carrying child	Yamashita Promenade
32	man photographing	Yamashita Promenade
33	park walkways	Marine tower in distance
34	people & ship	Hikawa Maru
35	garden & fountain	Guardian of the Water
36	parent & child	Grand Staircase

Table 7.1. Yokohama: Photo Criteria—photo pairs

PHOTO#	AGE OF APPEARANCE	HISTORICAL AMBIANCE Test 1	HISTORICAL AMBIANCE Test 2	HISTORICAL AMBIANCE Test 3
1	Modern	Not	Not	Not
2	other	other	other	other
3	Modern	Not	Not	Not
4	Modern	Not	Not	Not
5	Adaptive	Not	Not	Ambiance
6	Pseudo	Not	Ambiance	Ambiance
7	Modern	Not	Not	Not
8	Modern	Not	Not	Not
9	Modern	Not	Not	Not
10	Modern	Not	Not	Not
11	other	other	other	other
12	Adaptive	Not	Not	Ambiance
13	other	other	other	other
14	Modern	Not	Not	Not
15	Modern	Not	Not	Not
16	Modern	Not	Not	Not
17	Adaptive	Not	Not	Ambiance
18	other	other	other	other
19	Adaptive	Not	Not	Ambiance
20	Adaptive	Not	Not	Ambiance
21	Modern	Not	Not	Not
22	Adaptive	Not	Not	Ambiance
23	Adaptive	Not	Not	Ambiance
24	other	other	other	other
25	Adaptive	Not	Not	Ambiance
26	other	other	other	other
27	Restored	Ambiance	Ambiance	Ambiance
28	Restored	Ambiance	Ambiance	Ambiance
29	Restored	Ambiance	Ambiance	Ambiance
30	Restored	Ambiance	Ambiance	Ambiance
31	Modern	Not	Not	Not
32	Modern	Not	Not	Not
33	other	other	other	other
34	Adaptive	Not	Not	Ambiance
35	Modern	Not	Not	Not
36	Pseudo	Not	Ambiance	Ambiance

Table 7.2. Yokohama: Photo Criteria—ambience

PHOTO#	GREENERY IN VIEW	WATER IN VIEW	PHOTO ORIENTATION	PHOTO EXPOSURE
1	none	Water	Horizontal	normal
2	MAXIMUM	No Water	Horizontal	Dark
3	Moderate	Water	Horizontal	normal
4	minimal	Water	Horizontal	normal
5	none	Water	Horizontal	normal
6	none	Water	Horizontal	normal
7	none	Water	Horizontal	normal
8	minimal	No Water	Horizontal	normal
9	minimal	Water	vert	normal
10	none	No Water	Horizontal	normal
11	other	other	other	other
12	none	Water	Horizontal	normal
13	none	Water	Horizontal	Dark
14	none	Water	vert	Dark
15	minimal	No Water	Horizontal	normal
16	none	No Water	Horizontal	normal
17	none	No Water	vert	normal
18	other	other	other	other
19	none	No Water	vert	normal
20	none	No Water	vert	normal
21	Moderate	Water	Horizontal	normal
22	none	Water	vert	normal
23	minimal	Water	Horizontal	normal
24	none	Water	Horizontal	normal
25	minimal	Water	Horizontal	normal
26	none	Water	Horizontal	Dark
27	minimal	No Water	vert	normal
28	Moderate	No Water	Horizontal	normal
29	none	Water	Horizontal	normal
30	Moderate	No Water	Horizontal	normal
31	minimal	Water	Horizontal	normal
32	minimal	Water	Horizontal	normal
33	MAXIMUM	No Water	vert	Dark
34	none	Water	Horizontal	normal
35	Moderate	No Water	Horizontal	normal
36	Moderate	No Water	Horizontal	Dark

Table 7.3. Yokohama: Photo Criteria—other

Selections Overall

The following comparisons are in the manner done in the Philadelphia Survey. The percentages of a characteristic occurring in the overall selected photos is compared to the percentage occurring in the original photoset.

Age of Appearance	- Selected -		- Photoset -	
	(N)	**Prob.**	**(N)**	**Prob.**
Restored	(87)	18 %	(4)	14 %
Pseudo	(34)	7 %	(2)	7 %
Adaptive	(205)	42 %	(9)	31 %
Modern	(162)	33 %	(14)	48 %
Total	**(488)**	**100 %**	**(29)**	**100 %**

Table 7.4. Yokohama: Age of Appearance

In "Age of Appearance," a strong preference (+11%) is shown for structures that are "Adaptive." Also of note is a strong lack of preference (-15%) is shown for "Modern."

Historical Ambience: Test 1	- Selected -		- Photoset -	
	(N)	**Prob.**	**(N)**	**Prob.**
Historical Ambience	(87)	18 %	(4)	14 %
No Historical Ambience	(401)	82 %	(25)	86 %
Total	**(488)**	**100 %**	**(29)**	**100 %**

Table 7.5. Yokohama: Historical Ambience Test 1

Historical Ambience: Test 2	- Selected -		- Photoset -	
	(N)	**Prob.**	**(N)**	**Prob.**
Historical Ambience	(121)	25 %	(6)	21 %
No Historical Ambience	(367)	75 %	(23)	79 %
Total	**(488)**	**100 %**	**(29)**	**100 %**

Table 7.6. Yokohama: Historical Ambience Test 2

Historical Ambience: Test 3	- Selected -		- Photoset -	
	(N)	Prob.	(N)	Prob.
Historical Ambience	(326)	67 %	(15)	52 %
No Historical Ambience	(162)	33 %	(14)	48 %
Total	(488)	100 %	(29)	100 %

Table 7.7. Yokohama: Historical Ambience Test 3

No strong preference is revealed either way for "Historical Ambience: Test 1 and Test 2." In "Test 3," a strong preference (+15%) is shown for structures that contain this definition of "Historical Ambience." A comparable lack of preference is shown for those with "No Historical Ambience."

Greenery in Image	- Selected -		- Photoset -	
	(N)	Prob.	(N)	Prob.
Maximum	(15	3 %	(2)	6 %
Moderate	(123)	22 %	(6)	18 %
Minimum	(135)	25 %	(9)	26 %
None	(278)	50 %	(17)	50 %
Total	(551)	100 %	(34)	100 %

Table 7.8. Yokohama: Greenery in Image

"Greenery in Image" reveals no strong preference either way.

Water in Image	- Selected -		- Photoset -	
	(N)	Prob.	(N)	Prob.
Yes	(394)	72 %	(20)	59 %
No	(157)	28 %	(14)	41 %
Total	(551)	100 %	(34)	100 %

Table 7.9. Yokohama: Water in Image

In "Water in Image," a strong preference (+13%) is shown for images that contain "Water." A comparable lack of preference is shown for those with "No Water."

Photo Orientation	- Selected -		- Photoset -	
	(N)	Prob.	(N)	Prob.
Horizontal	(413)	75 %	(26)	76 %
Vertical	(138)	25 %	(8)	24 %
Total	(551)	100 %	(34)	100 %

Table 7.10. Yokohama: Photo Orientation

Photo Exposure	- Selected -		- Photoset -	
	(N)	Prob.	(N)	Prob.
Normal	(474)	86 %	(28)	82%
Dark	(77)	14 %	(6)	18 %
Total	(551)	100 %	(34)	100 %

Table 7.11. Yokohama: Photo Exposure

In the stability tests, "Photo Orientation" and "Photo Exposure," no strong preference is revealed either way. The location of the photographs chosen compared to the location where the respondents were surveyed did not strongly affect the choice of photographs. Sites in the immediate vicinity of the locations where the surveys were taken were not strongly favored.

Survey Demographics

A broad range of ages was included in the Yokohama Survey. The mix of ages in both the Yokohama and Philadelphia Survey populations coincidentally included the same proportion (35%) of respondents under age 35. The highest proportion (24%) of Yokohama respondents in a 10 year category lies within the 15-24 year olds. This is assuming that the twenty year category of 45-64 year olds comprises to roughly equal ten year groupings of about 18% a piece.

Gender within the surveyed population was weighted slightly towards males. 58% of respondents were male, 37% female. The remainder did not provide this information. Of all those surveyed, 69% were locals (living or working in Yokohama), while 31% were visitors to the area (neither living nor working in Yokohama).

OVERALL DEMOGRAPHICS of Yokohama Survey

AGE (6 groups)	<=14	15-24	25-34	35-44	45-64	65+	unknown	Total
(n)		24	11	14	36	14	3	102
%		24%	11%	14%	36%	14%	3%	100%

EDUCATION (5 groups)	Some HS	Grad HS	Some Col	Grad Col	Post Grad		unknown	Total
(n)	-	-	-	-	-		-	-
%	-	-	-	-	-		-	-

GENDER		Female	Male		unknown	Total
(n)		38	59		5	102
%		37%	58%		5%	100%

LOCAL / VISITOR (4 groups)	Resident & Worker	Yoko. Resident	Yoko. Worker	Visitor		unknown	Total
(n)	-	-	-	-		-	-
%	-	-	-	-		-	-

LOCAL / VISITOR (2 groups)	Local (Resid. or Worker)	Visitor	unknown	Total
(n)	70	32	0	102
%	69%	31%	0%	100%

Note:
Percentages may not total to 100% due to rounding errors.
Percentage rows are highlighted.

Table 7.12. Yokohama: Overall Survey Demographics

Selections by Demographics

Summary of Demographic Analysis

In this survey of the Yokohama waterfront, age has shown a significant correlation within the evaluative category of "Age of Appearance." Those under 35 showed a preference for "Modern" structures compared to those 35 and over. A corresponding preference for structures with "No Historical Ambience" as defined in "Test 3" was also shown. This is the test that directly equates these two characteristics. Those 35 and over showed a preference for "Pseudo-Historical" structures compared to those younger. A corresponding preference for "Historical Ambience" as defined by "Test 2" and "Test 3" was also shown.

Gender has shown a significant correlation in the category of "Water in image." Males have shown a preference for images that contained "Water" in them, compared to females' preferences for "Water."

Local/visitor status has shown significant correlation in only one evaluative category, "Greenery in Image." Locals have shown a preference for images with "Minimal Greenery" compared to visitors. Visitors have shown a preference for "No Greenery" compared to locals. Images with "Maximum" and "Moderate" amounts of greenery did not reveal demographic patterns of preference.

Analysis of Findings

The overall survey group demonstrates a strong preference for "Adaptive Use" and "Historical Ambience" as defined in "Test 3." "Adaptive Use" did not show significant demographic differences and, therefore, may be reflecting a cross-demographic preference of the respondents.

"Historical Ambience" as defined in "Test 3" includes "Pseudo-Historical" structures in its definition. Those respondents 35 and over have shown a significant preference for "Pseudo-Historical" structures. Therefore, the overall preference shown for "Historical Ambience" in "Test 3" reflects its demographics, and cannot assume to represent a more cross-demographic preference.

The overall survey group demonstrates a strong lack of preference for "Modern" and "No Historical Ambience" as defined in "Test 3." Those respondents 35 and over have shown a significant lack of preference for

"Modern." This age group represents 65% of the overall respondents. Therefore, the overall lack of preference shown for "Modern" reflects its demographics, and cannot assume to represent a more cross-demographic preference.

The overall survey group demonstrates a strong lack of preference for "No Historical Ambience" as defined in "Test 3." This test equates "Modern" with "No Historical Ambience" and therefore its evaluation mimics that of "Modern" above.

The overall survey group demonstrates a strong preference for "Water in Image." Male respondents have shown a significant preference for these images. The overall survey population contained a slightly greater percentage of males than females. Therefore, the preference for "Water in Image" and corresponding lack of preference for images with "No Water" may be reflecting the demographics, and cannot be assumed to represent a more cross-demographic preference.

'Pseudo-Hist' by Age

N(Pseudo) By Younger than 35

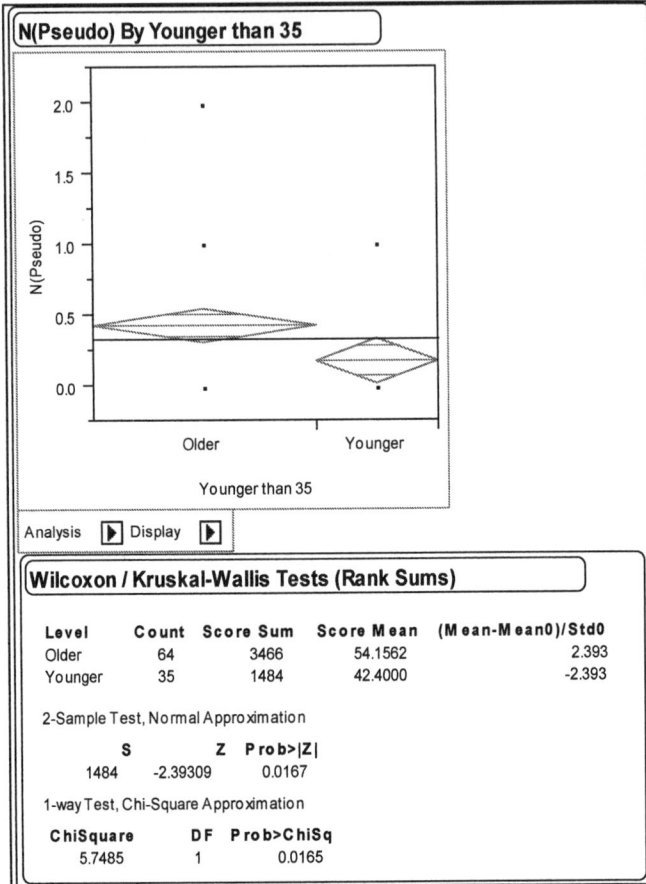

Wilcoxon / Kruskal-Wallis Tests (Rank Sums)

Level	Count	Score Sum	Score Mean	(Mean-Mean0)/Std0
Older	64	3466	54.1562	2.393
Younger	35	1484	42.4000	-2.393

2-Sample Test, Normal Approximation

S	Z	Prob>|Z|
1484	-2.39309	0.0167

1-way Test, Chi-Square Approximation

ChiSquare	DF	Prob>ChiSq
5.7485	1	0.0165

Figure 7.5. Yokohama: Age of Appearance—pseudo by age

'Modern' by Age

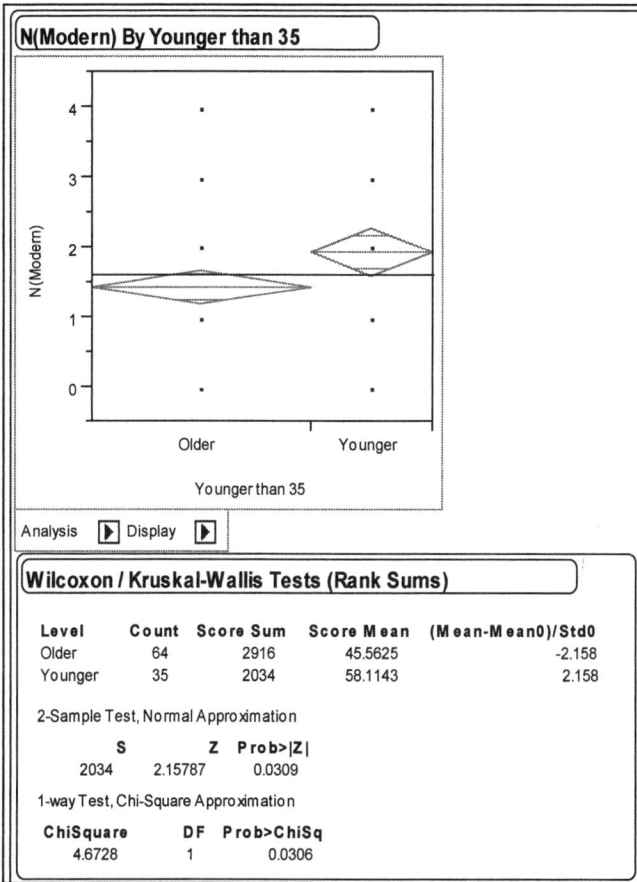

N(Modern) By Younger than 35

Wilcoxon / Kruskal-Wallis Tests (Rank Sums)

Level	Count	Score Sum	Score Mean	(Mean-Mean0)/Std0
Older	64	2916	45.5625	-2.158
Younger	35	2034	58.1143	2.158

2-Sample Test, Normal Approximation

S	Z	Prob>|Z|
2034	2.15787	0.0309

1-way Test, Chi-Square Approximation

ChiSquare	DF	Prob>ChiSq
4.6728	1	0.0306

Figure 7.6. Yokohama: Age of Appearance—modern by age

'Hist Ambiance' by Age

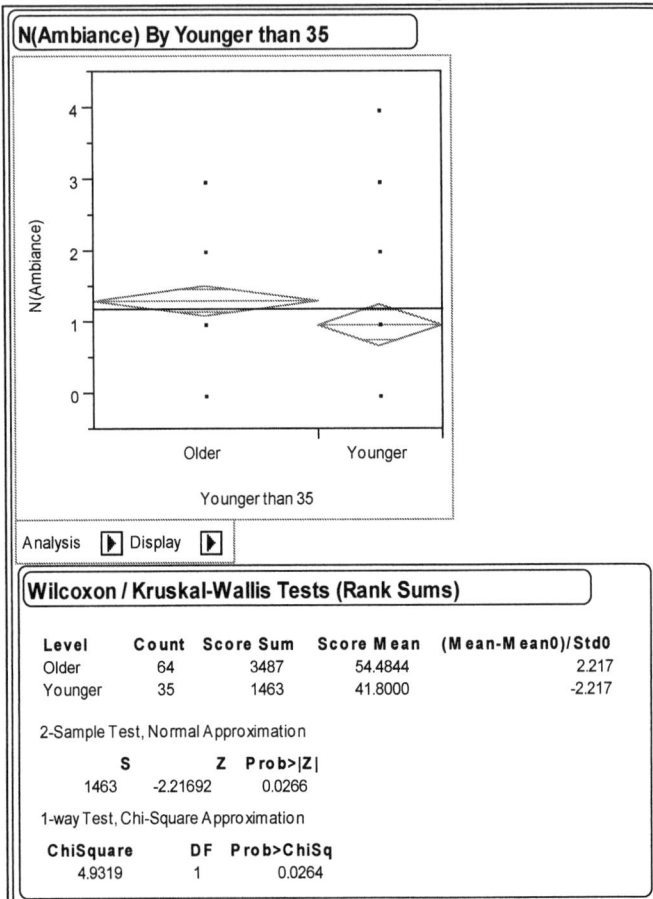

Figure 7.7. Yokohama: Ambience Test 2—ambience by age

'Hist Ambiance' by Age

N(Ambiance) By Younger than 35

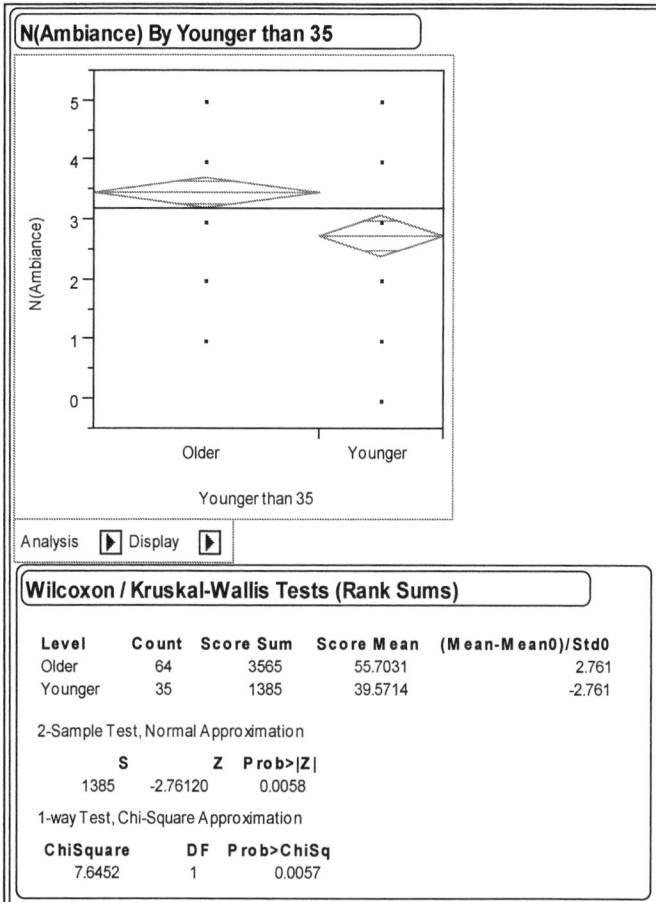

Wilcoxon / Kruskal-Wallis Tests (Rank Sums)

Level	Count	Score Sum	Score Mean	(Mean-Mean0)/Std0
Older	64	3565	55.7031	2.761
Younger	35	1385	39.5714	-2.761

2-Sample Test, Normal Approximation

S	Z	Prob>|Z|
1385	-2.76120	0.0058

1-way Test, Chi-Square Approximation

ChiSquare	DF	Prob>ChiSq
7.6452	1	0.0057

Figure 7.8. Yokohama: Ambience Test 3—ambience by age

'No Hist Ambiance' by Age

N(Not) By Younger than 35

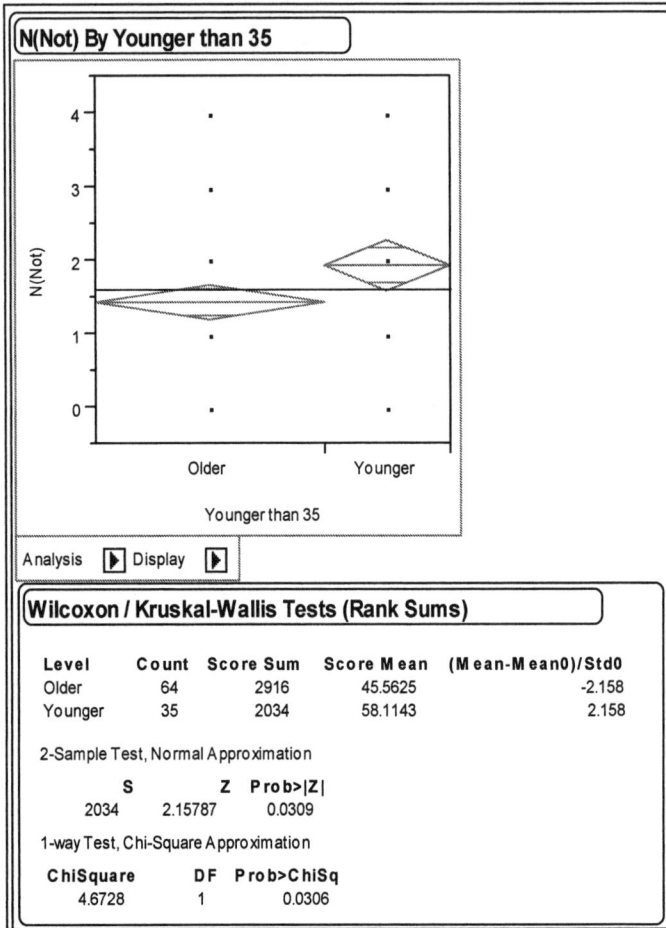

Level	Count	Score Sum	Score Mean	(Mean-Mean0)/Std0
Older	64	2916	45.5625	-2.158
Younger	35	2034	58.1143	2.158

2-Sample Test, Normal Approximation

S	Z	Prob>|Z|
2034	2.15787	0.0309

1-way Test, Chi-Square Approximation

ChiSquare	DF	Prob>ChiSq
4.6728	1	0.0306

Figure 7.9. Yokohama: Ambience Test 3—no by age

'Min Greenery' by Local/Visitor

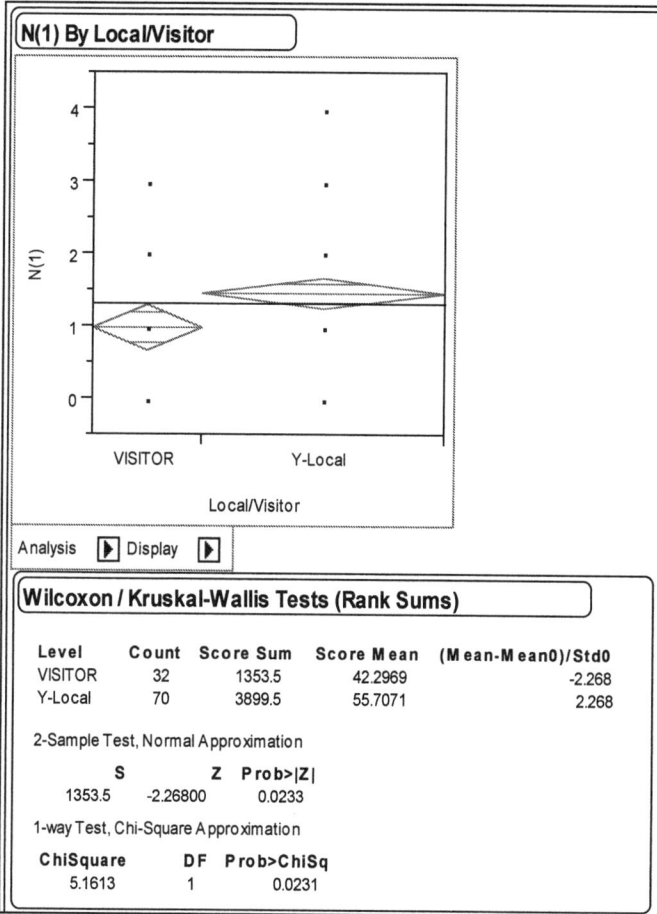

Figure 7.10. Yokohama: Greenery—min by local

'No Greenery' by Local/Visitor

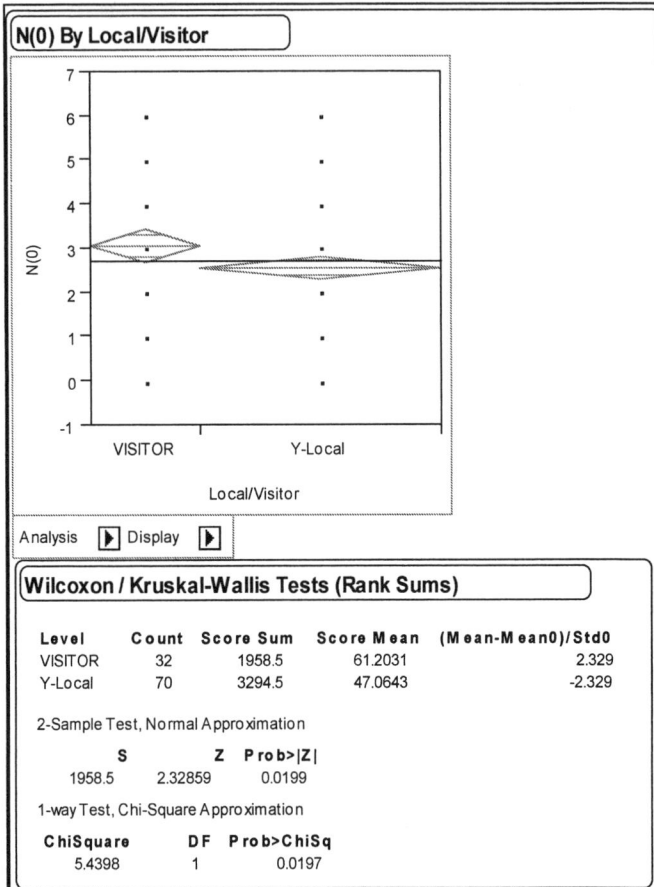

N(0) By Local/Visitor

Analysis ▶ Display ▶

Wilcoxon / Kruskal-Wallis Tests (Rank Sums)

Level	Count	Score Sum	Score Mean	(Mean-Mean0)/Std0
VISITOR	32	1958.5	61.2031	2.329
Y-Local	70	3294.5	47.0643	-2.329

2-Sample Test, Normal Approximation

S	Z	Prob>|Z|
1958.5	2.32859	0.0199

1-way Test, Chi-Square Approximation

ChiSquare	DF	Prob>ChiSq
5.4398	1	0.0197

Figure 7.11. Yokohama: Greenery—none by local

'Water in View' by Gender

N(Water) By 4. Gender

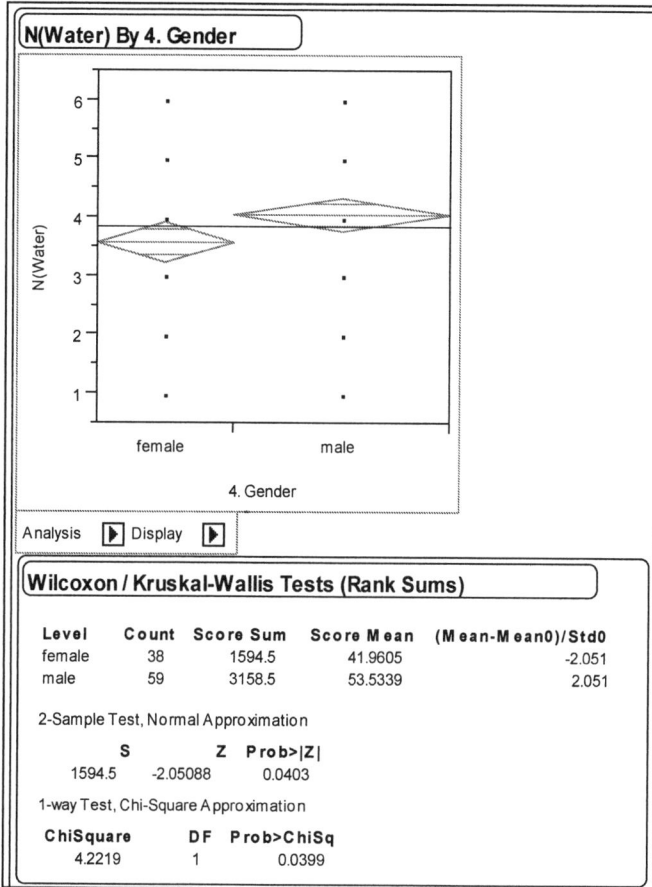

4. Gender

Analysis ▶ Display ▶

Wilcoxon / Kruskal-Wallis Tests (Rank Sums)

Level	Count	Score Sum	Score Mean	(Mean-Mean0)/Std0
female	38	1594.5	41.9605	-2.051
male	59	3158.5	53.5339	2.051

2-Sample Test, Normal Approximation

S	Z	Prob>|Z|
1594.5	-2.05088	0.0403

1-way Test, Chi-Square Approximation

ChiSquare	DF	Prob>ChiSq
4.2219	1	0.0399

Figure 7.12. Yokohama: Water—water by gender

'Horizontal' by Gender

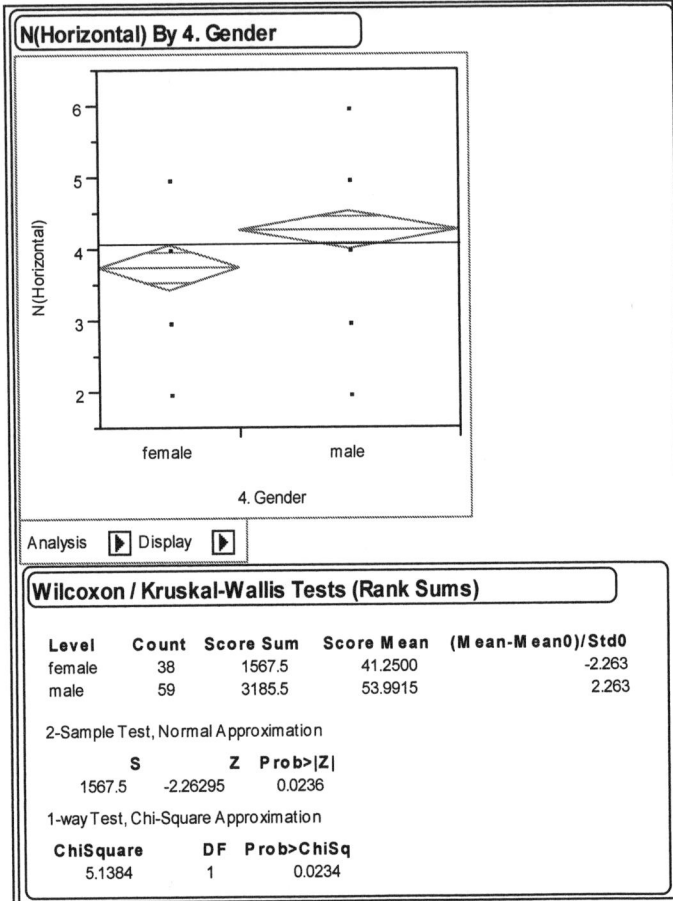

N(Horizontal) By 4. Gender

Wilcoxon / Kruskal-Wallis Tests (Rank Sums)

Level	Count	Score Sum	Score Mean	(Mean-Mean0)/Std0
female	38	1567.5	41.2500	-2.263
male	59	3185.5	53.9915	2.263

2-Sample Test, Normal Approximation

S	Z	Prob>|Z|
1567.5	-2.26295	0.0236

1-way Test, Chi-Square Approximation

ChiSquare	DF	Prob>ChiSq
5.1384	1	0.0234

Figure 7.13. Yokohama: Orientation—horiz by gender

SUMMARY OF SIGNIFICANCE - Yokohama

Overall Survey Population		Demographic Groups Within		Age	Educ	Gend	Local/Vis
Age of Appearance		**Age of Appearance**					
	Restored		Restored		x		
	Pseudo-Hist		**Pseudo-Hist**	**35+**	x		
	Adaptive Use (+)		Adaptive Use		x		
	Modern (-)		**Modern**	**<35**	x		
Hist Ambiance		**Hist Ambiance**					
(Test 1)	Hist Ambiance	**(Test 1)**	Hist Ambiance		x		
	Not		Not		x		
Hist Ambiance		**Hist Ambiance**					
(Test 2)	Hist Ambiance	**(Test 2)**	**Hist Ambiance**	**35+**	x		
	Not		Not		x		
Hist Ambiance		**Hist Ambiance**					
(Test 3)	**Hist Amb (+)**	**(Test 3)**	**Hist Ambiance**	**35+**	x		
	Not (-)		**Not**	**<35**	x		
Greenery in Image		**Greenery in Image**					
	Maximum Greenery		Maximum Greenery		x		
	Moderate Greenery		Moderate Greenery		x		
	Minimal Greenery		**Minimal Greenery**		x		**Local**
	No Greenery		**No Greenery**		x		**Visitor**
Water in Image		**Water in Image**					
	Water (+)		**Water**		x	**Male**	
	No Water (-)		No Water		x		

Note:
Characteristics in 'Overall' are highlighed when % of selected exceeds % of photoset by 10% or more.
(+) or (-) indicates a strong pos. or neg. relationship with a difference greater or equal to 10%.
Characteristics in 'Demographic' are highlighted when P-values =<0.050
The relevant demographic group favoring that characteristic is described.
Education is not a tested demographic category for this analysis.

Table. 7.13. Yokohama: Summary of Significance

Chapter Eight

Conclusions

The implications of this research are two-fold. The first deals with the specific findings of these surveys. They are discussed at length within the Philadelphia and Yokohama Survey chapters, as well as the following section comparing these findings. The second, and possibly more important implication lies in the validity and potential usefulness of this survey technique in the future. This will also be discussed in the remaining pages.

Comparison: Philadelphia and Yokohama

A direct comparison of overall survey population preferences between the Philadelphia and Yokohama Surveys should probably not be made. As was explained previously, the overall preferences may be primarily capturing the preferences of heavily represented demographic groups within. These surveys alone cannot confirm the existence of larger, cross-demographic preferences of evaluative characteristics.

A method of comparison that can be made between the two cities is within a demographic category. In particular, the preferences demonstrated for particular evaluative characteristics can be made within age, gender or local/visitor groupings of the respondents. Data on education level was not gathered in Yokohama, so cannot be used in this comparison.

One key similarity has been found in both the Philadelphia and Yokohama Surveys. Increasing age appears to correspond to increasing preference for some level of historical ambience in both survey groups.

The characteristics within "Age of Appearance" have been laid out in a continuum. "Restored" is used as the most extreme example of "Historical Ambience." "Modern" takes the opposite extreme, anchoring the definition of "No Historical Ambience." Between the two lies "Pseudo-Historical" which is contemporary construction that draws heavily on pre-modern architectural styles. Also within this continuum is "Adaptive Use" which is defined for this analysis as a pre-modern structure with external signs of a new use occurring within it.

In "Age of Appearance" the 15-24 age group in Philadelphia has a significant lack of preference for "Restored" and a significant preference for "Modern." The 45-64 age group has the reverse, a preference for "Restored" and lack of preference for "Modern." When age was broken into a simple two way split, a strong preference for "Restored" was still shown for those 35 and over compared to under 35.

These selections of the 15-24 age group compared to the 45- 64 age group in Philadelphia translate into a preference for "No Historical Ambience" in "Tests 1 and 3" for the 15-24 age group. They also translate into a preference for "Historical Ambience" in the 45-64 age group for "Tests 1 and 3."

In Yokohama, significant differences did not appear when the age groups were divided into five categories. When age was divided into a two-way split, however, differences in preferences were significant. They followed a similar pattern of increasing age equating to increasing preference for historical ambience. The specifics varied, however.

In Yokohama, those under 35 showed a preference for "Modern" structures compared to those 35 and over. Those 35 and over demonstrated a preference for "Pseudo-Historical" structures. Comparing this "Age of Appearance" category in the two studies just using the two age group split shows an interesting variation that may be based on cultural differences between the Japanese and Americans. Where those in the 35 and over category in the USA demonstrated a preference for "Restored" properties, this same demographic in Yokohama showed a preference for "Pseudo-Historical."

In Yokohama, those under 35 showed a corresponding preference for "No Historical Ambience" as defined in "Test 3." Those 35 and over showed a significant preference for Historical Ambience" as defined in "Test 2 and 3." Again, somewhat similar to findings in Philadelphia, but no identical matches of significant categories.

The vast majority of respondents of the Yokohama Survey were Japanese. Most respondents of the Philadelphia Survey were living in the

USA and were likely American citizens, though the specific cultural backgrounds are not known. One potentially interesting result of these surveys of Philadelphia and Yokohama is any light they might bring to a comparison of Japanese and American sensibilities. They include only one survey in one city of each country and cannot claim to capture the preferences across their entire respective countries. However, some speculation can be made on some underlying differences in cultural sensibilities between the respondent groups.

Most of the "Restored," "Pseudo-Historical," and "Adaptive Use" structures were stylistically imported from Western Architecture. The "Pseudo-Historical" may provide that preferred image of Historical Western architecture without the deterioration of age.

Authenticity of a structure may have less meaning in the context of Western Architecture in Japan. This may be in the same spirit of synthetic materials being used to simulate natural ones in a number of Japanese structures (e.g. metal panels simulating wood in a hotel lobby, or stucco simulating stone in a contemporary structure designed to look like a French Chateau).

It is as though a preference for historical ambience roughly increases in older age groups for both Americans and Japanese. However, their definition of Historical Ambience differs. The Americans may be exposed to more variations of pre-modern structures in various states of repair and reuse. The Japanese may have had less exposure to the roots that the "Pseudo-Historical" are based on, those classified as "Restored" in this survey. They may differentiate less between "Restored" and "Pseudo-Historical" because of a different understanding of authenticity.

Another possibility is a difference in cultural attitudes for preservation. The Japanese tradition of rebuilding shrines rather than restoring them in the Western sense of trying to retain the existing structure demonstrates this difference. Historical ambience, as captured in a rebuilt shrine may be appreciated without concern for the actual age of the building materials.

The demographic category of gender yields no simple comparisons. Male and female preferences only demonstrated significant differences in Japan. "Water in Image" was the evaluative characteristic that was significantly more preferred by male than female. In all other evaluative tests in both surveys, gender was not a significant factor in determining preference. The underlying reasons behind these gender preferences are not understood at this time.

The final demographic category of comparison is that of local/visitor status. In Yokohama, only the category of "Greenery in Image" demonstrates significance within the local/visitor demographic. Locals showed a preference for "Minimal Greenery" compared to visitors. Visitors showed a preference for "No Greenery" compared to locals. The results are ambiguous with no explanations readily available for the local/visitor preferences.

In Philadelphia, locals showed a preference compared to visitors, for "Modern" structures and for the equivalent "Test 3" definition of modern, "No Historical Ambience." Visitors preferred "No Historical Ambience" in "Test 3" over locals. No easy comparison between cultures can be made here.

In Philadelphia, however, an explanation for the differences in preferences can be speculated upon that incorporates several concepts discussed in earlier chapters. In Philadelphia, the locals are surrounded by historical ambience, whether "Restored," "Pseudo-Historical," or "Adaptive Use." They are the predictable in the area and the lives of the locals who experience them regularly. "Modern" structures are the distinct and the surprise for locals.

Visitors to Philadelphia may be familiar with buildings with these historical characteristics, but not likely with the frequency and density that exists in Philadelphia. The distinctness and surprise for visitors to this very same portion of Philadelphia is the historical ambience. This lure of the distinct can help explain these particular differences between the preferences of locals and visitors.

SUMMARY by Demographics - Philadelphia vs. Yokohama

PHILADELPHIA				YOKOHAMA			
P-value	Age	Gend	Where	P-value	Age	Gend	Where

Age of				**Age of**			
Appearance				**Appearance**			
0.0057 **Restored**	35 & Over			Restored			
Pseudo-Hist				0.0165 **Pseudo-Hist**	35 & Over		
Adaptive Use				Adaptive Use			
0.016 **Modern**			Local	0.0306 **Modern**	Under 35		

Hist Ambiance				**Hist Ambiance**			
(Test 1)				**(Test 1)**			
0.0057 **Hist Ambiance**	35 & Over			Hist Ambiance			
0.0057 **Not**	Under 35			Not			

Hist Ambiance				**Hist Ambiance**			
(Test 2)				**(Test 2)**			
Hist Ambiance				0.0264 **Hist Ambiance**	35 & Over		
Not				Not			

Hist Ambiance				**Hist Ambiance**			
(Test 3)				**(Test 3)**			
0.016 **Hist Ambiance**			Visitor	0.0057 **Hist Ambiance**	35 & Over		
0.016 **Not**			Local	0.0306 **Not**	Under 35		

Greenery				**Greenery**			
in Image				**in Image**			
Maximum Greenery				Maximum Greenery			
Moderate Greenery				Moderate Greenery			
Minimal Greenery				0.0231 **Minimal Greenery**			Local
No Greenery				0.0197 **No Greenery**			Visitor

Water				**Water**			
in Image				**in Image**			
Water				0.0399 **Water**		Male	
No Water				No Water			

Photo				**Photo**			
Orientation				**Orientation**			
Horizontal				0.0234 **Horizontal**		Male	
Vertical				Vertical			

Photo				**Photo**			
Exposure				**Exposure**			
Dark				Dark			
normal				normal			

Note:
P-values =<0.050 are highlighted, with the relevant demographic group favoring that characteristic described.
P-values =<0.010 are highlighted & have a black border.
'Education' is not a tested demographic category for this analysis.
'Age' is only tested in a 2 group split, 'under 35' & '35 and Over.'
'Where' is only tested in a 2 group split, 'Visitor' or 'Local' (which includes any local resident or local worker).
Data not fitting the definition of category characteristics, have been removed from that particular analysis.
P-values may vary within a two characteristic category (e.g., Yoko-Test 3) because of this removed extraneous data.

Table. 8.1. Philadelphia vs. Yokohama: Summary

Critique of Methods

The survey methodology can be looked at and critiqued in terms of how data is gathered and how it is evaluated.

In terms of the population sampled, the actual locations where the interviews take place does not appear to encourage preference for nearby locations. However, sampling people at multiple locations or even at only a few well traveled intersections, will likely yield a more accurate cross section of people in the area.

The use of a pair of photos for each site in question, appears to be a simple method of representing sites in the photoset. The average variance of selections within each of the 11 photo pairs of single sites is 1.5. That is, of the two different photos of a site, one was chosen an average of 1.5 times as frequently as the other. Not that extreme, but it still points out a possible risk of using a single photo to represent a site.

Though there is the possibility that one of each of the pair of photos is accurately representing an individual's preference for the site, and the other photo is not, it is difficult to know which is which. It also can not be known if the two photos were reduced to one, whether that single photo would capture those individuals who would have chosen either photo, or those who would have chosen only that specific photo.

Additional photos representing the site would likely offer a more accurate judgement from a respondent of their preference for a particular site. Likely the precision gained by additional photos would come at a progressively smaller and smaller rate. The respondent's patience at looking at multiple photos is continually at play as well, so high numbers of photos of the same site are not particularly realistic.

The pair of photos seems a simple compromise, removing some of the imbalances that a particularly strong or weak image may have over a particular individual's preference for a site. It should help offset the unknowns of preference that may be embodied within an image itself, and result in a more trustworthy interpretation for site preference.

"Photo Orientation" is part of the stability analysis for this survey. A male preference for photos oriented "Horizontally" was found. This may be due to an unintended overlap of the horizontal or vertical photos with a gender preferred category. It also may just be a false positive reading, an incorrect reading 5% of the time when using a P-value of 0.05. If it is proven valid in subsequent surveys, it then indicates an unintended factor within the survey instrument itself influencing preferences.

In either case, it does not negate the other findings which analyze separate evaluative characteristics. It may however, point to a need to increase consistency of presentation format of the photographs to reduce unintended effects. It also suggests multiple surveys to reduce possible false readings.

If a more high tech method of this survey method was chosen employing computers, an existing technology known as a "Quicktime" movie could be employed. This allows the respondent to click on an image (and move the cursor) to gain a panoramic view from a fixed location. Another related method could embed a video that allows a viewer to circle around a fixed location. This would allow an individual to highlight a singular image on a computer screen, and be given a more wide ranging view of the site in question from different viewpoints.

These computer techniques do require additional costs in time to set them up and scan in the images. They also mean higher costs during the actual survey. The number of survey takers becomes directly limited to the number of portable computers available.

So at the present time, if the budget is limited in implementing a survey, the simpler method of photos displayed on a presentation board remains most realistic. It will, of course, need to be continually refined, to improve its effectiveness. The expansion of the number of surveys taken at different times of the year, analyzing more waterfronts and broader populations, will likely be the most effective way to verify the correlations shown in this exploratory study.

Any number of evaluative categories with different characteristics may be applied in the analysis stage. It depends on the goals of the survey. An advantage of using data that was selected using very general criteria (i.e., liked or interesting) is that the evaluative categories may be refined or even switched after the data is gathered. Images may be reclassified by different characteristics or simply removed from the data set if they do not fit that particular category. Though ideally the evaluative categories will be known in advance, this flexibility without needing to gather additional data may be useful.

The background data gathered does not have that flexibility. Background information of education level was found to have strong correlations with preference in a number of evaluative categories in the Philadelphia Survey. Any future surveys should incorporate this as part of the data gathered. Additional data on cultural background and ethnicity might also prove informative, and should become standard in future surveys.

The analysis done by overall selections for these surveys are effective in gaining a general sense of preferences shown for the surveyed population. Since it is only representative of that particular sample group, much effort must be made to make it representative of the population intended to be surveyed. Since it has been shown that differences do exist in preferences according to demographic makeup, the meaningfulness of the overall selections are directly related to the demographic representation of the sample group. These intercept interviews will inherently skew the sample populations (e.g., those already in the survey area, those with enough time to take the survey, etc.). The overall selections, therefore, have somewhat limited meaningfulness on their own.

The analysis by demographic category provides the richest evaluations. The population comprising the sample set still is a key concern. However, the internal comparisons within a demographic category (such as age), allow results to be gathered independent of the demographic make-up of the sample set. It also allows comparisons to be made across survey areas and across cultures.

Ordering the photos from most to least selected is useful for site specific (not evaluative category) comparisons. It is intimately tied to the overall sample set. While selections that lie close together in preference might not be that informative, those at the extremes can provide much insight. This information is site (and waterfront) specific, and cannot be easily used for comparisons to other waterfronts.

Paired comparisons of photos offer similar value as overall photos ordered by preference. The photo pair comparisons are more descriptive than statistical. The analysis of photo pairs does not effectively compare evaluative categories, since they are direct comparisons of single sites. Preferences for different evaluative categories within these sites can not be deciphered as this analysis method now stands.

Though this paired comparison method should not be used to imply broader generalizations than the particular sites being looked at, still it does offer some use. It provides a simple visual identity to the more conceptual evaluative categories and characteristics explicated elsewhere. It may serve more effectively as a tool for speculation than for drawing conclusions.

Implications

The particular evaluative categories of this survey analysis were developed as a means of expanding traditional definitions of historical preservation. The valued sites (and exteriors of these sites) that are designated as historically significant and then conserved in some manner, are generally selected using formal criteria. Criteria used to judge the value of a site or series of sites includes rarity of form, fame of the designer, or significance of an event that occurred at that location. Are we preserving the properties that are truly significant for a wide cross section of the public, or are they chosen for criteria that are only important for a very select group of people?

This survey method, or likely any number of other easily created, accessible and relatively inexpensive survey methods, would allow this awareness of a broad spectrum of public opinions to be easily accessed by the designers working in the public realm of urban design.

Ideally, more than one method will be used to develop knowledge about the area.[1] This can cross-check results and help gather information that a particular survey method may not be suited to retrieve. Possibly this photo method which surveys a wide number of people could be balanced by a smaller number of less structured, in-depth interviews, as well as first hand observation.

Community meetings are good sounding boards as well, but only a select subset of the population at large might typically attend such a meeting. When relying exclusively on the reactions within a public meeting, anecdotal evidence from a small, select group of respondents may be gathered. This value should not be underestimated, yet it still comes from a particularly limited, and likely vocal cross section of people.[2] A user survey would sample a broader audience.

These methods are being suggested particularly in cases of larger scale urban design or historic preservation, particularly involving multiple sites. With certain variations this survey method could be applied at both larger and smaller scales as well. Larger scale surveys could study an entire region for preferences by its users. This might ground and guide future planning decisions.[3] At a smaller scale, versions of the survey might focus on an individual structure and the internal and external spaces and details that comprise it. It might serve a similar purpose as the data/impression gathering of a post-occupancy evaluation.

With only minor variations, these photo surveys may serve different purposes at different times. One is to deal with a scenario where redevelopment is about to occur in a specific location. Area residents and visitors would then be asked about which places have meaning to them. Following the general concept of sacred places discussed by Randolph Hester, meaningful locations for locals would be sought.[4] The knowledge of experts of what it architecturally important, or historically important, may or may not correspond to the meaningfulness of sites for local inhabitants, but in either case, the preferences of the public would be better understood.

This survey method can also be used as part of a post-occupancy evaluation of the larger urban environment, as a method of learning from an existing environment. The information gathered could then be used to better prepare guidelines for new construction being done there or elsewhere.

Though one or two surveys will not come close to revealing any universal tendencies, still they may be useful within their own particular contexts. A large number of these surveys executed in a wide number of U.S. Waterfront areas may reveal more convincing patterns of preference by their respective users. Studies in a number of waterfronts within different nations will allow a cross-cultural comparison of preferences.

When using the photo survey method with the public, empirical data will be gathered. Decisions might then be more easily guided and defended using the results of the process, on the grounds that they represent the popular demands of a broad section of the public. They also might be defended on the grounds that they represent a common preference of a particular subgroup of the population. The (cautiously) quantifiable results of this process can encourage participants to visualize and define what otherwise might be described only in more ambiguous qualitative terms.[5]

This study has shown a strong tie between demographics and preferences for a series of specific evaluative categories of urban design in the waterfront areas of Philadelphia and Yokohama. The particular evaluative categories tested and found significant in this study may offer some guidance in future planning and design decisions in urban waterfronts.

That significant correlations are found to exist within demographic groups for these evaluative categories at all, may prove equally important. This suggests the importance of planning not just for a general public in these areas. Rather, for this particular Philadelphia example, it suggests that age, education, and mix of visitors and locals of the target population, are key components.

Individual preferences always exist. That they also follow some basic demographic lines means that urban design in an area might be guided to potentially increase the number of preferred sites for those using the area, if their demographic mix is known (or can be approximated) in advance. It might affect the economic success of an area as well, though future studies would need to be done to search for links between economic success and level of preference.

This study and survey technique are intended as tools to assist planners, urban designers and preservation specialists in the decision making process. If further studies support findings of a more cross demographic preferences for an evaluative characteristic (e.g., Restored), it might prove useful in cases where the target population demographics cannot be known. Ideally though, the demographics of the target population would be known, and could, therefore, be better planned and designed for.

Planning and designing in an urban waterfront area should consider the demographics of the target population, both the existing and intended users of the area. When the planning and urban design of an area is done without understanding the demographics of the target population, or when it ignores it, the general preference of the overall population using the area may be needlessly diminished.

In a redesign of the Philadelphia waterfront, for example, "Restored" structures could be emphasized if the majority of the target population is intended to be 35 and over. If the location were Yokohama, "Pseudo-Historical" might be emphasized over "Modern" if the intent is to better satisfy that audience. Looking deeper into what qualities of the "Restored" or "Pseudo-Historical" individuals are drawn to might be the next logical step of analysis.

This survey highlights the need for urban design and physical planning incorporating preservation as an integral part of it. The age of appearance of a structure (Historical Ambience) is a significant factor in various demographic groups" preferences and should always be considered within physical planning decisions. It does not mean preservation should always be implemented. Nor does it mean contemporary design should necessarily mimic a public preference for "Pseudo-Historical," "Modern," or any other style. Rather, the public preferences should always be considered and reflected on as affecting the appreciation of the intended audience.

An area combining a mix of different ages of appearance may provide the most flexibility and leeway for being (at least partially) preferred by the widest number of demographic groups. But it will not necessarily be strongly preferred by any of them.

Cities often contain more focused areas within them, sometimes these were developed incrementally over time, sometimes more deliberately planned, designed or preserved. These areas often gain identities that include names, reputations and certain internal consistencies (physical, functional or social) holding them together. An area's identity, as discussed in earlier chapters, is a useful device to shrink and organize a large city from a perceptual point of view.

These more distinct areas and what they are known for, may attract certain demographic groups. This audience can then be further built upon by addressing their particular preferences in regard to urban design.

That the strategic planning of an area should take "Age of Appearance" into account, does not necessarily mean it should be a tight focus (exclusively "Adaptive Use," exclusively "Restored," etc.) It also doesn't mean that the intended audience will definitely end up using the area. There are too many other factors involved. However, "Age of Appearance" can serve as a supporting factor in guiding the conservation and change of the physical fabric of the city.

Appendix A

Philadelphia

SORTED PHOTO#	PHOTO DESCRIPTION	PHOTO PAIR	TIMES CHOSEN	% OF RESPONDENTS
6	Main Alleyway	Elfreth's Alley	61	48
14	Couple Looking Out	Penn's Landing (river)	48	38
26	Older Rowhouses	Society Hill (residential)	42	33
31	Cobblestone St	Headhouse Square	42	33
30	Sidewalk	Headhouse Square	40	31
15	Full Building	Greek Revival (Bank)	39	31
23	Walnut St.	Pedestrian Walkway	37	29
13	Boat on Water	Penn's Landing (river)	32	25
33	Sailboat	Ship & Skyline	32	25
16	Front Facade	Greek Revival (Bank)	28	22
12	Promenade	Penns Landing (plaza)	26	20
11	Plaza & Canopies	Penns Landing (plaza)	24	19
32	Steamship	Ship & Skyline	24	19
34	Colorful Facades	South St	23	18
36	South St	Pedestrian Walkway	23	18
28	Tree & Tower	Society Hill Towers	22	17
27	New Rowhouses	Society Hill (residential)	21	17
3	Doorway	Painted Bride	19	15
22	Full Building	City Tavern	19	15
29	Full Buildings	Society Hill Towers	18	14
35	Controlled Signage	South St	17	13
4	Full Building	Painted Bride	15	12
24	Overlooking Water	Seaport Museum	15	12
5	Hidden Alcove	Elfreth's Alley	13	10
21	Sidewalk	City Tavern	13	10
2	Rock Lobster	Delaware Ave	12	9
7	Front Elevation	Old City Galleries	9	7
19	Sidewalk	Ritz 5	9	7
1	Dave & Buster's	Delaware Ave	6	5
10	Full Building	Greek Revival (lunch)	6	5
17	Tower	Visitors Center	5	4
20	Front Elevation	Ritz 5	5	4
25	Front Facade	Seaport Museum	5	4
8	Sidewalk	Old City Galleries	4	3
9	Front Elevation	Greek Revival (lunch)	4	3
18	Reflective Glass	Visitors Center	4	3

Table A.1. Philadelphia: Sorted Photos

6

14

26

31

30

15

23

13

33

16

12

11

Figure A.1. Philadelphia: 12 Most Preferred Photos

32

34

36

28

27

3

22

29

35

4

24

5

Figure A.2. Philadelphia: 12 Mid Preferred Photos

Figure A.3. Philadelphia: 12 Least Preferred Photos

PHILADELPHIA WATERFRONT FIELD STUDY (11/5/98)

(read)   "Thank you very much for taking the time to do this survey. It is being given in order to find out how people perceive this general area. The map shows the bounds of this particular study. I will show you 36 photos. The locations of the photos are noted on the map."

(read)   "Please pick out 6 photos that show what you like most or think interesting about this area. For example: views, places, or people. They can include sites you have visited already, or want to visit in the future."

(As they pick each photo, put a post-it on it, and immediately mark down the Photo No. (column 2) and whether the map was glanced at prior to each choice (column 3). Then ask the questions in the remaining columns for each of the 6 photos chosen.)
(Repeat process until all 6 photos are selected.)

(do for all 6 choices)			(then for each photo, READ)	"What are your main reasons for choosing this photo?" (√ 1 or 2 boxes)											
Order of Choice	Photo No.	Did they glance at MAP or PHOTO first?	Have you seen this view or site in person? (Yes or No)	Building	Walkway	Water	Monument /Object	Boat/ Bridge	People	Lawn / Greenery	Signage / Decoration	Resting area	Amphitheater	Contrast	Other
1st Choice															
2nd Choice															
3rd Choice															
4th Choice															
5th Choice															
6th Choice															

Figure A.4. Philadelphia: Questionnaire Front

1. HOW MANY TIMES HAVE YOU BEEN TO THIS PART OF PHILADELPHIA, INCLUDING TODAY?
(read choices & circle)   1   2   3   4 or more

2. ARE YOU AWARE THIS AREA CONTAINS FORMER URBAN RENEWAL SITES?   yes / no

3. WHY DID YOU COME HERE TODAY? *(read choices & circle all that apply)*
relaxation | sightseeing | meet friend(s) | eating | shopping | education | other (_____)

4. WITH WHOM DID YOU COME? *(read choices & circle all that apply)*
alone | with spouse | with children | with friend(s) | with tour | other (_____)

5. WHERE ARE YOU COMING FROM TODAY? *(read choices & circle)*
work | school | home | hotel | other (_____)

6. DO YOU WORK OR GO TO SCHOOL IN PHILADELPHIA?   yes / no

    6a. If yes (to WORK), ZIPCODE of WORK location? _____
                                               (street address ok if don't know zip)

    6b. If yes (to SCHOOL), ZIPCODE of SCHOOL location? _____
                                               (school name ok if don't know zip)

7. ZIPCODE of CURRENT HOME ADDRESS? _____   _____
                                   (zipcode)   country (if not U.S.A.)

    7a. PERMANENT ADDRESS (if not same as current address)?

                  _____   _____
                                   (zipcode)   country (if not U.S.A.)

8. WHAT IS YOUR PRESENT OCCUPATION? _____

9. AGE BRACKET? *(read choices & circle)*   under 15   15-24   25-34   35-44   45-64   65 or over

10. WHAT IS THE HIGHEST LEVEL OF EDUCATION YOU HAVE COMPLETED?
(read choices & circle)
    some high school | graduated high school | some college | graduated college | post-grad work

(The following is to be filled out by the INTERVIEWER, without asking subjects)
==

1. GENDER of SUBJECT?   male / female
2. Time of day that survey is given? _____
3. Specific Location at time of survey? _____
4. Survey Takers Names? _____   _____
                             team member #1   team member #2

Figure A.5. Philadelphia: Questionnaire Back

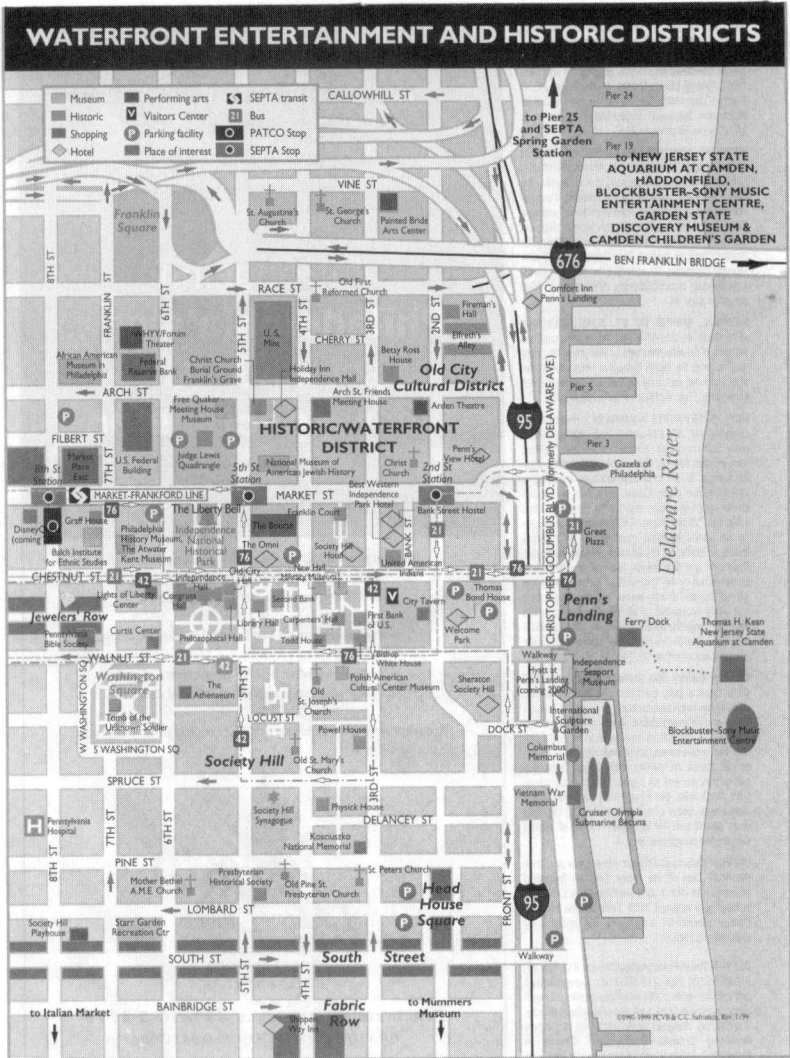

Figure A.6. Philadelphia: Tourist Map

General Survey Location By LOCATION ▶

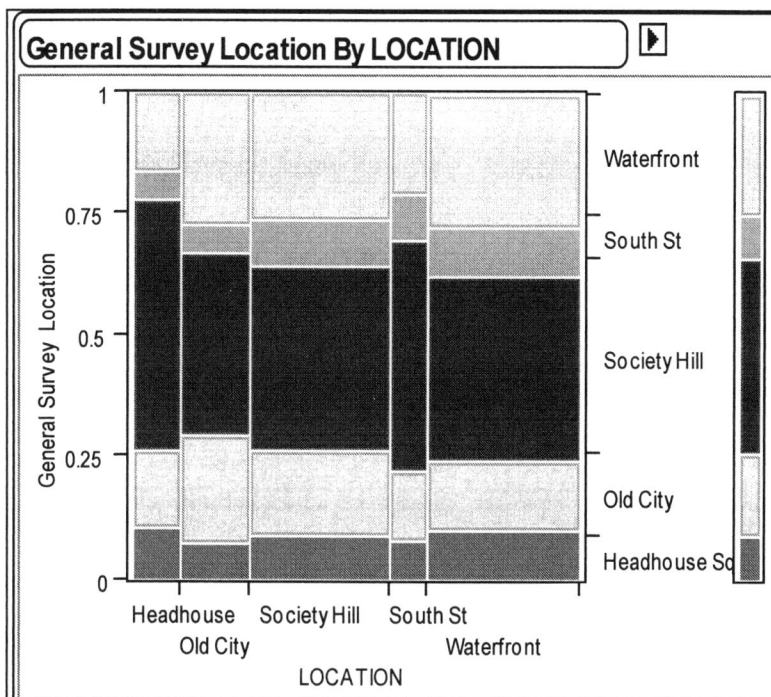

Tests

Source	DF	-LogLikelihood	RSquare (U)
Model	16	7.8856	0.0072
Error	742	1094.0408	
C Total	758	1101.9264	
Total Count	762		

Test	ChiSquare	Prob>ChiSq
Likelihood Ratio	15.771	0.4690
Pearson	15.518	0.4871

Figure A.7. Philadelphia: Survey Location vs. Photo Location

Paired Comparisons

This section looks at specific pairings of images from the Philadelphia survey. Each major site is shown with a pair of photos. Some paired photos show different images of a single site. Other paired photos attempt to divide a site into two different categories (e.g. eighteenth century Society Hill Rowhouses vs. twentieth century Society Hill Rowhouses). In this second set of comparisons, the preference for one category over the other is analyzed.

In a few cases, a pair of photos representing a single site are then judged against a pair of photos representing a comparative site (e.g., Greek Revival First Bank vs. Greek Revival Restaurant). These scenarios also try to compare preferences for sites with much in common, but also with distinct differences.

The pairings were chosen with the intent of reducing the set of variables between comparative sites. Though this analysis method was not the main focus of my survey, the approach may provide some further insight into preferences of the public.

23   36

Figure A.8. Philadelphia: Pedestrian Bridge Comparison Photos

Pedestrian Bridges

Photo #23 (Walnut St Walkway) vs. Photo #36 (South Street Walkway)

The following comparison is between photo #23 (Walnut St. Pedestrian Bridge) and photo #36 (South St. Pedestrian Bridge). They were both designed in the past few years in a manner that is extremely contextual, using historical materials and allusions from the surrounding area.

Noticeable differences lie within the preferences of these two images by those surveyed overall. Where the Walnut St. Bridge was the seventh most preferred image (selected thirty-seven times), the South St. Bridge was only the fifteenth most preferred (selected twenty-three times). Therefore, of the times either of the two images were selected, the Walnut St. bridge was selected at a slightly more than 3:2 ratio.

There was a significant difference found in only one demographic category, gender. Those choosing the Walnut St. Bridge photo were 68% female, 30% male. Those choosing the South St. Bridge photo were split the other way, 35% female, 61% male. This may owe something to the bridge's location. South St. Bridge, at the foot of South St., leads to a parking lot along Delware Ave. The bridge is used more as a terminus and scenic overlook for pedestrians walking along South St. Those selecting the images of South Street (Photo #34 and #35) were 75% male.

However, it still does not explain the high proportion of women selecting the Walnut St. Bridge. The Walnut St. Bridge, at the foot of Walnut St., leads to Penn's Landing which has a more balanced breakdown of people selecting those sites. Therefore, factors causing the differences in preference by gender may lie in the design features of the bridges themselves. No other significant differences were noted between these photos.

Within the Walnut St. Pedestrian Bridge (photo #23), the breakdown for reasons is led by "walkway" (21%) and "monument" (19%). Within the South St. Pedestrian Bridge (photo #36), the breakdown for reasons is led by "walkway" (34%) and "people" (14%). The reasons selected shows an expected preference of "walkway," since that is a prime function of these pedestrian bridges. Within the Walnut St. Bridge, the selection of "monument" demonstrates the lure of the monumental pylons framing the view beyond.

Category	Walnut St. Walkway Photo #23		South St. Walkway Photo #36	
	(N)	Prob.	(N)	Prob.
Total Times Chosen	(37)	62 %	(23)	38 %
Age				
<14	(2)	5 %	(0)	---
15-24	(7)	19 %	(8)	35 %
25-34	(7)	19 %	(2)	9 %
35-44	(7)	19 %	(8)	35 %
45-64	(12)	32 %	(5)	22%
65+	(2)	5 %	(0)	---
Unknown	(0)	---	(0)	---
Education				
Some HS	(3)	8 %	(0)	---
Grad HS	(7)	19 %	(2)	9 %
Some College	(12)	32 %	(8)	35 %
Grad College	(9)	24 %	(10)	43 %
Post Grad	(5)	14 %	(3)	13 %
Unknown	(1)	3 %	(0)	---
Local				
Both	(22)	60 %	(13)	57 %
Reside	(4)	11 %	(1)	4 %
Work	(6)	16 %	(4)	17 %
Visitor	(5)	14 %	(5)	22 %
Unknown	(0)	---	(0)	---
Seen				
No	(11)	30 %	(10)	43 %
Yes	(22)	59 %	(10)	43 %
Unknown	(4)	11 %	(3)	13 %
Gender				
Female	(25)	68 %	(8)	35 %
Male	(11)	30 %	(14)	61 %
Unknown	(1)	3 %	(1)	4 %

Table A.2. Philadelphia: Pedestrian Bridges—percentages
(Continued on next page)

Category	Walnut St. Walkway Photo #23		South St. Walkway Photo #36	
	(N)	Prob.	(N)	Prob.
Reasons				
Building	(4)	9 %	(1)	3 %
Walkway	(10)	21 %	(10)	34 %
Water	(2)	4 %	(1)	3 %
Monument/Object	(9)	19 %	(1)	3 %
Boat	(0)	---	(0)	---
Bridge	(1)	2 %	(1)	3 %
People	(1)	2 %	(4)	14 %
Lawn/Greenery	(0)	---	(0)	---
Signage/Decoration	(0)	---	(0)	---
Resting Area	(0)	---	(0)	---
Amphitheater	(0)	---	(0)	---
Contrast	(5)	11 %	(3)	10 %
Other: arrange of scenery	(0)	---	(1)	3 %
Other: architecture	(1)	2 %	(0)	---
Other: background	(1)	2 %	(0)	---
Other: brick	(1)	2 %	(0)	---
Other: clean	(1)	2 %	(0)	---
Other: composition	(1)	2 %	(0)	---
Other: cosmopolitan	(1)	2 %	(0)	---
Other: design	(1)	2 %	(0)	---
Other: familiar	(1)	2 %	(0)	---
Other: historic	(0)	---	(1)	3 %
Other: historic arch.	(0)	---	(1)	3 %
Other: interest	(0)	---	(1)	3 %
Other: interesting	(1)	2 %	(0)	---
Other: pedestrian haven	(0)	---	(1)	3 %
Other: roof	(1)	2 %	(0)	---
Other: scenery	(1)	2 %	(0)	---
Other: sculpt was his idea	(0)	---	(1)	3 %
Other: sky	(1)	2 %	(0)	---
Other: streets	(0)	---	(1)	3 %
Other: towers	(1)	2 %	(0)	---
Other: view	(2)	4 %	(9)	27 %
Other: well designed view	(0)	---	(1)	3 %

Note: Percentages may not total 100% due to rounding errors.

Table A.2—Continued

PEDESTRIAN BRIDGES   Photo #23 - Photo #36

	p-value				
AGE (5 groups)		15-24	25-34	35-44	45-64	65+
	0.23				

EDUCATION (5 groups)		Some HS	Grad HS	Some Col	Grad Col	Post Grad
	0.34				

GENDER		Female	Male
	0.01		

LOCAL / VISITOR (4 groups)		Resident & Worker	Phila. Resident	Phila. Worker	Visitor
	0.72				

Note: There were a small number of missing demographic responses on the actual surveys. These respondents have been temporarily removed from the relevant analysis P-values =<0.05 are highlighted, and further analyzed on the following pages.

Table A.3. Philadelphia: Pedestrian Bridges—overview

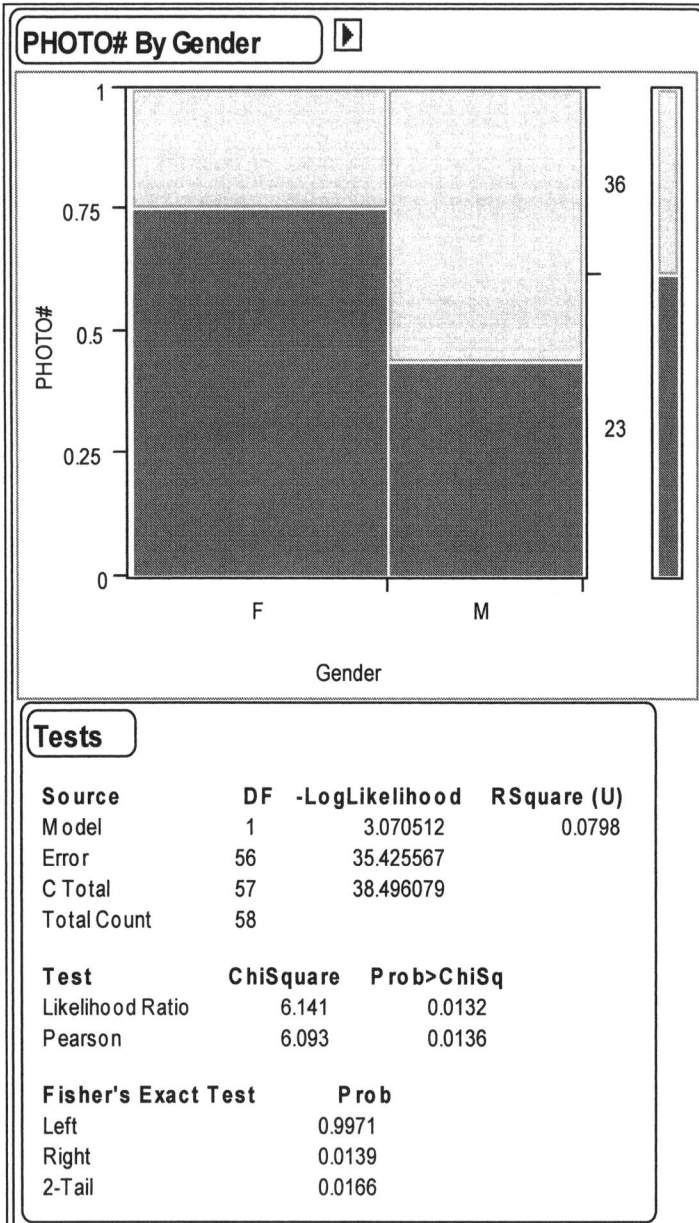

Figure A.9. Philadelphia: Pedestrian Bridges—photo by gender

26   27

Figure A.10. Philadelphia: Society Hill Comparison Photos

Society Hill Residential

Photo #26 (Older Rowhouses) vs. Photo #27 (Newer Rowhouses)

This comparison is between two photos of Society Hill rowhouses, taken on the opposite side of the same street. Photo #26 shows rowhouses originally constructed in the late eighteenth, early nineteenth century.

Photo #27 shows rowhouses designed in the 1960s. Both use brick, small paned windows and low scaled structures. Where the eighteenth century rowhouses have ornate lintels, shutters and marble stoops, the twentieth century rowhouses have simpler facades, along with ironwork balconies. Both have a substantial amount of greenery surrounding them.

Dramatic differences lie within the preferences of these two images among those surveyed overall. Where the older rowhouses were the third most preferred image (selected forty-eight times), the newer rowhouses were only the seventeenth most preferred (selected twenty-one times). Therefore, of the times either of the two images were selected, the older rowhouses were selected 2:1.

The two photos are similar in composition (though opposites), and show roughly similar amounts of building, sidewalk and greenery. It is interesting that where photo #26 is most frequently selected for the reasons of "building" (41%) followed by "walkway" (14%) and "history" (6%), photo #27 is most favored for the "walkway" (32%) followed by the "building" (18%) and "greenery" (18%). This could be suggesting the lure of brick paving and street trees along the walkway in general, as being a draw in themselves. When the rowhouses appear to have eighteenth century detailing, the buildings themselves take priority as the lure, and the paving and greenery fall behind as less selected reasons.

There was a significant difference found in two demographic categories, age and education. When age is aggregated into two groups, those under 35 and those 35 and over, a strong difference in preference is revealed. Similarly when education is aggregated into those who have not graduated from college, and those who have, another significant difference in preferences is shown.

Those choosing the older rowhouses were 22% under age 35 and 78% age 35 and over. Those choosing the newer rowhouses were 52% under age 35 and 48% age 35 and over. Where the newer rowhouses did not elicit a strong difference in preference by age, the older rowhouses showed a very strong preference by those 35 and over.

Those choosing the older rowhouses were 31% with less than a college education and 69% with a college degree or more. Those choosing the newer rowhouses were 57% with less than a college education and 43% with a college degree or more. As with age, the newer rowhouses did not elicit a strong difference in preference by education level, where the older rowhouses did. A very strong preference for the older rowhouses was shown by those with a college education or more.

Category	Older Rowhouses Photo #26		Newer Rowhouses Photo #27	
	(N)	Prob.	(N)	Prob.
Total Times Chosen	(42)	67 %	(21)	33 %
Age				
<14	(0)	---	(0)	---
15-24	(3)	7 %	(5)	24 %
25-34	(6)	14 %	(6)	29 %
35-44	(11)	26 %	(4)	19 %
45-64	(18)	43 %	(5)	24%
65+	(3)	7 %	(1)	5 %
Unknown	(1)	2 %	(0)	---
Education				
Some HS	(0)	---	(1)	5 %
Grad HS	(5)	12 %	(3)	14 %
Some College	(8)	19 %	(8)	38 %
Grad College	(19)	45 %	(4)	19 %
Post Grad	(10)	24 %	(5)	24 %
Unknown	(0)	---	(0)	---
Local				
Both	(19)	45 %	(9)	43 %
Reside	(4)	10 %	(3)	14 %
Work	(7)	17 %	(2)	10 %
Visitor	(12)	29 %	(7)	33 %
Unknown	(0)	---	(0)	---
Seen				
No	(9)	21 %	(1)	62 %
Yes	(25)	60 %	(6)	29 %
Unknown	(8)	19 %	(2)	10 %
Gender				
Female	(18)	43 %	(9)	43 %
Male	(23)	55 %	(11)	52 %
Unknown	(1)	2 %	(1)	5 %

Table A.4. Philadelphia: Society Hill Residential—percentages
(Continued on next page)

Category	Older Rowhouses Photo #26		Newer Rowhouses Photo #27	
	(N)	Prob.	(N)	Prob.
Reasons				
Building	(21)	41 %	(5)	18 %
Walkway	(7)	14 %	(9)	32 %
Water	(0)	---	(0)	---
Monument/Object	(0)	---	(1)	4 %
Boat	(0)	---	(0)	---
Bridge	(0)	---	(1)	3 %
People	(1)	2 %	(4)	14 %
Lawn/Greenery	(2)	4 %	(0)	---
Signage/Decoration	(0)	---	(0)	---
Resting Area	(0)	---	(0)	---
Amphitheater	(0)	---	(0)	---
Contrast	(1)	2 %	(2)	7 %
Other: architecture	(1)	2 %	(0)	---
Other: clean	(1)	2 %	(0)	---
Other: colonial	(1)	2 %	(1)	4 %
Other: familiar	(1)	2 %	(0)	---
Other: graciousness/hist.	(1)	2 %	(0)	---
Other: historic	(3)	6 %	(1)	4 %
Other: historic arch.	(1)	2 %	(0)	---
Other: historical	(1)	2 %	(0)	---
Other: houses	(1)	2 %	(0)	---
Other: just like Phila.	(1)	2 %	(0)	---
Other: neighborhood	(1)	2 %	(0)	---
Other: quiet	(1)	2 %	(1)	4 %
Other: residential	(1)	2 %	(1)	4 %
Other: scale bldg./street	(1)	2 %	(0)	---
Other: street rowhouses	(1)	2 %	(0)	---
Other: streetscape	(1)	2 %	(0)	---
Other: view of city	(1)	2 %	(0)	---

Note: Percentages may not total 100% due to rounding errors.

Table A.4—Continued

SOCIETY HILL RESIDENTIAL Photo #26 - Photo #27

	p-value				
AGE (5 groups)		15-24	25-34	35-44	45-64	65+
	0.18				

		<=34	35+
AGE (2 groups)			
	0.02		

		Some HS	Grad HS	Some Col	Grad Col	Post Grad
EDUCATION (5 groups)						
	0.15					

		<= Some Col	Grad Col+
EDUCATION (2 groups)			
	0.05		

		Female	Male
GENDER			
	0.94		

		Resident & Worker	Phila. Resident	Phila. Worker	Visitor
LOCAL / VISITOR (4 groups)					
	0.82				

Note: There were a small number of missing demographic responses on the actual surveys. These respondents have been temporarily removed from the relevant analysis P-values =<0.05 are highlighted, and further analyzed on the following pages.

Table A.5. Philadelphia: Society Hill Residential—overview

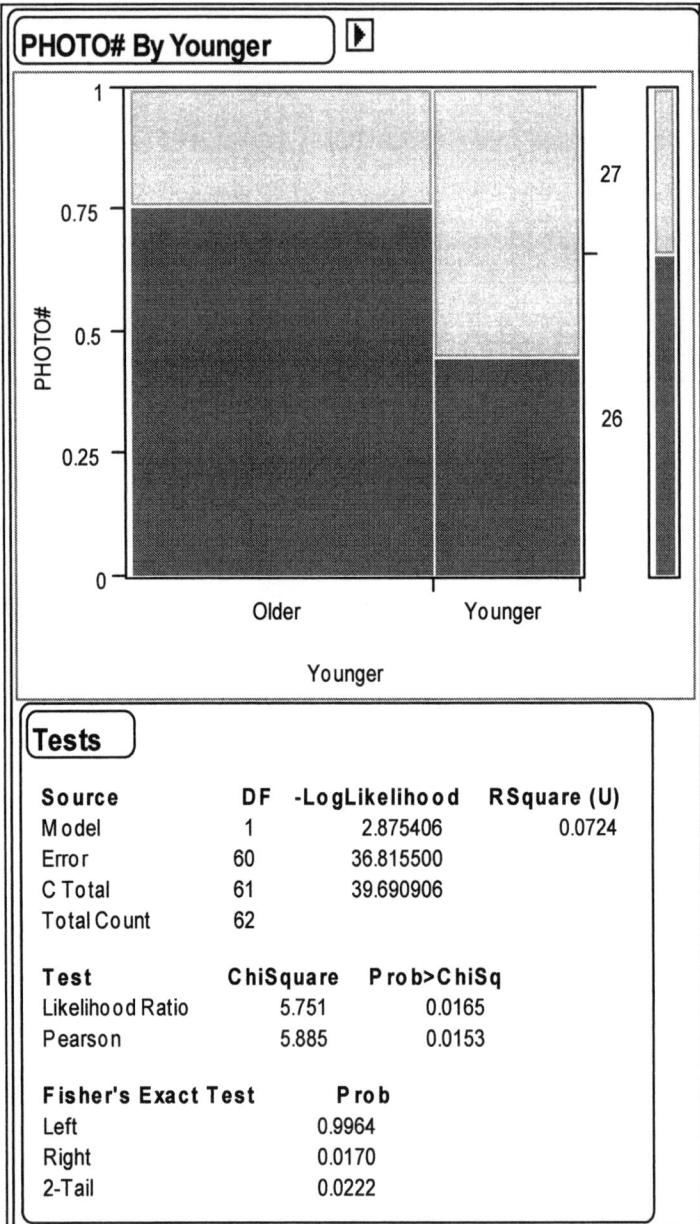

Figure A.11. Philadelphia: Society Hill Residential—photo by younger

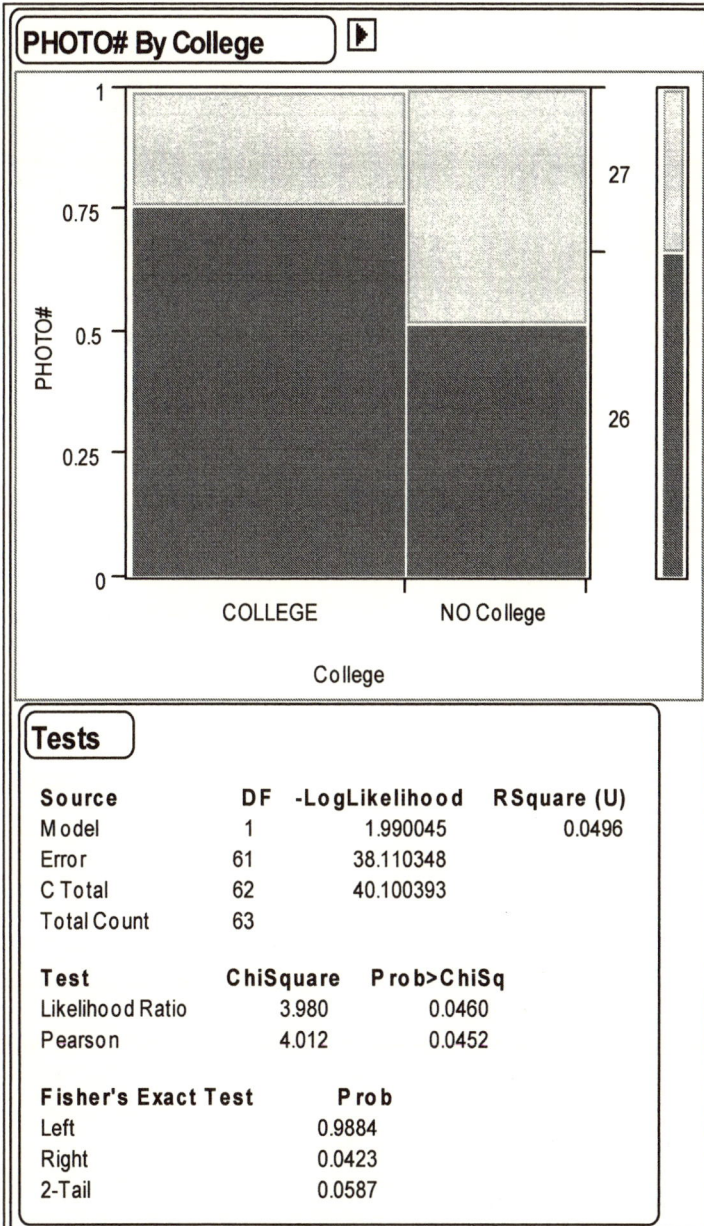

PHOTO# By College ▶

Tests

Source	DF	-LogLikelihood	RSquare (U)
Model	1	1.990045	0.0496
Error	61	38.110348	
C Total	62	40.100393	
Total Count	63		

Test	ChiSquare	Prob>ChiSq
Likelihood Ratio	3.980	0.0460
Pearson	4.012	0.0452

Fisher's Exact Test	Prob
Left	0.9884
Right	0.0423
2-Tail	0.0587

Figure A.12. Philadelphia: Society Hill Residential—photo by college

34   35

Figure A.13. Philadelphia: South Street Comparison Photos

South Street

Photo #34 (Colorful Signage) vs. Photo #35 (Refined Signage)

The following comparison is between photo #34 (Storefronts with colorful signage) and photo #35 (Storefronts with refined signage). The structures in both photos lie one block apart along South Street. They were built originally in the late eighteenth and early nineteenth centuries, and have been adapted to new uses over the years. Photo #34 shows a series of these storefronts with colorfully painted facades and unrestrained signage. Photo #35 shows a calmer, more restrained treatment of the facades and signage.

Noticeable differences lie within the preferences of these two images among those surveyed overall. Where the colorful storefronts were the fourteenth most preferred image (selected twenty-three times), the restrained storefronts were the twenty-first most preferred (selected seventeen times). Therefore, the colorful storefronts were selected at slightly less than a 3:2 ratio.

That the overall preferences are not dramatically different, and that they even slightly favor the colorful storefronts is of note here. The restrained signage (which might be described as the more tasteful of the two) was not selected as frequently as the less controlled, more playful treatment. Possibly the shear distinctiveness of these colorful facades within the context of a red brick city provides some relief or attraction to those who selected this photo. These colorful facades may also be more representative of the image people associate with "South Street." It is known as an area that attracts and caters to a very young clientele.

The most popular reasons for choosing both photos were similar as well, "buildings" being most common and "signage" being the second choice. There were no significant demographic differences found between the people selecting these photographs.

Category	Colorful Signage Photo #34		Refined Signage Photo #35	
	(N)	Prob.	(N)	Prob.
Total Times Chosen	**(23)**	**58 %**	**(17)**	**43 %**
Age				
<14	(0)	---	(0)	---
15-24	(1)	4 %	(2)	12 %
25-34	(7)	30 %	(2)	12 %
35-44	(6)	26 %	(7)	41 %
45-64	(8)	35 %	(4)	24%
65+	(1)	4 %	(1)	6 %
Unknown	(0)	---	(1)	6 %
Education				
Some HS	(2)	9 %	(1)	6 %
Grad HS	(2)	9 %	(3)	18 %
Some College	(2)	9 %	(5)	29 %
Grad College	(11)	48 %	(6)	35 %
Post Grad	(6)	26 %	(2)	12 %
Unknown	(0)	---	(0)	---
Local				
Both	(9)	39 %	(7)	41 %
Reside	(2)	9 %	(2)	12 %
Work	(4)	17 %	(3)	18 %
Visitor	(8)	35 %	(5)	29 %
Unknown	(0)	---	(0)	---
Seen				
No	(8)	35 %	(4)	24 %
Yes	(13)	57 %	(9)	53 %
Unknown	(2)	9 %	(4)	24 %
Gender				
Female	(6)	26 %	(4)	24 %
Male	(17)	74 %	(13)	76 %
Unknown	(0)	---	(0)	---

Table A.6. Philadelphia: South Street—percentages
(Continued on next page)

Category	Colorful Signage Photo #34		Refined Signage Photo #35	
	(N)	Prob.	(N)	Prob.
Reasons				
Building	(10)	34 %	(7)	32 %
Walkway	(0)	---	(1)	5 %
Water	(0)	---	(0)	---
Monument/Object	(0)	---	(0)	---
Boat	(0)	---	(1)	5 %
Bridge	(0)	---	(0)	---
People	(2)	7 %	(1)	5 %
Lawn/Greenery	(0)	---	(0)	---
Signage/Decoration	(5)	17 %	(4)	18 %
Resting Area	(0)	---	(0)	---
Amphitheater	(0)	---	(0)	---
Contrast	(3)	10 %	(1)	5 %
Other:	(2)	7 %	(0)	---
Other: atmosphere	(0)	---	(1)	5 %
Other: business owner	(0)	---	(1)	5 %
Other: busy	(1)	3 %	(0)	---
Other: color	(2)	7 %	(0)	---
Other: colors	(2)	7 %	(0)	---
Other: familiar	(0)	---	(1)	5 %
Other: familiarity	(1)	3 %	(0)	---
Other: fun	(0)	---	(1)	5 %
Other: historic	(0)	---	(1)	5 %
Other: quaint	(0)	---	(1)	5 %
Other: vibrant colors	(1)	3 %	(0)	---

Note: Percentages may not total 100% due to rounding errors.

Table A.6—Continued

Appendix A

SOUTH STREET		Photo #34 - Photo #35				
	p-value					
AGE		15-24	25-34	35-44	45-64	65+
(5 groups)						
	0.50					

EDUCATION		Some HS	Grad HS	Some Col	Grad Col	Post Grad
(5 groups)						
	0.34					

GENDER		Female	Male
	0.85		

LOCAL / VISITOR		Resident	Phila.	Phila.	Visitor
(4 groups)		& Worker	Resident	Worker	
	0.98				

Note: There were a small number of missing demographic responses on the actual surveys. These respondents have been temporarily removed from the relevant analysis P-values =<0.05 are highlighted, and further analyzed on the following pages.

Table A.7. Philadelphia: South Street—overview

9 10

Figure A.14. Philadelphia: Greek Revival Restaurant Comparison Photos

15 16

Figure A.15. Philadelphia: Greek Revival Bank Comparison Photos

Greek Revival

Photo #9+10 (Restaurant) vs. Photo #15+16 (First Bank)

The following comparison is between photos #9 & #10 (Greek Revival Structure - Restaurant) and photos #15 & #16 (Greek Revival Structure - First Bank). The goal of this comparison of two sites with Greek Revival facades is to look at preferences for restoration of a site compared to adaptive use. The sites are about one block from each other. The use of similar, Greek Revival facade removes the possible preference for the style itself as a factor. The photo compositions of pictures of both sites are similar, though not identical.

The restaurant is pictured in photo #9+10. It has a formal Greek Revival Facade outside (frequently associated with banks, courts, etc.), but a slightly incongruous use inside as a restaurant. It actually was originally constructed as a bank in 1830s. The new use of the structure is made apparent by the external signage proclaiming "lunch" wrapped around the entry columns and a colorful mural on the side of the building. Two tables with chairs and umbrellas also flank the front doorway on the exterior.

The First Bank is pictured in photos #15+16. It is more pristine in appearance, with no commercial signage whatsoever. It is part of Independence National Park and appears from the outside to be restored as it originally existed. It was constructed in the 1790s. It displays no visible signs of contemporary times or incongruous uses inside.

Dramatic differences lie within the preferences of these two sites among those surveyed overall. The First Bank images were the sixth and tenth most preferred images, selected a total of sixty-seven times. The Greek Revival Restaurant photos were the thirtieth and thirty-fifth most preferred, selected a total of ten times. Therefore, the restored Greek Revival First Bank was selected more than six times as often. "Building" is the most favored reason in both the Restaurant and the First Bank photos, while "monument" and "historic" follow.

Comparing the demographics of those choosing the First Bank photos against those choosing the Greek Revival Restaurant yields no significant differences in terms of age, education, gender or local/visitor status. There are at least two strong possibilities for underlying factors behind the differences in preference by the overall survey respondents, which might work independently or in tandem.

The restaurant facade had more signs of natural deterioration due to time, which might be perceived as a sign of neglect. The grafitti-like mural on the side of the restaurant may have contributed to this perception. The First Bank, in contrast seemed extremely well maintained, with everything including the surrounding greenery, well manicured.

Another, is that the strong split in preference between the two sites implies a preference for sites (apparently) consistent in structure and expected use. The restaurant, however, had a more dissonant appearance between structure and expected use. A "Restored" structure was therefore chosen over one employing "Adaptive Use" (with signs of this use visible externally).

Category	Gr. Rev. Rest. (front) Photo #9		Gr. Rev. Rest. (full bldg.) Photo #10	
	(N)	Prob.	(N)	Prob.
Total Times Chosen	**(4)**	**40 %**	**(6)**	**60 %**
Age				
<14	(0)	---	(0)	---
15-24	(0)	---	(1)	17 %
25-34	(1)	25 %	(2)	33 %
35-44	(1)	25 %	(2)	33 %
45-64	(2)	50 %	(0)	---
65+	(0)	---	(0)	---
Unknown	(0)	---	(1)	17 %
Education				
Some HS	(0)	---	(0)	---
Grad HS	(1)	25 %	(1)	17 %
Some College	(1)	25 %	(3)	50 %
Grad College	(2)	50 %	(2)	33 %
Post Grad	(0)	---	(0)	---
Unknown	(0)	---	(0)	---
Local				
Both	(2)	50 %	(5)	83 %
Reside	(1)	25 %	(0)	---
Work	(0)	---	(0)	---
Visitor	(1)	25 %	(1)	17 %
Unknown	(0)	---	(0)	---
Seen				
No	(1)	25 %	(0)	---
Yes	(3)	75 %	(6)	100 %
Unknown	(0)	---	(0)	---
Gender				
Female	(1)	25 %	(1)	17 %
Male	(3)	75 %	(5)	83 %
Unknown	(0)	---	(0)	---

Table A.8. Philadelphia: Greek Revival Restaurant—percentages
(Continued on next page)

Category	Gr. Rev. Rest. (front) Photo #9		Gr. Rev. Rest. (full bldg.) Photo #10	
	(N)	Prob.	(N)	Prob.
Reasons				
Building	(2)	40 %	(3)	50 %
Walkway	(0)	---	(0)	---
Water	(0)	---	(0)	---
Monument/Object	(1)	20 %	(1)	17 %
Boat	(0)	---	(0)	---
Bridge	(0)	---	(0)	---
People	(0)	---	(0)	---
Lawn/Greenery	(0)	---	(0)	---
Signage/Decoration	(0)	---	(0)	---
Resting Area	(0)	---	(0)	---
Amphitheater	(0)	---	(0)	---
Contrast	(0)	---	(0)	---
Other: bar	(0)	---	(1)	17 %
Other: familiar	(0)	---	(1)	17 %
Other: historic	(1)	20 %	(0)	---
Other: historic arch	(1)	20 %	(0)	---

Note: Percentages may not total 100% due to rounding errors.

Table A.8—Continued

Category	Gr. Rev. Bank (full bldg.) Photo #15		Gr. Rev. Bank (front) Photo #16	
	(N)	Prob.	(N)	Prob.
Total Times Chosen	(39)	58 %	(28)	42 %
Age				
<14	(0)	---	(1)	4 %
15-24	(4)	10 %	(4)	14 %
25-34	(8)	21 %	(5)	18 %
35-44	(7)	18 %	(7)	25 %
45-64	(16)	41 %	(11)	39 %
65+	(4)	10 %	(0)	---
Unknown	(0)	---	(0)	---
Education				
Some HS	(2)	5 %	(4)	14 %
Grad HS	(2)	5 %	(3)	11 %
Some College	(11)	28 %	(5)	18 %
Grad College	(14)	36 %	(7)	25 %
Post Grad	(10)	26 %	(9)	32 %
Unknown	(0)	---	(0)	---
Local				
Both	(17)	44 %	(14)	50 %
Reside	(4)	10 %	(1)	4 %
Work	(5)	13 %	(4)	14 %
Visitor	(13)	33 %	(9)	32 %
Unknown	(0)	---	(0)	---
Seen				
No	(9)	23 %	(10)	36 %
Yes	(28)	72 %	(17)	61 %
Unknown	(2)	5 %	(1)	4 %
Gender				
Female	(17)	44 %	(17)	61 %
Male	(22)	56 %	(10)	36 %
Unknown	(0)	---	(1)	4 %

Table A.9. Philadelphia: Greek Revival Bank—percentages
(Continued on next page)

Category	Gr. Rev. Bank (full bldg.) Photo #15		Gr. Rev. Bank (front) Photo #16	
	(N)	Prob.	(N)	Prob.
Reasons				
Building	(23)	51 %	(18)	55 %
Walkway	(1)	2 %	(1)	3 %
Water	(2)	4 %	(0)	---
Monument/Object	(8)	18 %	(6)	18 %
Boat	(0)	---	(0)	---
Bridge	(0)	---	(0)	---
People	(0)	---	(0)	---
Lawn/Greenery	(0)	---	(2)	6 %
Signage/Decoration	(0)	---	(0)	---
Resting Area	(0)	---	(0)	---
Amphitheater	(0)	---	(0)	---
Contrast	(0)	---	(0)	---
Other:	(1)	2 %	(0)	---
Other: architecture	(0)	---	(1)	3 %
Other: familiarity	(0)	---	(1)	3 %
Other: historic	(1)	2 %	(1)	3 %
Other: historic arch.	(1)	2 %	(0)	---
Other: historical	(1)	2 %	(0)	---
Other: history	(1)	2 %	(1)	3 %
Other: impressive	(1)	2 %	(0)	---
Other: landmark	(1)	2 %	(0)	---
Other: light	(1)	2 %	(0)	---
Other: steps	(0)	---	(1)	3 %

Note: Percentages may not total 100% due to rounding errors.

Table A.9—Continued

Appendix A

GREEK REVIVAL	(Photo #9+10) - (Photo #15+16)				
p-value					
AGE		15-24	25-34	35-44	45-64	65+
(5 groups)						
0.76						

EDUCATION		Some HS	Grad HS	Some Col	Grad Col	Post Grad
(5 groups)						
0.18						

GENDER	Female	Male
0.06		

LOCAL / VISITOR	Resident	Phila.	Phila.	Visitor
(4 groups)	& Worker	Resident	Worker	
0.41				

Note: There were a small number of missing demographic responses on the actual surveys. These respondents have been temporarily removed from the relevant analysis P-values =<0.05 are highlighted, and further analyzed on the following pages.

Table A.10. Philadelphia: Greek Revival—overview

11   12

Figure A.16. Philadelphia: Penn's Landing Plaza Comparison Photos

13   14

Figure A.17. Philadelphia: Penn's Landing River Comparison Photos

Penn's Landing

Photo #11+12 (Great Plaza) vs. Photo #13+14 (Secluded Seating)

  This comparison of two sites at Penn's Landing is being made to look at preferences for different portions of this site. Photo #11+12 show the Great Plaza, which is a large amphitheater shaped set space that overlooks the water. During certain weekends of the summer it is used as an event space with performers at its base. Photo #13+14 is a view of the same area closer to the water's edge, showing some secluded seating overlooking the water.

  Only slight differences lie within the preferences of these two sites among those surveyed overall. The Secluded Seating images were the second and eighth most preferred images, selected a total of eighty times. The Great Plaza photos were the eleventh and twelfth most preferred, selected a total of fifty times. Therefore, the restored Secluded Seating was selected at a slightly more than 3:2 ratio.

"Water" is the most favored reason in both sites and all four photos. Comparing the demographics of those choosing the Great Plaza photos against those choosing the Secluded Seating yields no significant differences in terms of age, education, gender or local/visitor status.

The implication of these findings are fairly tenuous. One possibility might deal with the view of the water. The larger the amount of water in the image, and the less distracting the other elements, the more it is favored. Within the Secluded Seating photos, Photo #14 was more frequently selected. It shows a view of the water with the least distracting foreground. Photo #13 shows a slightly more distracting foreground of tri-colored paving and is selected less often.

The Great Plaza photos both show some of the river in them as well. The foregrounds of both, however are even more complex and distracting compared to the view of the river itself. Both these photos are selected less frequently again. This may then be interpreted as an indication that the view of water is prime, and the setting is secondary, with the less distractions and obstructions, the better.

Category	Penn's Landing (Canopies) Photo #11		Penn's Landing (Plaza) Photo #12	
	(N)	Prob.	(N)	Prob.
Total Times Chosen	**(24)**	**48 %**	**(26)**	**52 %**
Age				
<14	(0)	---	(1)	4 %
15-24	(2)	8 %	(8)	31 %
25-34	(2)	8 %	(4)	15 %
35-44	(10)	42 %	(7)	27 %
45-64	(7)	29 %	(5)	19 %
65+	(3)	13 %	(1)	4 %
Unknown	(0)	---	(0)	---
Education				
Some HS	(1)	4 %	(3)	12 %
Grad HS	(7)	29 %	(5)	19 %
Some College	(6)	25 %	(10)	38 %
Grad College	(7)	29 %	(6)	23 %
Post Grad	(3)	13 %	(2)	8 %
Unknown	(0)	---	(0)	---
Local				
Both	(17)	71 %	(16)	62 %
Reside	(1)	4 %	(4)	15 %
Work	(2)	8 %	(3)	12 %
Visitor	(4)	17 %	(3)	12 %
Unknown	(0)	---	(0)	---
Seen				
No	(1)	4 %	(4)	15 %
Yes	(22)	92 %	(21)	81 %
Unknown	(1)	4 %	(1)	4 %
Gender				
Female	(15)	63 %	(13)	50 %
Male	(9)	38 %	(13)	50 %
Unknown	(0)	---	(0)	---

Table A.11. Philadelphia: Penn's Landing Plaza—percentages
(Continued on next page)

Category	Penn's Landing (Canopies) Photo #11		Penn's Landing (Plaza) Photo #12	
	(N)	Prob.	(N)	Prob.
Reasons				
Building	(0)	---	(1)	2 %
Walkway	(4)	12 %	(9)	22 %
Water	(20)	61 %	(13)	32 %
Monument/Object	(0)	---	(1)	2 %
Boat	(0)	---	(0)	---
Bridge	(0)	---	(0)	---
People	(1)	3 %	(1)	2 %
Lawn/Greenery	(0)	---	(0)	---
Signage/Decoration	(0)	---	(1)	2 %
Resting Area	(0)	---	(0)	---
Amphitheater	(0)	---	(2)	5 %
Contrast	(0)	---	(0)	---
Other: aesthetic, pleasing	(0)	---	(1)	2 %
Other: design	(1)	3 %	(0)	---
Other: interesting shapes	(0)	---	(1)	2 %
Other: open	(0)	---	(1)	2 %
Other: open space	(0)	---	(1)	2 %
Other: orchestra	(1)	3 %	(0)	---
Other: pattern	(0)	---	(1)	2 %
Other: relaxing	(0)	---	(1)	2 %
Other: rest area & amph.	(0)	---	(1)	2 %
Other: riverside	(1)	3 %	(0)	---
Other: sky	(0)	---	(1)	2 %
Other: view	(1)	3 %	(0)	---

Note: Percentages may not total 100% due to rounding errors.

Table A.11—Continued

Category	Penn's Landing (boat) Photo #13		Penn's Landing (couple) Photo #14	
	(N)	Prob.	(N)	Prob.
Total Times Chosen	**(32)**	**40 %**	**(48)**	**60 %**
Age				
<14	(0)	---	(1)	2 %
15-24	(6)	19 %	(7)	15 %
25-34	(5)	16 %	(8)	17 %
35-44	(10)	31 %	(17)	35 %
45-64	(8)	25 %	(14)	29 %
65+	(3)	9 %	(1)	2 %
Unknown	(0)	---	(0)	---
Education				
Some HS	(0)	---	(2)	4 %
Grad HS	(7)	22 %	(6)	13 %
Some College	(6)	19 %	(17)	35 %
Grad College	(13)	41 %	(15)	31 %
Post Grad	(6)	19 %	(7)	15 %
Unknown	(0)	---	(1)	2 %
Local				
Both	(16)	50 %	(30)	63 %
Reside	(4)	13 %	(2)	4 %
Work	(5)	16 %	(7)	15 %
Visitor	(7)	22 %	(9)	19 %
Unknown	(0)	---	(0)	---
Seen				
No	(2)	6 %	(8)	17 %
Yes	(26)	81 %	(38)	79 %
Unknown	(4)	13 %	(2)	4 %
Gender				
Female	(14)	44 %	(18)	38 %
Male	(18)	56 %	(29)	60 %
Unknown	(0)	---	(1)	2 %

Table A.12. Philadelphia: Penn's Landing River—percentages
(Continued on next page)

Category	Penn's Landing (boat) Photo #13		Penn's Landing (couple) Photo #14	
	(N)	Prob.	(N)	Prob.
Reasons				
Building	(3)	8 %	(4)	6 %
Walkway	(0)	---	(0)	---
Water	(27)	69 %	(41)	65 %
Monument/Object	(0)	---	(0)	---
Boat	(3)	8 %	(0)	---
Bridge	(0)	---	(0)	---
People	(0)	---	(3)	5 %
Lawn/Greenery	(0)	---	(0)	---
Signage/Decoration	(0)	---	(0)	---
Resting Area	(2)	5	(5)	8 %
Amphitheater	(0)	---	(0)	---
Contrast	(1)	3 %	(1)	2 %
Other: accessibility	(1)	3 %	(0)	---
Other: activities	(0)	---	(1)	2 %
Other: Camden	(1)	3 %	(1)	2 %
Other: riverside	(0)	---	(1)	2 %
Other: sentimental	(1)	3 %	(1)	2 %
Other: sky	(0)	---	(1)	2 %
Other: view	(0)	---	(1)	2 %
Other: view of river	(0)	---	(1)	2 %

Note: Percentages may not total 100% due to rounding errors.

Table A.12—Continued

PENN'S LANDING	(Photo #11+12) - (Photo #13+14)				
p-value					
AGE (5 groups)	**15-24**	**25-34**	**35-44**	**45-64**	**65+**
0.93					

EDUCATION (5 groups)	**Some HS**	**Grad HS**	**Some Col**	**Grad Col**	**Post Grad**
0.32					

GENDER	**Female**	**Male**
0.09		

LOCAL / VISITOR (4 groups)	**Resident & Worker**	**Phila. Resident**	**Phila. Worker**	**Visitor**
0.61				

Note: There were a small number of missing demographic responses on the actual surveys. These respondents have been temporarily removed from the relevant analysis P-values =<0.05 are highlighted, and further analyzed on the following pages.

Table A.13. Philadelphia: Penn's Landing—overview

Summary of Photo Pair Comparisons

The photo pair comparisons are more descriptive than statistical, with broad conclusions difficult to draw.

The comparison of Pedestrian Bridges gave an unexplained gender preference (the only of the study). The Society Hill Residential comparison of late eighteenth and early nineteenth century rowhouses with 1960's rowhouses mimics the age and education preferences that appeared in the category "Age of Appearance." However, as a single side by side comparison it might be more a comment on the specific design of each set of structures than a reaction to their age of appearance.

The South St. comparison showed a general preference for the image of the more colorful facades, but again the reason behind the preference cannot be pinpointed with this single comparison.

The Greek Revival comparison showed an extremely strong preference for the First Bank, which is a restored structure, pristine in outward appearance. The lesser preferred was the Greek Revival building adaptively used as a restaurant.

It could be the preference of a restored structure compared to an adaptively used one. It also could be a preference for pristine compared to a less maintained exterior.

Lastly, the Penn's Landing comparison hints that views of water are more appreciated with less distracting foregrounds. In all these cases, broader interpretations of the conclusions must be made warily. They are comparisons of single sites, and do not inherently provide enough data to determine the underlying reasons behind the differences in preferences.

Appendix B

Yokohama

SORTED PHOTO#	PHOTO DESCRIPTION	PHOTO PAIR	TIMES CHOSEN	% OF RESPONDENTS
23	view along bridge	kishamichi	39	39
18	mall atrium	Landmark Plaza	37	37
34	people & ship	Hikawa Maru	36	36
14	ferris wheel	Pacifico Yokohama	31	31
25	bridge & tower	Kishamichi / Tower	31	31
28	field foreground	Red Brick Warehouses	30	30
6	marine terminal	Pukari Sanbashi Pier	29	29
3	anchor monument	Rinko Park	28	28
30	monu. & walkers	India Monument	28	28
5	men on mast	Training Vessel	27	27
21	berm & skyline	Maritime Museum	27	27
4	walkway	Rinko Park	24	24
26	river reflections	River lined with buildings	24	24
24	sleek & old	Pacifico Yoko./Old Warehouse	22	22
19	view from base	DryDock2 / Tower	21	21
11	indoor arcade	Queen's Square	20	20
22	water & ship	NipponMaru / DryDock1	20	20
27	street view	Customs House	20	20
17	looking down	DryDock2 / Tower	15	15
1	pedestrian bridge	Rinko Park	14	14
9	walkers	Waterfront Promenade	11	11
20	ship & skyscraper	NipponMaru / Tower	10	10
33	park walkways	Marine tower in distance	10	10
29	water foreground	Red Brick Warehouses	9	9
7	men fishing	Waterfront Promenade	6	6
12	bridge in distance	Kishamichi/Highrise	6	6
31	man carrying child	Yamashita Promenade	6	6
2	open field	Rinko Park	5	5
35	garden & fountain	Guardian of the Water	5	5
36	parent & child	Grand Staircase	5	5
10	outdoor entry	Queen's Square	3	3
16	performance	entryway amphitheatre	3	3
13	old warehouse	Cosmo World	2	2
32	man photographing	Yamashita Promenade	2	2
8	festival	Pacifico Yokohama	1	1
15	performance	entryway amphitheatre	1	1

Table B.1. Yokohama: Sorted Photos

23

18

34

14

25

28

6

3

30

5

21

4

Figure B.1. Yokohama: 12 Most Preferred Photos

26

24

19

11

22

27

17

1

9

20

33

29

Figure B.2. Yokohama: 12 Mid Preferred Photos

7

12

31

2

35

36

10

16

13

32

8

15

Figure B.3. Yokohama: 12 Least Preferred Photos

横浜ウォーターフロント現地調 YOKOHAMA WATERFRONT FIELD STUDY

はじめに
TO BEGIN WITH

「今日は調査にご協力いただき、ありがとうございます。この調査は、人々が調査対象区域を
どのようにとらえているかを調べるものです。対象区域は、この地図のとおりです。ここに、
この区域で撮影した３６枚の写真があります。それぞれの撮影地点は地図に示されています。」
"Thank you very much for taking the time to do this survey. It is being given in order to find
how people perceive the study area. The map shows the bounds of the study area. On the table
are 36 pictures taken in this area. The locations of the photos are noted on the map."

写真を見せながら
SHOWING THE PHOTOS

「これらの写真の中から、あなたが好きな、あるいは面白いと思うもの、例えば景色、場所、
人、そしてあなたが気がついた点などを写した写真を６枚選んでください。今までに行った
ことのある場所からでも、将来行ってみたい場所からでも結構です。」
"Please pick out 6 photos that show what you like most or think interesting about the study area.
--- for example, views, places, or people ---. and what you have noticed in this area.
They can include sites you have visited or want to visit in the future."

６枚選び終えたら
AFTER ALL 6 PHOTOS ARE CHOSEN

「では、この６枚の写真についてお伺いします。」
"Then, let me ask the related questions for each of these 6 photos."

写真番号 PHOTO NO.	選んだ順序 Order of choice	ここ(この風景の見える場所)に行ったことがありますか Have you seen this view or site in person?		コメント Comments	この写真を選んだ理由は何ですか？ 次の選択肢から、1つか2つ選んでください。 What are your main reasons to choose this photo? (1 or 2)												
		ある YES	ない NO		建物 building	歩道 walkway	水・水面 water	オブジェ monument /object	ボート boat	橋 bridge	人々 people	芝生植木草 lawn/ greenery	看板サイン signage/decoration	休憩場所 resting area	円形劇場 amphi-theater	コントラスト contrast	その他 other
1																	
2																	
3																	
4																	
5																	
6																	
7																	
8																	
9																	
10																	
11																	
12																	
13																	
14																	
15																	
16																	
17																	
18																	
19																	
20																	
21																	
22																	
23																	
24																	
25																	
26																	
27																	
28																	
29																	
30																	
31																	
32																	
33																	
34																	
35																	
36																	

Figure B.4. Yokohama: Questionnaire Front

もし、あなたがこれら36枚に加えてもう一枚写真を撮るなら、何を撮りますか？それは何故ですか。
If you were to take a picture in addition to these 36 photos. what would you like to take? And why?

この地域には他に何があればよいですか。
What would you like to have in the study area in addition to what existing?

〈あなたのプロフィールについてお聞かせください〉
Please tell me about your background

1. この地域に来られるのは何回目ですか。
   How many times have you been to this location including today?
   1   2   3   4 回以上 (more)

2. 今日来られた目的は何ですか。（複数回答可）
   Why did you come here today? (Circle all that apply)

   | くつろぎ | 観光 | 友人と会う | 食事 | 買い物 | 教養 | その他 ( ) |
   | relaxation | sightseeing | meet friend(s) | eating | shopping | education | other ( ) |

3. この近所にお勤めですか。あるいは、この近所の学校に通学していらっしゃいますか。
   Do you work or go to school nearby?   はい YES   いいえ NO

4. 今日、ここへ来られたのは？
   *どこから？   自宅   勤務先   学校   ホテル   その他 ( )
   From where to here today?   home   work   school   hotel   other ( )

   *どんな交通手段で？   徒歩   バス   電車   車   その他 ( )
   What transportation method(s)? foot   bus   train   car   other ( )

   *所要時間は？   15分以内   15－30分   30－60分   60分以上
   How long did it take?   <15 minutes 15-30 minutes 30-60 minutes 60 minutes<

   *旅行者の方なら、どこから？   （日本人なら地方名、外国人なら国名）   (   )
   If you are a tourist. where from? (Region for Japanese. Country for foreigners)

5. よろしければご自宅の住所を教えてください。   (県   市   区)
   Please give us your home address. if possible.   pref.   city   ward

   そこには何年お住まいですか。   (年)
   How long have you lived there?   year

6. ご職業は何ですか。   学生   会社員(管理職) 会社員   パート   フリーター・テンポ゛ラリー 主婦   その他
   What is your occupation? student   managerial   non-managerial part-time temporary   housewife other

---

<調査の記録 Questionnaire Record>   質問をしないで調査員が記入(to be filled out without questioning the subjects.)

| 1. 調査日・調査時間帯
Date & Time | [12/ | /'97] | | | | | | | | |
| | 9 | 10 | 11 | 12 | 13 | 14 | 15 | 16 | 17 | 18 |

2. 調査場所   ミュージアム   その他 ( )
   Place   museum   other

3. 天気 Weather	晴れ sunny	曇り cloudy	雨 rainy	雪 snowy
体感温度（調査員感覚） Temperature as felt by Survey Taker		とても寒い very cold	肌寒い chilly	快適 comfortable
4. 性別 Gender	男性 male	女性 female				
5. 年齢層 Age	-15	15-24	25-34	35-44	45-64	65-
6. 誰と With whom	一人 alone	カップル couple	友人と with friends	子供連れ with children	ツアーで with a tour	

7. NAME _____

8. NATIONALITY _____

Figure B.5. Yokohama: Questionnaire Back

Site Descriptions

Rinko Park (MM21) - photo #1, #2, #3, #4

This is the largest green space in MM21. It contains 9.3 ha. total area, 5.3 of which are presently open to the public. It fronts the water and consists primarily of lawns and a long terraced embankment overlooking the water and the Yokohama Bay Bridge.[1] A sculpture/monument of an anchor is located at one point along the embankment. An artificial inlet and tidal pool has been created at another point. It is lined with a paved path and a seating area stepping down along its banks.

Training Vessel (MM21) - photo #5

This current sail training vessel was docked nearby the Marine Terminal.

Marine Terminal (MM21) - photo #6

Pukari Sanbashi Pier comprises four berths and a two story building on a floating pier. Pukari Sanbashi means floating pier. It is the access point for Tokyo Bay excursion cruises and water shuttles to the subway station and Yamashita Park. A restaurant is housed within the building, as is a ticket booth for the boats. The dock and building sitting on it are of recent construction.

Waterfront Promenade (MM21) - photo #7, #9

A series of walkways line the waterfront. Used for walking and viewing, it is also sometimes used for informal fishing.

Outdoor Plaza at Pacifico Yokohama (MM21) - photo #8

This space is sometimes used for temporary outdoor festivals. This space was photographed during one of those festivals.

Queen's Square (MM21) - photo #10, #11

This development within MM21 contains business, commercial, cultural and hotel facilities. Of particular interest to the visitor are the retail facilities along the internal arcade of this complex. In essence, a retail mall.

Kishamichi Promenade (MM21) - photo #12, #23, #25

Kishamichi Promenade consists of reused railroad tracks converted to pedestrian use. This 500 meter long section crosses over the water on narrow strips of land, as well as a series of small historic steel bridges manufactured abroad.

This section of tracks was first opened around the turn of the century primarily for trains moving freight. Since the 1960s, its use to transport freight was no longer needed so it focused exclusively passengers. More recently, the use of these railroad lines to transport passengers has also become obsolete. Rather than be razed, however, this structure has been converted to pedestrian use. A boardwalk has been built along it leaving the original rails exposed and at grade.

Cosmo World (MM21) - photo #13, #14

This amusement park contains what is billed as the largest ferris wheel in the world, as well as other rides.

Staircase/Amphitheatre up to Landmark Plaza - photo #15, #16

This set of stairs is occasionally used as an amphitheatre by street performers. The performer stands at the base of the stairs (the stage) and the audience sits and stands along the steps. This space was photographed during a performance. It is located adjacent to Dry Dock #2.

Dry Docks (MM21) - photo #17, #19, #22

The original function for a dry dock is to serve as a location to repair or build a ship. It can be filled with water so the ship can float in or out, and drained of water so the ship's hull becomes exposed and can then be worked on. The dry docks are the oldest sites still existent in this area. They were built at the turn of the century to serve the shipping industry of this area. They were built in the manner of Japanese castles and survived the 1923 earthquake.

Dry Dock #1 has been filled with water and now permanently berths the sail ship Nippon-maru, which is part of the adjacent Maritime Museum. Dry Dock #2 has been drained and left exposed. It serves as a forecourt to Landmark Plaza and Tower. Public events are occasionally held within this plaza, though it also has tables and chairs set up at other times for more informal use by the general public. This dry dock did not simply remain untouched during construction of the tower, but rather was disassembled and then reassembled.

Landmark Tower and Plaza (MM21) - photo #17, #18, #19, #20, #25

This is the tallest building in Japan. It is 70 stories (296 meters) high. It has a slightly stepped and very distinctive profile. Landmark Plaza is an indoor retail mall at the base of the building. It contains a large central atrium.

Nippon-maru (MM21) - photo #20, #22

This tall masted ship was previously used as a sail training ship between 1930-1984. It is now permanently moored at this location. Tours of the ship are typically allowed along its decks. The ship, dry dock, and museum work together within an area designated Nippon-maru Memorial Park.

Yokohama Maritime Museum (MM21) - photo #21

The Maritime Museum is subdued in its exterior design and partially bermed beneath ground level. The roof of the museum slopes down towards the water and is covered with grass and a grid of pathways. It is readily accessible to the public.

Customs House - photo #27

From early this century, the architecture is distinctly different from the surrounding structures.

Red Brick Warehouses (MM21) - photo #28, #29

These two red brick warehouses were built between 1907-1913. Warehouse #2 survived the Great Kanto Earthquake of 1923. Warehouse #1 sustained major damage and was rebuilt to half its original length. Most early brick buildings did not survive the 1923 earthquake. From that point on, brick was rarely, if ever used within this area. This makes the warehouses one of the few remaining examples of brick architecture in the city.

Old Warehouse - photo #24

This old warehouse lies near Kishamichi Promenade. It does not appear renovated, but rather in a state of slight disrepair.

River View - photo #26

View of the adjacent river within the original part of town. It is lined with older buildings. Many small passenger boats are moored along its shores.

India Monument (Yamashita Park) - photo #30

Within Yamashita Park are several focal points with additional historical connections. One is the India Monument which was built after the Great Kanto Earthquake. Yokohama and the surrounding area had many Indian residents at the time of the earthquake. The Indian citizens were grateful for the help they received following the earthquake. They donated and built this monument to commemorate their appreciation.

Promenade and Walkways (Yamashita Park) - photo #31, #32, #33

A long continuous promenade lines the shoreline of the park.

Marine Tower - photo #33

It is located in the Kannai District and nearby Yamashita Park. It can be seen throughout much of the surrounding area. There is a viewing platform at the top of this tower that is open to the public with an admission charge.

Hikawa-maru (Yamashita Park) - photo #34

Another historical focal point along Yamashita Park is the ocean liner, Hikawa-maru. Formerly operating as a passenger ship between Japan and the U.S.A. between 1930-1960, it is permanently moored alongside the park. This ship allows access for a small fee and also has a restaurant and beer garden on board.

Fountain (Yamashita Park) - photo #35

This fountain representing the 'Guardian of the Water' was donated by San Diego, a sister port of Yokohama. It was installed in the 1960s and is a replica of a fountain in front of the San Diego City Hall at that time.

Grand Staircase (Yamashita Park) - photo #36

The railings of these stairs are covered with colorful mosaics. The stairs lead to the 'Plaza of the World.' The plaza itself is a representation of six paths representing trading routes to six continents. It is of recent construction.

Bibliography

Alexander, Christopher. "A City is Not a Tree." In *The City Reader*, ed. Richard T. LeGates and Frederic Stout. London: Routledge, 1996.

Alexander, Christopher. *The Timeless Way of Building*. New York: Oxford University Press, 1979.

Alpern, Andrew and Seymour Durst. *Holdouts!* New York: McGraw-Hill, 1984.

Basso, Keith H. "Wisdom Sits in Places: Notes on a Western Apache Landscape." In *Senses of Place*, ed. Steven Feld and Keith H. Basso, 53-87. Santa Fe: School of American Research Press, 1996.

Boniface, Priscilla and Peter J. Fowler. *Heritage and Tourism in "the global village"*. London: Routledge, 1993.

Boorstin, Daniel. *The Image: A guide to pseudo-events in America*. New York and Evanston: Harper Colophon Books, 1961.

Boyer, M. Christine. *The City of Collective Memory: Its Historical Imaagery and Architectural Entertainments*. Cambridge: MIT Press, 1994.

DeBlieu, Jan. "Mapping the Sacred Places," *Orion* 13 (Spring 1994): 18-23.

Gallery, John Andrew, ed. *Philadelphia Architecture: A guide to the City* 2d ed. Philadelphia: The Foundation for Architecture, 1994.

Garreau, Joel. *Edge City: Life on the new frontier*. NY: Doubleday, 1991.

Goldsteen, Joel B. and Cecil D. Elliott. *Designing America: Creating Urban Identity*. New York: Van Nostrand Reinhold, 1994.

Hayden, Dolores. *Power of Place*. Cambridge, Mass.: The MIT Press, 1995.

Herbert, David T. "Conclusions." In *Heritage, Tourism and Society*, ed. David T. Herbert, 212-222. London: Mansell, 1995.

Herbert, David T. "Heritage Places, Leisure and Tourism." In *Heritage, Tourism and Society*, ed. David T. Herbert, 1-20. London: Mansell,

1995.

Hiss, Tony. *The Experience of Place.* New York: Alfred A. Knopf, 1990.

Hough, Michael. *Out of Place: Restoring Identity to the Regional Landscape.* New Haven: Yale University Press, 1990.

Hughes, George. "Authenticity in Tourism." *Annals of Tourism Research* Vol. 22, No. 4 (1995): 781-803.

Jackson, John Brinckerhoff. *Discovering the Vernacular Landscape.* New Haven: Yale University Press, 1984.

Jackson, John Brinckerhoff. *The Necessity for Ruins, and Other Topics.* Amherst: University of Massachusetts Press, 1980.

Jacobs, Allan B. *Great Streets.* Cambridge, Mass.: MIT Press, 1993.

Kaplan, Rachel. "The Analysis of Perception via Preference: A Strategy for Studying How the Environment is Experienced," *Landscape Planning* 12 (1985): 161-176.

Larkham, Peter J. *Conservation and the City.* London; New York: Routledge, 1996.

Light, Duncan. "Heritage as Informal Education." In *Heritage, Tourism and Society,* ed. David T. Herbert, 117-145. London: Mansell, 1995.

Limmer, Ruth. *Six Heritage Tours of Lower East Side: a Walking Guide.* New York: New York University Press, 1997.

Lippard, Lucy. *The Lure of the Local: Senses of Place in a Multicentered Society.* New York: The New Press, 1997.

Littrell, Mary Ann, Luella F. Anderson and Pamela J. Brown. "What Makes a Craft Souvenir Authentic?" *Annals of Tourism Research* Vol. 20, No. 1 (1993): 197-215.

Lowenthal, David. *The Past is a Foreign Country.* Cambridge: Cambridge Univ. Press, 1985.

Lowenthal, David. *Possessed by the Past: The Heritage Crusade and the Spoils of History.* New York: Free Press, 1996.

Lynch, Kevin. *Image of the City.* Cambridge: M.I.T. Press, 1960.

Lynch, Kevin. *Managing the Sense of a Region.* Cambridge: M.I.T. Press, 1976.

Lynch, Kevin. *What Time is this Place.* Cambridge: M.I.T. Press, 1972.

MacCannell, Dean. *The Tourist: A New Theory of the Leisure Class.* New York: Schocken Books, 1976.

Malmaison Hotel - Edinburgh (Self Published Brochure, 1998).

Moscardo, Gianna. "Mindful Visitors: Heritage and Tourism." *Annals of Tourism Research* Vol. 23, No. 2 (1996): 376-397.

Mostafavi, Hohsen and David Leatherbarrow. *On Weathering: The Life of*

Buildings in Time. Cambridge: MIT Press, 1993.

Moughtin, Cliff, Taner Oc, Steven Tiesdell. *Urban Design: Ornament and Decoration*. Oxford, Boston: Butterworth Architecture, 1995.

Murphy, Peter E. "Urban Tourism and Visitor Behavior." *American Behavioral Scientist* Vol. 36, No. 2 (1992): 200-211.

Nasar, Jack L. *The Evaluative Image of the City*. London: Sage Publications, 1998.

National Park Service. "Criteria for Evaluation." Available: *http://www.cr.nps.gov/nr/criteria/crieria.html*. 2 April 1999.

Norberg-Schulz, Christian. *Genius Loci: Towards a Phenomenology of Architecture*. New York: Rizzoli, 1980.

Nuryanti, Wiendu. "Heritage and Postmodern Tourism." *Annals of Tourism Research* Vol. 23, No. 2 (1996): 249-260.

Philadelphia Access. New York: Access Press, 1994.

Rapoport, Amos. *The Meaning of the Built Environment: A Nonverbal Communication Approach*. Beverly Hills: Sage Publications, 1982.

Saito, Ren. *The Story of Yokohama: a History of a Port in Asia*. Trans. Mariko Yokoyama and Carol R. Kimmel. Tokyo: Libro-Port Pub. Co., 1989.

Sall, John and Ann Lehman, *JMP Start Statistics*. Belmont, California: Duxbury Press, 1996.

Sorkin, Michael. "See You in Disneyland." In *Variations on a Theme Park: The New American City and the End of Public Space*. Ed. Michael Sorkin. New York: Hill and Wang, 1992.

Stamps, Arthur III. "Use of photographs to simulate environments: a meta-analysis." *Perceptual and Motor Skills* (Dec 1990): 907-913.

Steele, Fritz. *The Sense of Place*. Boston, Mass.: CBI Publishing Company, Inc., 1981.

Stewart, Susan. *On Longing: Narratives of the Miniature, the Gigantic, the Souvenir, the Collection*. Durham: Duke University Press, 1993.

Taylor, S.M. and V.A. Konrad. "Scaling Dispositions Towards the Past." *Environment and Behavior* Vol. 12, No. 3 (1980): 283-307.

Teo, Peggy and Shirlena Huang. "Tourism and Heritage Conservation in Singapore." *Annals of Tourism Research* Vol. 22, No. 3 (1995): 589-615.

Tuan, Yi-Fu. *Space and Place: The Perspective of Experience*. Minneapolis: University of Minneapolis Press, 1977.

Tuan, Yi-Fu. *Topophilia: A Study of Environmental Perception, Attitudes, and Values*. Englewood Cliff, N.J.: Prentice-Hall, 1974.

Tunbridge, J. E. and G. J. Ashworth. "From History to Heritage." Chap. in
    *Dissonant Heritage: The Management of the Past as a Resource in
    Conflict.* Chichester; New York: Wiley, 1996.
Tunbridge, J. E. and G. J. Ashworth. "Leisure Resource Development in
    City Revitalisation: The Tourist-Historic Dimension." In *European
    Port Cities in Transition*, ed. B. S. Hoyle and D. A. Pinder, 176-200.
    London: Belhaven, 1992.
Urry, John. *Consuming Places*. London: Routledge, 1995.
Urry, John. *The Tourist Gaze: Leisure and Travel in Contemporary
    Societies*. London: Sage Publications, 1990.
Urry, John. "The Tourist Gaze "Revisited"." *American Behavioral
    Scientist* Vol. 36, No. 2 (1992): 172-186.
Willis, Susan. *A Primer for Daily Life*. London and New York: Routledge,
    1991.
"Yamashita Park." Available:
    *http://www.city.yokohama.jp/me/yoke/theyoke/yscene/y.park/park.ht
    ml*. 2 April 1999.
"City of Yokohama: Geography." Available:
    http://www.city.yokohama.jp/ne/info/map/indexE.html 1998.
Yokohama Minato Mirai 21 Corporation and Minato Mirai 21 Department,
    Urban Planning Bureau, Yokohama City. *Overview of Minato Mirai
    21 Planning and Individual Operations*. Japan: Self Published, 1996.
Zeisel, John. *Inquiry by Design: tools for environment-behavior research*.
    Cambridge: Cambridge University Press, 1985.

Notes

Introduction

1. Amos Rapoport, *The Meaning of the Built Environment: A Nonverbal Communication Approach* (Beverly Hills: Sage Publications, 1982), 16.

Chapter One

1. Christopher Alexander, *The Timeless Way of Building* (New York: Oxford University Press, 1979), xv.
2. Christopher Alexander, *The Timeless Way of Building* (New York: Oxford University Press, 1979), 144.
3. *Oxford English Dictionary*, 2d ed., s.v. "Tourist."
4. John Urry, *Consuming Places* (London: Routledge, 1995), 140.
5. Dean MacCannell, *The Tourist: A New Theory of the Leisure Class* (New York: Schocken Books, 1976), 13.
6. Dean MacCannell, *The Tourist: A New Theory of the Leisure Class* (New York: Schocken Books, 1976), 44.
7. John Urry, *The Tourist Gaze: Leisure and Travel in Contemporary Societies* (London: Sage Publications, 1990), 100.
8. John Urry, *The Tourist Gaze: Leisure and Travel in Contemporary Societies* (London: Sage Publications, 1990), 11.
9. John Urry, "The Tourist Gaze 'Revisited'," *American Behavioral Scientist*, Vol. 36, No. 2 (1992): 182.
10. J. E. Tunbridge and G. J. Ashworth, "Leisure Resource Development in City Revitalisation: The Tourist-Historic Dimension," in *European Port Cities in Transition*, ed. B. S. Hoyle and D. A. Pinder (London: Belhaven, 1992), 181.
11. Priscilla Boniface and Peter J. Fowler, *Heritage and Tourism in 'the global village'* (London: Routledge, 1993), 61.
12. *Oxford English Dictionary*, 2d ed., s.v. "Unique."
13. *Oxford English Dictionary*, 2d ed., s.v. "Distinct."

14. John Brinckerhoff Jackson, *Discovering the Vernacular Landscape* (New Haven: Yale University Press, 1984), 32.

15. Kevin Lynch, *Image of the City* (Cambridge: M.I.T. Press, 1960), 8.

16. Christian Norberg-Schulz, *Genius Loci: Towards a Phenomenology of Architecture* (New York: Rizzoli, 1980), 179.

17. Amos Rapoport, *The Meaning of the Built Environment: A Nonverbal Communication Approach* (Beverly Hills: Sage Publications, 1982), 121.

18. Michael Hough, *Out of Place: Restoring Identity to the Regional Landscape* (New Haven: Yale University Press, 1990), 3; John Urry, Consuming Places (London: Routledge, 1995), 132.

19. Mary Ann Littrell, Luella F. Anderson and Pamela J. Brown, "What Makes a Craft Souvenir Authentic?" *Annals of Tourism Research* Vol. 20, No. 1 (1993): 211.

20. George Hughes, "Authenticity in Tourism," *Annals of Tourism Research* Vol. 22, No. 4 (1995): 798.

21. Christopher Alexander, "A City is Not a Tree," in *The City Reader*, ed. Richard T. LeGates and Frederic Stout (London: Routledge, 1996), 129-130.

22. John Brinckerhoff Jackson, *Discovering the Vernacular Landscape* (New Haven: Yale University Press, 1984), 15; Amos Rapoport, *The Meaning of the Built Environment: A Nonverbal Communication Approach* (Beverly Hills: Sage Publications, 1982), 170.

23. Kevin Lynch, *Image of the City* (Cambridge: M.I.T. Press, 1960), 78.

24. Kevin Lynch, *Image of the City* (Cambridge: M.I.T. Press, 1960), 79.

25. John Urry, "The Tourist Gaze 'Revisited'," *American Behavioral Scientist* Vol. 36, No. 2 (1992): 173; John Urry, The Tourist Gaze: Leisure and Travel in Contemporary Societies (London: Sage Publications, 1990), 12.

26. Tony Hiss, *The Experience of Place* (New York: Alfred A. Knopf, 1990), xii.

27. Kevin Lynch, *Image of the City* (Cambridge: M.I.T. Press, 1960), 100.

28. Yi-Fu Tuan, *Space and Place: The Perspective of Experience* (Minneapolis: University of Minneapolis Press, 1977), 55.

29. Tony Hiss, *The Experience of Place* (New York: Alfred A. Knopf, 1990), 27.

30. John Brinckerhoff Jackson, *Discovering the Vernacular Landscape* (New Haven: Yale University Press, 1984), 147, 67.

31. Fritz Steele, *The Sense of Place* (Boston, Mass.: CBI Publishing Company, Inc., 1981), 23; Gianna Moscardo, "Mindful Visitors: Heritage and Tourism," *Annals of Tourism Research* Vol. 23, No. 2 (1996): 382.

32. Dolores Hayden, *Power of Place* (Cambridge, Mass.: The MIT Press, 1995), 16.

Chapter Two

1. Kevin Lynch, *Image of the City* (Cambridge: M.I.T. Press, 1960), 103.

2. Kevin Lynch, *Image of the City* (Cambridge: M.I.T. Press, 1960), 67-68.

3. Kevin Lynch, *Image of the City* (Cambridge: M.I.T. Press, 1960), 68.

4. Amos Rapoport, *The Meaning of the Built Environment: A Nonverbal Communication Approach* (Beverly Hills: Sage Publications, 1982), 30.

5. Amos Rapoport, *The Meaning of the Built Environment: A Nonverbal Communication Approach* (Beverly Hills: Sage Publications, 1982), 41.

6. Christopher Alexander, *The Timeless Way of Building* (New York: Oxford University Press, 1979), 521; Fritz Steele, *The Sense of Place* (Boston, Mass.: CBI Publishing Company, Inc., 1981), 8.

7. Christian Norberg-Schulz, *Genius Loci: Towards a Phenomenology of Architecture* (New York: Rizzoli, 1980), 184, 190.

8. Jack L. Nasar, *The Evaluative Image of the City* (London: Sage Publications, 1998), 71, 72.

9. Allan B. Jacobs, *Great Streets* (Cambridge, Mass.: MIT Press, 1993), 255, 257.

10. Andrew Alpern and Seymour Durst, *Holdouts!* (New York: McGraw-Hill, 1984), viii.

11. Andrew Alpern and Seymour Durst, *Holdouts!* (New York: McGraw-Hill, 1984), vii.

12. Amos Rapoport, *The Meaning of the Built Environment: A Nonverbal Communication Approach* (Beverly Hills: Sage Publications, 1982), 119.

13. Kay D. Weeks and Anne E. Grimmer, *Secretary of the Interior's Standards for the Treatment of Historic Properties with Guidelines for Preserving, Rehabilitating, Restoring and Reconstructing Historic Buildings* (Washington, D.C.: Heritage Preservation Services, 1995), 2, 17, 61.

14. Kay D. Weeks and Anne E. Grimmer, *Secretary of the Interior's Standards for the Treatment of Historic Properties with Guidelines for Preserving, Rehabilitating, Restoring and Reconstructing Historic Buildings* (Washington, D.C.: Heritage Preservation Services, 1995), 117.

15. David Lowenthal, *The Past is a Foreign Country* (Cambridge: Cambridge Univ. Press, 1985), 288.

16. Sheila Dyan, "Old candy factory is dandy digs," *Philadelphia Inquirer*, 13 December 1996.

17. Lucie Young, "Hotels Offer Surprises—Warehouse with Room Service," *New York Times*, 2 April 1998, sec. F, 3.

18. Malmaison Hotel - Edinburgh (self-published brochure, 1998).

Chapter Three

1. David T. Herbert, "Heritage Places, Leisure and Tourism," in *Heritage, Tourism and Society*, ed. David T. Herbert (London: Mansell, 1995), 18.

2. *Oxford English Dictionary*, 2d ed., s.v. "Packaging."

3. Dean MacCannell, *The Tourist: A New Theory of the Leisure Class* (New York: Schocken Books, 1976), 44.

4. Susan Stewart, *On Longing: Narratives of the Miniature, the Gigantic, the Souvenir, the Collection* (Durham: Duke University Press, 1993), 138.

5. Susan Willis, *A Primer for Daily Life* (London and New York: Routledge, 1991), 4.

6. Priscilla Boniface and Peter J. Fowler, *Heritage and Tourism in 'the global village'* (London: Routledge, 1993), 16; John Urry, *The Tourist Gaze: Leisure and Travel in Contemporary Societies* (London: Sage Publications, 1990), 3.

7. Dean MacCannell, *The Tourist: A New Theory of the Leisure Class* (New York: Schocken Books, 1976), 42; John Urry, "The Tourist Gaze 'Revisited'," *American Behavioral Scientist* Vol. 36, No. 2 (1992): 181.

8. Cliff Moughtin, Taner Oc, Steven Tiesdell, *Urban Design: Ornament and Decoration* (Oxford, Boston: Butterworth Architecture, 1995), 65.

9. Dean MacCannell, *The Tourist: A New Theory of the Leisure Class* (New York: Schocken Books, 1976), 132; Yi-Fu Tuan, *Topophilia: A Study of Environmental Perception, Attitudes, and Values* (Englewood Cliff, N.J.: Prentice-Hall, 1974), 204; Lucy Lippard, *The Lure of the Local: Senses of Place in a Multicentered Society* (New York: The New Press, 1997), 199.

10. Lucy Lippard, *The Lure of the Local: Senses of Place in a Multicentered Society* (New York: The New Press, 1997), 46.

11. Michael Hough, *Out of Place: Restoring Identity to the Regional Landscape* (New Haven: Yale University Press, 1990), 18.

12. John Urry, "The Tourist Gaze 'Revisited'," *American Behavioral Scientist* Vol. 36, No. 2 (1992): 173.

13. Susan Stewart, *On Longing: Narratives of the Miniature, the Gigantic, the Souvenir, the Collection* (Durham: Duke University Press, 1993), xii, xiii.

14. Lucy Lippard, *The Lure of the Local: Senses of Place in a Multicentered Society* (New York: The New Press, 1997), 93.

15. J. E. Tunbridge and G. J. Ashworth, "From History to Heritage," chap. in *Dissonant Heritage: The Management of the Past as a Resource in Conflict* (Chichester; New York: Wiley, 1996), 8.

16. David Lowenthal, *Possessed by the Past: The Heritage Crusade and the Spoils of History* (New York: Free Press, 1996), 156.

17. Priscilla Boniface and Peter J. Fowler, *Heritage and Tourism in 'the global village'* (London: Routledge, 1993), 64, 70.

18. Susan Willis, *A Primer for Daily Life* (London and New York: Routledge,

1991), 1.

19. Priscilla Boniface and Peter J. Fowler, *Heritage and Tourism in 'the global village'* (London: Routledge, 1993), 21; David T. Herbert, "Conclusions," in *Heritage, Tourism and Society*, ed. David T. Herbert (London: Mansell, 1995), 215; Dolores Hayden, *Power of Place* (Cambridge, Mass.: The MIT Press, 1995), 59.

20. Fritz Steele, *The Sense of Place* (Boston, Mass.: CBI Publishing Company, Inc., 1981), 149, 155.

21. M. Christine Boyer, *The City of Collective Memory: Its Historical Imaagery and Architectural Entertainments* (Cambridge: MIT Press, 1994), 2; Susan Willis, *A Primer for Daily Life* (London and New York: Routledge, 1991), 167.

22. Daniel Boorstin, *The Image: A guide to pseudo-events in America* (New York and Evanston: Harper Colophon Books, 1961), 55, 77-117.

23. *New York Times*, 9 July 1995.

24. Ruth Limmer, *Six Heritage Tours of Lower East Side: a Walking Guide* (New York: New York University Press, 1997).

25. Gianna Moscardo, "Mindful Visitors: Heritage and Tourism," *Annals of Tourism Research* Vol. 23, No. 2 (1996): 382, 384.

26. Priscilla Boniface and Peter J. Fowler, *Heritage and Tourism in 'the global village'* (London: Routledge, 1993), 7, 8.

27. Michael Sorkin, "See You in Disneyland" in *Variations on a Theme Park: The New American City and the End of Public Space*, ed. Michael Sorkin (New York: Hill and Wang, 1992), 217.

28. J. E. Tunbridge and G. J. Ashworth, "Leisure Resource Development in City Revitalisation: The Tourist-Historic Dimension," in *European Port Cities in Transition*, ed. B. S. Hoyle and D. A. Pinder (London: Belhaven, 1992), 198.

29. J. E. Tunbridge and G. J. Ashworth, "Leisure Resource Development in City Revitalisation: The Tourist-Historic Dimension," in *European Port Cities in Transition*, ed. B. S. Hoyle and D. A. Pinder (London: Belhaven, 1992), 199.

30. David T. Herbert, "Heritage Places, Leisure and Tourism," in *Heritage, Tourism and Society*, ed. David T. Herbert (London: Mansell, 1995), 217.

Chapter Four

1. Priscilla Boniface and Peter J. Fowler, *Heritage and Tourism in 'the global village'* (London: Routledge, 1993), 1, 184; Peter E. Murphy, "Urban Tourism and Visitor Behavior," *American Behavioral Scientist*, Vol. 36, No. 2 (1992): 1992, 200.

2. Dean MacCannell, *The Tourist: A New Theory of the Leisure Class* (New

York: Schocken Books, 1976), 1, 3.

3. David Lowenthal, *Possessed by the Past: The Heritage Crusade and the Spoils of History* (New York: Free Press, 1996), 6.

4. Wiendu Nuryanti, "Heritage and Postmodern Tourism," *Annals of Tourism Research* Vol. 23, No. 2 (1996): 257.

5. Oxford English Dictionary, 2d ed., s.v. "Ambience"; *Merriam-Webster's Collegiate Dictionary*, 10th ed., s.v. "Ambience."

6. Fritz Steele, *The Sense of Place* (Boston, Mass.: CBI Publishing Company, Inc., 1981), 131; Yi-Fu Tuan, *Space and Place: The Perspective of Experience* (Minneapolis: University of Minneapolis Press, 1977), 125.

7. David Lowenthal, *Possessed by the Past: The Heritage Crusade and the Spoils of History* (New York: Free Press, 1996), 134, 249.

8. Jack L. Nasar, *The Evaluative Image of the City* (London: Sage Publications, 1998), 69.

9. Yi-Fu Tuan, *Space and Place: The Perspective of Experience* (Minneapolis: University of Minneapolis Press, 1977), 6.

10. Kevin Lynch, *Image of the City* (Cambridge: M.I.T. Press, 1960), 1.

11. Lucy Lippard, *The Lure of the Local: Senses of Place in a Multicentered Society* (New York: The New Press, 1997), 85.

12. Kevin Lynch, *What Time is this Place* (Cambridge: M.I.T. Press, 1972), 171.

13. National Park Service, "Criteria for Evaluation," available: *http://www.cr.nps.gov/nr/criteria/crieria.html*, 2 April 1999.

14. Hohsen Mostafavi and David Leatherbarrow, *On Weathering: The Life of Buildings in Time* (Cambridge: MIT Press, 1993), 16, 32.

15. John Brinckerhoff Jackson, *Discovering the Vernacular Landscape* (New Haven: Yale University Press, 1984), 117.

16. Christopher Alexander, *The Timeless Way of Building* (New York: Oxford University Press, 1979), 153.

17. *Oxford English Dictionary*, 2d ed., s.v. "Patina."

18. Hohsen Mostafavi and David Leatherbarrow, *On Weathering: The Life of Buildings in Time* (Cambridge: MIT Press, 1993), 16, 72.

19. Kevin Lynch, *Image of the City* (Cambridge: M.I.T. Press, 1960), 44; Jack L. Nasar, *The Evaluative Image of the City* (London: Sage Publications, 1998), 65.

20. Yi-Fu Tuan, *Space and Place: The Perspective of Experience* (Minneapolis: University of Minneapolis Press, 1977), 55.

21. John Brinckerhoff Jackson, *The Necessity for Ruins, and Other Topics* (Amherst: University of Massachusetts Press, 1980), 98, 101.

22. J. E. Tunbridge and G. J. Ashworth, "From History to Heritage," chap. in *Dissonant Heritage: The Management of the Past as a Resource in Conflict* (Chichester; New York: Wiley, 1996), 16.

23. Michael Hough, *Out of Place: Restoring Identity to the Regional Landscape* (New Haven: Yale University Press, 1990), 18.

24. Priscilla Boniface and Peter J. Fowler, *Heritage and Tourism in 'the global village'* (London: Routledge, 1993), 73.

25. Yi-Fu Tuan, *Space and Place: The Perspective of Experience* (Minneapolis: University of Minneapolis Press, 1977), 187; David Lowenthal, *The Past is a Foreign Country* (Cambridge: Cambridge Univ. Press, 1985), xxiii.

26. Michael Hough, *Out of Place: Restoring Identity to the Regional Landscape* (New Haven: Yale University Press, 1990), 187.

27. Dolores Hayden, *Power of Place* (Cambridge, Mass.: The MIT Press, 1995), 46, 78.

28. Keith H. Basso, "Wisdom Sits in Places: Notes on a Western Apache Landscape," in *Senses of Place*, ed. Steven Feld and Keith H. Basso (Santa Fe: School of American Research Press, 1996), 61.

29. "Yamashita Park," available: *http://www.city.yokohama.jp/me/yoke/theyoke/yscene/y.park/park.html*, 2 April 1999.

30. Duncan Light, "Heritage as Informal Education," in *Heritage, Tourism and Society*, ed. David T. Herbert (London: Mansell, 1995), 139.

31. S.M. Taylor and V.A. Konrad, "Scaling Dispositions Towards the Past," *Environment and Behavior*, Vol. 12, No. 3 (1980): 304; Peter E. Murphy, "Urban Tourism and Visitor Behavior," *American Behavioral Scientist*, Vol. 36, No. 2 (1992): 209.

32. Jack L. Nasar, *The Evaluative Image of the City* (London: Sage Publications, 1998), 72.

33. Peggy Teo and Shirlena Huang, "Tourism and Heritage Conservation in Singapore," *Annals of Tourism Research* Vol. 22, No. 3 (1995): 589.

34. Kevin Lynch, *What Time is this Place* (Cambridge: M.I.T. Press, 1972), 1.

35. Christopher Alexander, *The Timeless Way of Building* (New York: Oxford University Press, 1979), 95.

36. David Lowenthal, *The Past is a Foreign Country* (Cambridge: Cambridge Univ. Press, 1985), 405.

37. Kevin Lynch, *What Time is this Place* (Cambridge: M.I.T. Press, 1972), 57.

38. Yi-Fu Tuan, *Space and Place: The Perspective of Experience* (Minneapolis: University of Minneapolis Press, 1977), 54.

39. David Lowenthal, *The Past is a Foreign Country* (Cambridge: Cambridge Univ. Press, 1985), 318.

Chapter Five

1. Rachel Kaplan, "The Analysis of Perception via Preference: A Strategy for Studying How the Environment is Experienced," *Landscape Planning* 12 (1985): 161-162.
2. Arthur Stamps, III, "Use of photographs to simulate environments: a meta-analysis," *Perceptual and Motor Skills* (Dec 1990): 907.
3. Jack L. Nasar, *The Evaluative Image of the City* (London: Sage Publications, 1998), 28; Dolores Hayden, *Power of Place* (Cambridge, Mass.: The MIT Press, 1995), 39.
4. Jack L. Nasar, *The Evaluative Image of the City* (London: Sage Publications, 1998), 79, 81.

Chapter Six

1. John Andrew Gallery, ed., *Philadelphia Architecture: A Guide to the City* 2d ed. (Philadelphia: The Foundation for Architecture, 1994), 162.
2. John Andrew Gallery, ed., *Philadelphia Architecture: A Guide to the City* 2d ed. (Philadelphia: The Foundation for Architecture, 1994), 160.
3. *Philadelphia Access* (New York: Access Press, 1994), 42.
4. *Philadelphia Access* (New York: Access Press, 1994), 40.
1. John Sall and Ann Lehman, *JMP Start Statistics*, (Belmont, California: Duxbury Press, 1996), 120.

Chapter Seven

1. Ren Saito, *The Story of Yokohama: a History of a Port in Asia*, trans. Mariko Yokoyama and Carol R. Kimmel (Tokyo: Libro-Port Pub. Co., 1989), 34-36; "City of Yokohama: Geography," available: *http://www.city.yokohama.jp/ne/info/map/indexE.html* 1998.
2. "Yamashita Park," available: *http://www.city.yokohama.jp/me/yoke/theyoke/yscene/y.park/park.html*, 2 April 1999.
3. Yokohama Minato Mirai 21 Corporation and Minato Mirai 21 Department, Urban Planning Bureau, Yokohama City, *Overview of Minato Mirai 21 Planning and Individual Operations* (Japan: Self Published, 1996), 6.

Chapter Eight

1. John Zeisel, *Inquiry by Design: tools for environment-behavior research* (Cambridge: Cambridge University Press, 1985), xi, 81.

2. Rachel Kaplan, "The Analysis of Perception via Preference: A Strategy for Studying How the Environment is Experienced," *Landscape Planning* 12 (1985) 175.

3. Kevin Lynch, *Managing the Sense of a Region* (Cambridge: M.I.T. Press, 1976), 28.

4. Jan DeBlieu, "Mapping the Sacred Places," *Orion* 13 (Spring 1994): 22.

5. John Zeisel, *Inquiry by Design: tools for environment-behavior research* (Cambridge: Cambridge University Press, 1985), 161.

Appendix B

1. Yokohama Minato Mirai 21 Corporation and Minato Mirai 21 Department, Urban Planning Bureau, Yokohama City. *Overview of Minato Mirai 21 Planning and Individual Operations* (Japan: Self Published, 1996), 22.

Index

About the Author

Richard W. Berman is a registered architect, having received his professional degree from the Rhode Island School of Design. He received his Ph.D. in City and Regional Planning from the University of Pennsylvania. He is currently a lecturer at Penn, teaching courses on urban design and sustainable design. He also runs a web business, ArchitectsTouch.com, which carries his smaller, product designs.